WITHDRAWN

James A. Herne

The Rise of Realism in the American Drama

HERBERT J. EDWARDS AND JULIE A. HERNE

University of Maine Press · Orono, Maine, 1964

Copyrighted by the University of Maine 1964

Printed by the University of Maine Press on
University Text, manufactured by the
S. D. Warren Paper Company, Cumberland Mills, Maine

University of Maine Studies, Second Series
No. 80

COMMITTEE ON PUBLICATIONS

of the

FACULTY OF GRADUATE STUDY

H. M. Fife *(English)*, Chairman
R. E. Armington *(Electrical Engineering)*
A. M. Caughran *(Education)*
F. P. Eggert, *Dean of Graduate Study*
A. F. Harrison, *Public Information*
F. Hyland *(Botany)*
J. C. MacCampbell, *University Librarian*
A. H. Raphaelson *(Business and Economics)*
D. B. Tolman, *Public Information*

Editors for this issue

| J. W. Barushok | H. J. Edwards |
| H. M. Fife | J. C. MacCampbell |

CONTENTS

Chapter		Page
1	Beginnings	1
2	The Western Sisters and The Old Melodrama	10
3	Little Miss Corcoran	19
4	Hearts of Oak	27
5	Boston	37
6	Hamlin Garland	45
7	Margaret Fleming	57
8	William Dean Howells	74
9	Shore Acres	85
10	Griffith Davenport	112
11	Sag Harbor	135
12	Farewell	150
	Notes	160
	Bibliography	172
	Index	177

To The Memory of
Chrystal Herne

PREFACE

A natural result of the increased interest in American literature and its elevation to a place of honor in our universities during the last three decades of the twentieth century has been the rediscovery of many "lost" writers. Some of these, such as Emily Dickinson and Edward Taylor the Puritan poet, had been almost unknown during their times. Others, such as John W. DeForest, the author of *Miss Ravenel's Conversion,* and a pioneer of realism in the American novel, had been slightly known, and in this group belongs also the great Herman Melville and his masterpiece, *Moby Dick.* Still others had been well known during their lifetimes, but had long been neglected and their real significance unappreciated. To this latter group belong such writers as Henry James, William Dean Howells, and James A. Herne.

Until Herne was past forty years of age he was known to the American public solely as a character actor distinguished for the naturalism of his acting. Then in the late eighties he began to write plays which were so different from the usual dramatic fare of the time in the realism of their character drawing and technique that the public refused to accept them. Herne and his actress wife, Katharine, were living in Boston when Hamlin Garland, then a struggling young writer just beginning his career, saw *Drifting Apart* and became an enthusiastic admirer of Herne's art. Through Garland, Herne was introduced to the plays of Ibsen, and wrote what was probably the first example of continental realism to appear on the American Stage, *Margaret Fleming,* a play that was highly praised by Howells and a small group of Boston intellectuals, but which no theatre owner of the time would sponsor, and which had its first showing in a small public hall in Boston. *Shore Acres,* which made some concessions to the popular taste of the time, was a financial success, and enabled Herne to write another play of uncompromising realism, *Griffith Davenport,* which was an artistic success but a financial failure. His last play, *Sag Harbor,* was a success in Boston, where Barrett Wendell saw in it a forerunner of the modern American drama, but it failed in New York, and its future career on the stage was cut short by Herne's untimely death.

The importance of Herne in the history of American drama was not fully realized until the publication of Arthur Hobson Quinn's history of the American drama in the second decade of the present century. As a result, scholarly interest in Herne was awakened, and in our own day this interest has resulted in a number of articles about him by students of the American drama. The present recognition of his importance in the history of the American drama is further indicated by the inclusion of his plays in anthologies of the American drama (*Margaret Fleming* in Quinn's *Representative American Plays,* and *Shore Acres* in Downer's recent (1960) *American Drama*). In the *Literary History of the United States,* Scully Bradley states: "Herne had brought realism to the theatre," and Alan S. Downer says in his *American Drama* that "it was James A. Herne who took the final step towards realism" in the American theatre of the late nineteenth century. Today, most scholars in the field of American drama would agree with the statement made by Henry Nash Smith and William M. Gibson in their *Mark Twain-Howells Letters* (1960) that Herne was "the ablest American playwright of the time."

The basis of the present work was a biography of her father written by Julie A. Herne, who died in 1955. I wish to acknowledge with deep gratitude the help received from the following persons and institutions: Alan S. Downer of Princeton University who kindly consented to read the manuscript, John T. Herne, the late William VanLennep, Curator of the Theatre Collection at Harvard University; Arthur Hobson Quinn; Mildred Howells and the late John Mead Howells for permission to quote from the letters of William Dean Howells; Mary Isabel Lord and Constance Garland Doyle for permission to quote from the books, articles, and letters of Hamlin Garland; Lars Ahnebrink of the University of Upsala; May Davenport Seymour, Curator of the Theatre Collection, Museum of the City of New York; Felicia Giffen, Assistant Secretary of the National Institute of Arts and Letters and Mrs. Matthew Josephson of the library of the Institute; George Freedley, Curator, Theatre Collection, New York Public Library; Robert W. Hill, Keeper of Manuscripts, New York Public Library, for permission to examine the Henry George and Paul Kester Collections; Albert M. Turner, former Head of the Department of English, University of Maine; John Erskine Hankins, Head of the Department of English, University of Maine; Donald Pizer of the University of California at Los Angeles; the Coe Fund of the University of Maine for financial assistance; Appleton Century Crofts, Inc., for permission to quote from Edith Wharton's *The Age of Innocence;* Columbia University Press for permission to quote from Edmond Gagey's *The San Francisco Stage;* Grace Enneking Young for material on her father, John J. Enneking; Richard Moody and the University of Indiana Press for permission to quote from *America Takes The Stage.*

1

BEGINNINGS

In the early fifties of the last century Edwin Forrest gave a performance of *The Gladiator* at a theatre in Albany, New York, called The Albany Museum. It was not his first visit to Albany, nor was it the first time he had appeared in the role of Spartacus, the leader of the rebellious Roman gladiators. Forrest had played in Albany in 1825 at the beginning of his career, and tonight was almost his thousandth performance of *The Gladiator*.

In that quarter century much had happened to Forrest.[1] He had become the leading American actor, at least in the opinion of the masses; he had accumulated a fortune; his feud with the famous English actor Macready had caused the Astor Place riot on the night of May 10, 1848, in which 22 were killed and several hundred wounded; he had sued his wife for divorce on the grounds of adultery in a case that had rocked the nation; he had lost the case and with it the friendship of all the distinguished New York people who had at one time cultivated him—such people as William Cullen Bryant and N. P. Willis. Later he had horsewhipped Willis on the street.

But he had not lost the adoration of the masses. The aristocrats might scorn him and his style of acting and prefer the intellectual style of William Macready, but the people loved Forrest and thronged to see him. His style was their idea of what acting should be, and in their eyes Edwin Forrest was the ideal actor. His tremendous physique with its bulging muscles, his dark and leonine head, his deep-chested voice that could shake the rafters and a moment later modulate itself to tones of softest music, his fiery vigor and enthusiasm—all these enthralled them. His parts ran the whole gamut of the emotions—he could lift the spectators from their seats in terror, make them tremble with fear or weep with grief, inspire them with lofty ideals or make them tense with anger.

It was the age of forensic eloquence; every school boy recited Daniel Webster's magnificent peroration of the Reply to Hayne, and Longfellow was the great American poet. Neither Forrest himself nor anyone in his audience could have been aware that the school of grandeur was already on its way out and that the slowly rising tide of realism and naturalism had already lapped at its foundations. Meanwhile the grand style was the accepted style of the age, and one met it everywhere—on the lecture platform, on the stage, in Congress, in the novels of Cooper and Dickens, in newspapers. Even the business letters of the day had an oratorical rhythm.

One of the most enthusiastic members of the audience that night in the Albany Museum was a fourteen-year-old boy high in the gallery. His name was James Ahern, and this was the first time he had ever been in a theatre. His father, Patrick Ahern, was a devout but narrow-minded Irish immigrant who regarded the theatre as the haunt of the devil, and Jim's visit tonight was a daring escapade undertaken with his brother Charles, who sat beside him. The penalty if they were caught might well be a terrible strapping.[2] One of Jim's brothers, after such a beating, had run away from home and had never been heard from. But now that Jim was making his own money (Patrick had taken him out of school the year before and put him to work in a brush factory) he was developing an independence of his father. Jim gave most of his small salary to his mother, a meek and affectionate woman, for the large family was always poor, Patrick being only an impecunious clerk in a hardware store; but Jim now had some money of his own.

For the past year, he had spent his small surplus on the novels of Scott and Dickens, and he read and re-read every novel by Dickens he could get. He did not merely read these books; he studied them. He delighted in memorizing entire scenes. He did this with ease, for he had a phenomenal memory. And his mother, her ear apprehensively cocked for the footstep of her husband on the front porch, listened with fond amazement at the boy's ability to mimic the characters. Somehow they seemed to come to life when Jim began to recite, whether they were old or young. To Jim it was all easy and natural and spontaneous. The idea of becoming an actor never occurred to him; he had never seen one, he had never been inside a theatre, he had never read a play.

And now, on this fateful night in his fourteenth year, he was actually in a theatre, and he was seeing and hearing the great Edwin Forrest. Even though Jim was high up in the gallery, he had no difficulty in hearing, for such was the range and pitch control of that marvellous voice that even a stage whisper carried to the remotest parts of the house.

Many years later Walt Whitman was to write in "November Boughs" of the first time he saw Forrest act. Whitman had seen him in John Howard Payne's *Brutus* at the Bowery Theatre in 1831. He wrote: "It affected me for weeks; or rather I might say, permanently filtered into my whole nature." Twenty years later, when Jim Ahern saw him, Forrest was still at the height of his powers, and the audience was still electrified when the great giant of a man, half-naked and in chains, stalked majestically upon the stage, and waiting for the thunderous applause to subside, darted a dark and fiery glance about him. Then in stentorian and reverberating tones that struck terror into every heart, he spoke: "Is it a thousand leagues away to Thrace?"

Jim Ahern was so entranced that he sat motionless and tensely silent in the midst of the applause. After the fall of the curtain he stumbled out into the dark street, only dimly aware of the crowds or of the talk of his brother beside him. Everything material or physical seemed insubstantial and unreal beside the glorious illumination that had swept over him. He had found his future career; he had discovered the great loyalty to which his life would be devoted. He had determined to be an actor, and nothing was ever to shake that resolution, neither poverty nor any other obstacle.

He did not dare mention his ambition to any of his brothers, for fear it might reach his father. He confided it only to his mother, his only safe refuge in that stormy household. But from that night on he saw, from a gallery seat, every star who came to Albany. Stars in those days did not travel with their own companies, but were supported by the actors playing in the local stock companies of the towns they visited. This system was to be in effect for a number of years. Whatever its disadvantages, it had the advantage of bringing the great stars of the day to every town that could boast a theatre. During the next few years, Jim saw many of them. But none of them could compare with Forrest. The early fifties was a period of interregnum on the American stage. Junius Brutus Booth had died in 1852, and his far greater son, Edwin, was still to win his laurels. Charlotte Cushman, the greatest of the tragediennes, had made a fortune and had temporarily retired to England. Fortunately, there was a good deal of Shakespeare, for there were few good contemporary dramas being written either in the United States or England during the fifties, and almost every actor or actress of any note aspired to play Shakespeare. In the dearth of contemporary drama, there were many dramatizations of Dickens' novels, and the boy in the gallery saw the characters he loved and heard the lines he knew by heart come to life on the stage.

Six years passed, six years of back-breaking drudgery in the brush factory, which Jim endured because his dream with each passing year became surer of realization. At twenty-one he would be his own master, and he saved his money for that glorious day. When he was twenty-one he had saved $165. He knew he must start at the bottom in realizing his great ambition, but in his excessive humility he aimed too low. At the Green Street Theatre, a small travelling company was playing in a crude melodrama called *The Butcher of Ghent and His Dog*. Probably the best trained member of the company was the dog, who, in the climatic scene when the hero was lost in the woods and called out, "This darkness is impenetrable! If I had but a lantern!" would come running out onto the stage with a lighted lantern in his mouth.

After the performance, Jim met the hero, part-owner, and manager of the company, Webb, and confided his ambition. Webb informed him that he was about to part company with his partner, Coney, and embark on a tour of the small towns of upper New York in *The Dog of Montargis*. Webb owned one of the two dogs in the company. He would be glad to take Jim with him, playing the part of the Seneschal, for $165. The company played Schenectady, Gloversville, Amsterdam, Rome, and Oneida, to increasingly smaller houses. Webb's small capital was soon exhausted, and he resorted to the expedient of quietly departing without paying the hotel bill. But he tried this once too often, and at Penn Yan the sheriff caught him and seized his dog. Without a star, the company was forced to disband and make its way back to Albany.

Luckily, they had no sooner arrived in the city than Webb met James Connor, manager of the Adelphi Theatre in Troy, who was looking for talent for his spring and summer season. Webb recommended Jim as a promising young actor, and Connor immediately engaged him, at a salary of $6 a week. Jim had been engaged to play "general utility business," which meant minor parts with only a few lines, but Connor, soon impressed with his ability, gave him the part of George Shelby in *Uncle Tom's Cabin* and in this part he opened the spring and summer season at the Adelphi in April, 1859.

The names of the principal members of the stock company have long been forgotten — Mr. and Mrs. Connor, Charlotte Crampton, T. M. Tyrrell, Charles Bishop — but they were all competent professionals, and from them Jim learned the rudiments of his art.³ He had an attractive personality; he made friends easily, and he kept them. The besetting sin of the actor — egotism — was notably absent from his make-up. All his life he was to make many friends, both in and out of the profession; all his life people seemed to be eager to go out of their way to help him. He was not handsome in the way the Drews or the Barrymores were handsome; he was rougher hewn and more ruggedly masculine. There was a humorous twinkle in his blue-gray eyes, and a determined chin that bespoke the fighting Irish. Later, he was to fight desperately for a cause in which he believed, but there are few instances of his fighting people — and then it was for a principle, not because of temper. When he was directing plays years later, he was noted for a patience, a coolness and a calmness that were conspicuous in a temperamental profession.

Uncle Tom's Cabin, in which he made his first appearance as a regular actor, was one of the most sensationally successful plays ever to appear on the American stage. Dramatized by the actor George L. Aiken in 1852, for his cousin's husband, George C. Howard, then manager of the Troy Museum, and featuring four-year-old Cordelia Howard as the "The Gentle Eva," it had moved to the National in New York City the next year for an unprecedented run of 325 consecutive performances. On tour, and in Great Britain, it had repeated its phenomenal success, and now, seven years later, it was still playing to packed houses.

Thus Jim Ahern made his debut in a strong and popular play. He tasted the heady intoxication of applause and was forever confirmed in his decision to make the theatre his life work. Years afterward, speaking of this time, he said, "I had reached the summit of earthly bliss. My dream was realized. Not a wish remained unsatisfied." His work became his life. When Connor said that he should change his name to Herne because it would look better on the playbills, he eagerly complied, and henceforth he was James A. Herne.

With all the energy and enthusiasm of youth he plunged into the business of learning the technique of his craft. He took fencing lessons, learned how to make effective entrances and exits, how to cross the stage, how to manage his hands, his feet, and his body without self-consciousness. He learned how to manage his voice, how to get the "range" of a theatre, how to pitch his voice so that even a whisper could be heard in the gallery. Clarity of diction was all-important, and he worked until he achieved the perfection in that respect for which he was always noted. He learned the art of timing, the value of a pause, a gesture, the way to get a laugh, how to hold the attention of an audience. He learned to use his wits, and to "fill in" or improvise speeches when someone forgot his lines or made "a stage wait."

The star system then in vogue may have had its disadvantages — Walt Whitman had criticized it severely in the pages of the *Brooklyn Eagle* in 1847 — but for a young actor it had the great advantage of enabling him to observe and study the methods of the leading actors of the day. Sooner or later, James A. Herne, as he was now known, had the opportunity of working with most of the leading actors and actresses of the time. Keenly observant, he watched them closely. A favorite topic of discussion among the actors of the stock company at the tavern to which they invariably went after the performance was "the validity of a reading" given by the visiting star, and the argument often lasted until the early hours of the morning. Herne was there with the rest, listening attentively, though he spoke little.

When the well-known Shakespearean actor J. B. Roberts arrived, Herne played Horatio to his Hamlet, Cassio to his Othello, Bassanio in *The Merchant of Venice,* and "doubled" the parts of Tressel, Oxford, and Buckingham in *Richard III*. The assignment of parts in the old stock company was largely governed by a complex system of tradition and precedent that seems strange to us today. There was, first of all, the leading man, who had his choice of parts, and a play could not be cast without consulting him. Then there was the first juvenile, who played all the lovers and heroic parts not considered of sufficient importance to be offered to the leading man. The second juvenile man took what might be left. The first heavy man had his choice of villain parts, and the second heavy man had second choice. So it went, through a long string of categories including the first walking gentleman, the second walking gentleman, the first singing walking gentleman, the second singing walking gentleman, the first old man, the second old man, the first comedian, the second comedian, respectable utility, general utility — and then the whole list of categories was repeated with the actresses.

Each actor or actress was engaged for his or her "line of business' and to play the entire range of characters which tradition and precedent associated with that particular line.[4] Obviously, poor casting often resulted. For instance, Stuart Robson, who was a born comedian, and who later became one of the leading comedians of the American stage, co-starring with William H. Crane in Bronson Howard's satirical play, *The Henrietta,* was, in his early stock days at Ford's theatre in Baltimore, always cast as Hastings, the conspirator, in *King Richard the Third.* He was absurdly miscast in this role, but under the prevailing system the part belonged to him. Occasionally, necessity forced a temporary departure from the system, and on these occasions Herne's remarkable memory, which enabled him to learn long parts on short notice, together with his natural acting ability, secured him a part outside his prescribed "line."

When the Civil War broke out, Herne was at the Gaiety in Albany. The theatre closed, and he thought seriously of enlisting. But just at this time, he received an offer from John T. Ford to join his stock company at the Holliday Street Theatre in Baltimore. Herne was faced with a difficult dilemma. Many of his friends had enlisted — even his father and his fourteen-year-old brother. The deep love of his native land that was to find expression later in such plays as *Griffith Davenport* was strong within him. But Ford was offering him a wonderful opportunity to progress in his life's work. Ford bore one of the finest reputations in the theatrical world. He engaged only the best actors; the most distinguished stars of the American stage were glad to play in his theatres. Of Herne it might almost be said, as Ellen Terry wrote of Henry Irving, "His work, his work! He has always held his life, and his death, second to his work." Herne chose his work. His father, Patrick, was killed in one of the early battles of the war, and the younger brother, after rising to the rank of captain, received wounds that made him a life-long invalid.

Herne found Baltimore seething with activity, the streets crowded with men in uniform, and business, including the theatrical business, booming. The audiences seemed warmer and more demonstrative than those in northern New York. In general, the people seemed more hospitable to actors. Herne was fascinated by their soft, slurred, leisurely speech, and also by the Negroes, who were quite different, both in speech and attitudes, from the Negroes of Mrs. Stowe. His quick ear readily caught the nuances of southern speech, both white and Negro, and the knowledge was stored away for possible later use.

The natural style of acting, for which Herne later became

famous, began to develop about this time. In that day of well-rounded eloquence and oratorical rhythm, Herne's developing naturalness was conspicuous enough to attract the attention of his fellow actors at Ford's. For the young actor who had originally taken Forrest as his ideal had been developing ideas of his own. He had an exceptionally sensitive ear, and he was keenly observant of gesture and facial expression. He had begun to study people of all classes in all kinds of situations — in taverns and hotel lobbies, on the street, at parties — listening acutely to catch their characteristic intonations of speech, the look on their faces as they spoke, the movements of their hands and bodies. On one occasion, Edwin Booth, as the visiting star, was struck with the way the young Herne read a certain line, and asked him where he had heard that reading. Herne admitted that he had never heard the line read in that way before; that it was his own reading, one which seemed to him to be the only right way to speak it. "Unusual — but very fine," Booth said.

During the next three years Herne advanced rapidly in the favor of the audiences and with Ford, who alternated him between his Baltimore and Washington theatres. When Ford's old Tenth Street Theatre in Washington was destroyed by fire, and he built a new one — the one where Fate was to lie in wait for Abraham Lincoln on the night of April 14, 1865 — it was Herne who was chosen to deliver the opening address, written by Thomas S. Donoho, of Washington, which began:

"As from the ashes Cinderella rose,
Rise we — all radiant from our night of woes."

Herne had become one of Ford's most promising young actors, but there was something about the young man's private life that seriously disturbed the manager. Ford, like many of the old time managers, was a highly respectable business man in his city — later he became mayor of Baltimore. His ideals were high, and his reputation unsullied. There were others like him in the theatre of the day — Field of Boston, accepted as an equal by the best of the Brahmins, and Rice and Beach of the same city. There was also J. H. McVicker of Chicago, who twice declined the office of mayor. Ford was a fatherly man who took a paternal interest in the welfare of his young actors. There was a tendency toward conviviality — and worse — that he had seen growing at an alarming rate in his young actor, along with his increasing ability in his profession, and he decided to speak to him about it.

Insensibly, the serious young student of his craft had been slipping into the free and easy life of the typical actor of his day. He had drifted into the way of life of a group of cronies who made the after-theatre suppers a carouse that lasted until the early hours of the morning. Herne, like a much greater actor, was "of an open, free, and generous nature," and he had the defects of those qualities. The ringleader of the group was John Wilkes Booth, handsome, magnetic, and erratic, and the others were Charles Bishop, Stuart Robson, Frank Mordaunt, and Charles Thorne — all talented, but all lacking the self-discipline that is prerequisite to greatness. Herne had been flattered by the friendship of Booth, the son of the great Junius Brutus, and not until later, when Booth had almost killed him in a violent outburst of temper, did their friendship wane.

Ford called Herne into his private office, and talked to him like a father. "If you will drop your present companions, and settle down and study, Jim," Ford said finally, "I'll guarantee to make you as big a star as Lester Wallack."

Herne was impressed. Lester Wallack was probably the most popular leading man on the American stage. Graceful, handsome, clever, he had won the applause of all in such plays as *The Three Musketeers,* in Sheridan's comedies, in contemporary comedies, in *The Winter's Tale,* in *As You Like It,* and in *Twelfth Night.* But Wallack was a genius — not only did the public say it but also great stars like Charlotte Cushman, Dion Boucicault, and Joseph Jefferson. And he belonged by right of birth to one of the royal families of the stage, one of the dynasties of English origin such as the Booths, the Drews, the Jeffersons. Jim Herne, with the excessive humility of the young, and too conscious of his lowly origins, felt that Ford was proposing the impossible. And "drop his present companions!" How could he drop his friends — the only friends he had? And "settle down and study!" As if he hadn't been studying — for years! With youthful folly, as he was to recognize later, he resented Ford's charge that he hadn't been studying. At that time he had no conception of the gruelling effort required to rise to the top of the ladder. He listened respectfully to Ford's words of wisdom — but he did not take his advice.[5]

2

THE WESTERN SISTERS AND
THE OLD MELODRAMA

Herne was not the handsome matinee idol type represented by Lester Wallack, and later in our theatre by John Drew, John Barrymore, and Nat Goodwin. Herne was the athletic type, rugged and masculine. Amy Leslie, the Louella Parsons of her day, wrote: "He stood straight as an arrow, brawny and spirited, with fine blue eyes and an odd, unruly crop of brown hair." He wore no jewelry except a seal ring, and he dressed conservatively, but his suits were tailor-made of the best woolens and his shoes made to order of fine quality leather. He loved all forms of outdoor exercise — swimming, tennis, bicycle and horseback riding. Although he could rarely get to bed before midnight he was usually up at dawn for a two-hour bicycle ride before breakfast. A photograph taken years later, when he was middle-aged, shows him standing in a small boat that has just reached the shore of his summer home on Long Island at Sayville. Herne is in his bathing suit, and he looks more like a prize-fighter than an actor. His chest is broad and deep, his arms and legs muscular, his waist trim. His features are regular, but he is not handsome and gives an impression of strength and masculinity.[6]

He was quiet, dignified, and gentlemanly in manner, rarely lost his temper, and in temperament resembled Joseph Jefferson more nearly than he did Edwin Forrest and James O'Neill. But that he could not escape entirely from the tempestuous environment in which he lived — that of the mid-nineteenth century American theatre — is revealed by the story of his association with the Western sisters — Lucille and Helen. Some of the most hectic years of their brief and flaming careers Herne was destined to share.

Their mother, the vivacious and pretty Jane Sharples, of an old and aristocratic Philadelphia Quaker family, had eloped with George Western, one of the best known comedians of his day, and her family had disowned her. With him she trouped across the country, sharing the hard life of the itinerant player. Lucille was born in New Orleans in 1840, and Helen two years later. Almost from babyhood the two girls were on the stage. Lucille was dancing and playing child parts at the National Theatre in Boston in 1849, and Helen appeared as Little Eva in *Uncle Tom's Cabin* at the Boston Mueum in 1852. As the girls entered their teens it was apparent that they would both be beautiful women. Both were tall, dark, and graceful, were clever soubrettes, could sing and dance well, and had obviously profited a great deal from the skillful coaching of their mother, a fine actress in her own right. When George Western died in 1857, the girls had already demonstrated their ability in such plays as *Charles the Second*.[7]

Soon after George Western's death, Jane Western married another actor, William B. English, who had considerable ability as an impressario and who saw in his two talented stepdaughters a potential gold mine. Shrewd and ambitious, he had noted the great attraction the girls had for the male portion of the audience in "breeches parts" and he decided to exploit their charms in a play especially adapted to his purpose. He bought a play called *The Three Fast Men, or The Female Robinson Crusoes,* and changed it to suit his purpose, which was primarily to exhibit the shapely legs of his stepdaughters both in and out of breeches. Beyond this, the play was principally distinguished for its dancing and singing numbers (the girls were good at both) and for its fund of broad low comedy. Their success in the play was phenomenal, and they played in it all over the country for several years. Other managers pirated the play, and English sued them in the courts, with an eye to the resulting publicity.

Jane English looked on, frightened at what had happened, but too timid to oppose her husband. She saw the girls feted and flattered, and constantly pursued by a crowd of gay young men. Too late, she saw that they had drifted away from her and that her protests about dissipation and dubious company were unavailing. She had allowed them to grow up in the theatre, almost without formal education. When they were little she had protected and counseled them; now they had eluded her and seemed wholly bent on a life of reckless pleasure.[8]

In appearance the two girls were similar — both were dark beauties. But Lucille had more intelligence, talent, and ambition than Helen. In manner and in character, Lucille was genial, generous, and openhearted, while Helen was secretive and designing. Lucille was ambitious to become a tragedienne, while Helen was destined to remain a soubrette. In St. Louis in 1859 Lucille met and married an actor, James A. Meade, who afterwards became her manager. In 1860 she tried the part of La Thisbe in Penn Smith's romantic tragedy *The Actress of Padua,* and failed, but the next year at the Holliday Street Theatre in Baltimore she had her first great success in a serious dramatic role, playing Cynthia in Buckstone's popular melodrama, *The Flowers of the Forest.* In the part of Cynthia, the noble-hearted gypsy girl who commits suicide rather than kill the man she loves, Lucille displayed unexpected qualities of fire and passion. Helen's acting during this engagement aroused little critical acclaim. In November she married a wealthy young Baltimore lawyer named Hoblitzell, and they went to live in Paris.

The "Star Sisters" never played together again; in fact, they later played against each other in similar plays at the same time in the same city. Helen had become increasingly envious of her more talented sister and tried to emulate her in everything. Lucille had married an actor, but Helen had shown her that she could outdo her by marrying a young man who was not only handsome but wealthy and socially prominent. Actually all Helen's attempts to emulate her sister turned out disastrously. The marriage with Hoblitzell was a failure. A year later, after she had given birth to an idiot girl baby, Hoblitzell deserted her in Paris. She went to England and persuaded a manager to star her in a popular melodrama, *The French Spy.* After a tour of the provinces, the play opened at Sadler's Wells on June 13, 1863, but English audiences were cold to her, and in October, probably with money received from Lucille, she set sail for Canada.

At the Holliday Street Theatre in Baltimore both girls had met Herne, who was a member of the stock company there. Lucille, though she was still married to Meade, fell in love with Herne, and he with her. With amazing rapidity, Lucille had developed into an emotional actress immensely popular with the public. In December, 1861, at the Holliday she was starred in *Camille.* Her emotional powers were astounding, and her fund of emotion apparently inexhaustible. Her Camille was not an elegant Parisenne, nor a *grande amoreuse,* nor a repentent Magdalen, nor an exquisite flower fading untimely, but a girl of the people, earthy, passionate, avid for life and love, who burned herself out in her love for Armand with a passion that was almost frightening in its frank fervor and unashamed ardor. She had little technique, little taste, no fastidiousness nor refinement, but the audiences — and Herne — were fascinated. Herne was in love with her, and she — in her way — very much in love with him. But James A. Meade, her husband, was very much in the picture, and he had no intention of retiring. It was Herne who withdrew. The principal reason for Herne's temporary withdrawal may have been his good Catholic upbringing and the deeply implanted sense of moral responsibility stemming from his youth. At any rate, we do know that there was a severe struggle with conscience and that for the moment conscience was victorious.

In October, 1862, Lucille opened at the Holliday in what was to prove one of her greatest popular successes — *East Lynne*. This masterwork of England's leading writer of the domestic sentimental school, Mrs. Henry Wood, had been a popular hit as a novel from the time of its publication in 1861. The dramatization by Clifford W. Tayleure, a young American journalist, was better than the book because the implausible motivation and the author's inferior style were not apparent in the play. The story was one to wring the heart of every woman.

Lucille was to present the play, for which she had paid Tayleure $100, over a thousand times, and always to crowded houses. The sophisticated New York critics might sneer, "profound ignorance of the art of acting, cheerful indifference to the laws of English grammar." (Odell v. 7, p. 479), but the American public loved her. The actors and actresses, and the managers likewise, did not agree with the fastidious critics. Harrison Grey Fiske, the husband and manager of the famous Minnie Maddern Fiske, called Lucille, "a wonderful child of genius, a powerful tornado, an irresistible magnetic force." While Lucille trouped across the country, winning fame and fortune in *East Lynne, Camille, Leah the Forsaken,* and *Lucrezia Borgia,* Herne remained, desolate and broken-hearted, with the stock company in Baltimore.

Then in the fall of 1864, Herne joined the stock company at the Walnut Street Theatre in Philadelphia, one of the oldest and most famous theatres in the country, then owned jointly by Edwin Booth and his brother-in-law, John Sleeper Clark. Here Herne played with such famous stars as the elder Sothern, John E. Owens, McKean Buchanan, E. L. Davenport, Matilda Heron, and the greatest of them all — Edwin Booth. And here one night, he actually played with Edwin Forrest, who twenty-five years ago had inspired his youthful dream. What had happened to that dream? The years had slipped by, and he was almost forty. As he watched the great Booth from the wings, or as he played Horatio to his Hamlet, he knew that he would never reach the heights. The great parts of Shakespeare were beyond his reach. He was experiencing the almost universal despondency of most men at middle age. Playing with these great men in the great plays seemed only to emphasize his own inadequacies, his own complete lack of genius.

Then Lucille appeared again, to open an engagement at the Walnut that was to last for three months. She was more beautiful than ever, and the terrible conflict in Herne's soul was renewed. She chose him to play opposite her, as Armand to her Camille, and as Count Henri de Beausoleil in *Satan In Paris*. On the night of January 20, 1865, there was a great benefit performance for E. L. Davenport with an all-star cast. The play was Joseph Jefferson's dramatization of *Oliver Twist,* with Davenport as Bill Sikes, Lucille as Nancy, and J. W. Wallack as Fagin. Lucille was a sensation as Nancy, and at the end of the performance Davenport added to the general acclaim by a graceful speech praising her performance. That night Lucille was accepted as an equal by one of the most famous actors of the American stage. Herne could no longer endure his torture, and at the end of the season he left for Montreal, where he joined the stock company of the Theatre Royal.

Meanwhile Helen had set out to emulate her famous sister on her own ground. Divorced from Hoblitzell, and leaving the idiot child with her mother, she had opened at the Bowery Theatre in New York in *The French Spy* on July 18, 1864. In the war boom, people were spending lavishly, and all the theatres were crowded. Helen had a moderate success, the secret of which was her astounding physical beauty, generously displayed. The next year — was it by chance or design? — she came to the Theatre Royal in Montreal, where she knew Herne was playing. Her opening play was *The Fate of a Coquette*. Three weeks later, Helen Western and James A. Herne were married in St. George's Church on St. Joseph Street.

Anthony Trollope, in his novel *The American Senator,* says: "There are for most of us moments of unhappiness, in which we are tempted by our misery to think that we are relieved, at any rate, from the burden of caution, because nothing that can occur to us can make us worse than we are . . . . But in a few months or weeks we have got a new footing amidst our troubles, and then we may find how terrible is the injury which our own indiscretion has brought on us." The motive of Helen in this amazing marriage is sufficiently clear — triumph over her sister. But what was Herne's? Was it the sheer recklessness of despair that Trollope describes? There is no way of answering the question, for in later life Herne never mentioned the name of Helen although he often spoke of Lucille's beauty and ability. A short time after he was married to Helen he learned that Lucille had divorced James A. Meade.

But, having taken the step, Herne seemed determined to make a success of the marriage. He became Helen's leading man in the melodramas that constituted her only possible repertoire, and he gave of the best that was in him in such plays as *The French Spy, A Devilish Good Joke, Satan In Paris, East Lynne, The Corsican Brothers,* and *Oliver Twist.* His playing of Bill Sikes was to attract widespread critical acclaim, and at this time he began to demonstrate the outstanding managerial capacity which was later to be much in demand. He and Helen came to New York and opened at the Academy of Music, in Brooklyn. Business was good in the great wave of post-war expansion in 1866, and Herne, who had always wanted a place that he could call home, bought a farm at Topsfield, Massachusetts.

But again and again Lucille crossed his path during the next three years. Exactly what happened we shall never know. We have only the bare facts that Helen and James Herne were divorced in 1868, that Herne left for California as Lucille's leading man, and that Helen died in December of that year of pneumonia. Amy Leslie thought she had died of a broken heart because she had lost Herne, but it is more likely that the real cause was her defeat in the great contest with her sister. It is difficult to place blame in a situation so confusing, but one fact is of considerable significance. In later years, old Mrs. English, the mother of the Western girls, had great affection for Herne, and her home was always open to him. He, in turn, treated her like a devoted son, and his children called her "grandma." In view of this fact, it seems unlikely that Herne could have been guilty of any wrong towards Helen.

Lucille Western and James A. Herne found the San Francisco of 1868 a theatrical paradise.[9] It was a large city, with a more or less permanent population approaching a hundred thousand, and its population was still largely men, with an abundance of money and eager for entertainment. It had more theatres, and finer theatres, than any city of its size in the West. It demanded the best and was willing to pay for it. Already, even though the Union Pacific was not completed, the city had attracted the best talent the country had to offer. The Booths, Matilda Heron, Laura Keene, John McCullough, Lawrence Barrett, James H. Hackett, Joseph Jefferson, Edwin Forrest, and others had all appeared in San Francisco before the completion of the railroad. Theatrical profits were extremely high — Adah Isaacs Menken accumulated $50,000 from her California engagement, according to Gagey, despite the lavish scale on which she lived.

At the close of a successful season in California, Herne, in the spring of 1869, was offered the post of manager of the Grand Opera House in New York by James Fisk. The salary offered by the notorious financier-owner was exceptionally large for those days — $10,000. Herne accepted immediately, and he and Lucille went back east. The Grand Opera House had cost a million dollars to build, and, now only a year old, it was the newest and finest theatre in the city. In June, Lucille opened there in her familiar repertoire for a successful engagement lasting a hundred nights. Herne, in addition to his duties as manager, appeared as her support in a distinguished company containing such actors as McKee Rankin and Charles Thorne. Odell calls this season "her apogee." Although E. L. Davenport had appeared at the Grand Opera House in a magnificently mounted production of *The Tempest,* the Lucille Western-Herne engagement was the first really profitable one in the new theatre.

Herne was at first attracted by the undeniably magnetic personality of his new employer. Fisk was, admittedly, dissolute and unscrupulous, but he had the fascination of all colorful geniuses, and this was Herne's first encounter with a financial wizard. Up to this time, Herne's world had been that of the theatre, and he had shown little interest in anything that lay outside. His reading had been largely confined to novels and plays, mostly Dickens, Scott, and Dumas. Social and economic problems had concerned him little, and he had manifested small interest in politics. The machinations of Jay Gould and Fisk, whereby they had manipulated the stock of the Erie Railroad and won millions for themselves but had wrecked the road in the process, disturbed him little, for he had not been among the ruined stockholders, and the consequences to the nation of uncontrolled capitalism made little impression on one whose interests were solely in the theatre.

But when thousands of persons were ruined on "Black Friday," September 24, 1869, by Gould and Fisk's corner of the market in gold, Herne became seriously concerned with problems of social justice. Later such problems were to occupy an important place in his thinking. He must have severed his connection with Fisk at the close of Lucille's summer engagement, since she and Herne played at Niblo's in October, and at the Park Theatre, Brooklyn, in November of 1869 in *Oliver Twist,* Herne playing the part of Bill Sikes.

In May, 1870, Herne returned to the Theatre Royal, Montreal, in the double capacity of manager of the theatre and leading man for Lucille. What must have been his feelings when he returned to the theatre where he had met and married Helen can only be imagined. Here, in addition to other plays, he performed in *Rip Van Winkle* for the first time. The next spring he and Lucille were in New York, in the familiar *East Lynne, Leah the Forsaken, Oliver Twist,* and *The Child Stealer.* But in the relations between Lucille and Herne the usual pattern of the theatre was about to be repeated. Why they were never married, we do not know. Amy Leslie said they were, and that in 1874 they quarreled violently, and that there was a divorce. But there is no record of either marriage or divorce. All we know with certainty is that they came to the parting of the ways about 1874, that Herne was supplanted in Lucille's affections by a young actor named Arthur Cambridge, that she soon married Cambridge, and he became her manager. Herne left by ship for California.

Scarcely three years later, on January 11, 1877, Lucille, a few days after her thirty-fourth birthday, died of pneumonia in her room at the Pierrepont House, watched over, mercifully, by her husband Arthur Cambridge. She had been playing Nancy Sikes the day before at the Park Theatre, although carrying a high fever. At five o'clock on that Thursday she awakened from a fitful sleep and asked Cambridge what time it was. When he told her, she said, "It's time to go to the theatre. Has the basket boy come yet?" In the old days of the theatre a boy called late every afternoon at the actor's hotel room, and carried the costumes to be worn that night to the theatre in a champagne basket. When Cambridge told her that an understudy was taking her part, she sank back in her pillow, murmuring, "Yes, I remember now." She grew suddenly worse, and at seven breathed her last in her husband's arms, whispering, "You have been kind and true. Goodbye." A few days later she was buried beside Helen in Mt. Auburn cemetery, near Boston. James A. Meade, her first husband, was one of the mourners at her funeral, and another mourner, though far away, was James A. Herne. All his life he was to remember her beauty, her generosity, her impulsive warm-heartedness, her talent, and her goodness. For four years after they had parted his heart lay empty, until in a little Irish girl, Katharine Corcoran, he at last found a love that endured.

3

LITTLE MISS CORCORAN

When Herne reached San Francisco in 1874 he became manager of Tom Maguire's New Theatre, and two years later of his Baldwin. Tom Maguire, known as the "Napoleon of Managers," had established a theatrical empire on the West Coast, and owned a chain of fine theatres. As early as 1851, he had built the magnificent Jenny Lind Theatre with a seating capacity of 2000. His rise had been meteoric. He had been a bartender in New York, and later the owner of a bar near City Hall. When he came to California in the golden year of 1849, he opened a hotel and gambling saloon called the Parker House. A year later he opened a theatre above the Parker House. He proved to be a shrewd and enterprising manager who brought to California the leading actors and actresses of the East. His tastes were catholic. In 1863, he presented the notorious Adah Isaacs Menken in *Mazeppa,* with its famous scene in which the curvesome form of Adah, encased in pink tights, was bound to the back of a horse. Later he offered minstrel shows, opera, and Shakespeare. Gagey says that he lost $20,000 on an Italian opera troupe and that he later presented the celebrated tragedienne, Adelaide Ristori, and the great Adelaide Neilson in *As You Like It, Cymbeline,* and *Romeo and Juliet.* Maguire's fall was as rapid as his rise. In 1882 he became bankrupt and left for New York, where during his declining years he was supported by the Actors' Fund.

In 1874, when Herne became Maguire's manager at the New Theatre, the great impressario, entrepreneur, and gambler was at the height of his career. Tall, well built, with luxuriant white hair and mustache and with a handsome florid face, Maguire was one of the best dressed men in the city. His manner was courtly, his speech soft and courteous. Kindly by nature, he had the generosity of the gambler, and Herne was not the first of his actors and managers to become his life-long friend.

It was at the New Theatre that Herne first tried his hand at playwriting. His beginning was humble, consisting of adaptations of Charles Lever's novel, *Charles O'Malley,* of *Oliver Twist,* and of one of the several versions of *Rip Van Winkle* that had appeared on the stage. Maguire was enthusiastic about Herne's adaptations and his performances in them. He later stated in *The Anaconda Standard* that Herne as Rip was "the greatest impersonator of the part," and added, "I have seen great performances of certain characters by great actors, but no such indelible impression on my memory was ever made by any other like that of Bill Sikes by James A. Herne." Maguire's stage manager at the New Theatre, David Belasco, was later to write of Herne's role in *Rip Van Winkle:* "I have seen three Rips — that of Jefferson, that of Robert McWade, and finally that of James A. Herne. This last was a wonderful characterization, with all the softness and pathos of the part. But Fate chose to thrust forward Jefferson as the only Rip that ever was or could be. I happen to know better. Jefferson was never the Dutchman; he was the Yankee impersonating the Dutchman. But James A. Herne's Rip was the real thing."

In San Francisco about this time, Herne met the remarkable woman who later became his wife, Katharine Corcoran.

Katharine Corcoran was born in Ballyleeks, County Cork, Ireland, on December 8, 1856, the first child of Michael and Mary Nolan Corcoran. When the baby was two weeks old, Mary made an offering of the child to the Virgin Mary, and as soon as little Katharine was old enough to understand, impressed upon her that she was under the special protection of the Holy Mother. Michael was a school teacher, and Mary had a good convent education in Dublin. Their first child resembled her father. Later there were three other children, Edward, Elizabeth, and Mollie.[10]

In 1860, the family emigrated to the United States, settling in New York City. When the Civil War broke out the next year, Michael volunteered. He served through several campaigns, was wounded and honorably discharged in 1863, but reenlisted, was captured by the enemy and sent to Libby Prison. Eventually he managed to escape, but the prison privations had wrecked his health, and he died in a Washington military hospital a few months before the close of the war.

Mary Corcoran was left with three small children, with no money, with no relatives in New York; and having always depended upon Michael for guidance and support, she was confused and frightened. Finally, there came a day when there was no food in the house and the children were crying with hunger. Mary did not know what to do. It was little Katharine, eight years old, who took over, ran to a boarding house across the street, burst into the dining room where the boarders were just sitting down to their Sunday dinner, and exclaimed in her clear, childish voice, "We're hungry and we have nothing to eat! Please give us some food." The response of her audience was immediate. She carried home a basket loaded with food. But the effect of little Katharine's act was disastrous. Someone notified the authorities, and the children were sent to an orphanage. Little Katharine was never to forget the horror of that day on which she was separated from her mother. And it shocked Mary into action. She determined to find work, since she had been promised by the authorities that the children would be returned to her as soon as she could show that she could support them. She had had a good education, but in her fear and desperation, she took the first work she could find, forewoman in a hoopskirt factory. The hours were long and the pay small, but it enabled her to reclaim her children.

The poverty of the little family was pitiful. In the next few years the children were often out of school because of lack of decent clothing, and Mary tried to teach them herself in the evening. Katharine tried to take care of the other children, but she and the others were often out on the streets trying to make money.[11] They sold newspapers and shoveled snow. They sold flowers in front of the Hoffman House and the Fifth Avenue Hotel. Inevitably, in this hard school they became wise beyond their years in the ways of the world. Little Katharine soon became adept at judging human nature from external appearance and could tell at a glance which man would give her more than her button-hole bouquet was worth. At noon they would seek out Pursell's Bakery, always crowded with women shoppers having lunch. Here it was often possible, because of the crowd, to slip from counter to counter, and snatch a bun here and a cake there. Sometimes in the evening they would proudly hand to their care-worn mother as much as a whole dollar.

Katharine soon became an avid reader. She could never pass a bookstore without gazing hungrily through the windows at the books displayed there. She would read the open pages until she knew them by heart, and would come back the next day hoping that by some miracle the proprietor had turned a page overnight. Somehow Mary managed to get copies of the novels of Scott, Dickens, and Thackeray and the poems of Byron, Shelley, and Tennyson, and Katharine surprised her mother by her facility in learning poems by heart.

Katharine was an adventuresome little girl. One day, with a favorite novel clutched in her hands, she boarded a horse car and rode far uptown to a lonely wooded spot near Harlem. There, high up on the cliffs was an old stone fort dating back to Revolutionary times. She climbed up to the ramparts, and spent the day there reading her book.

But, even better than reading, she loved the theatre. She became adept at stealing past the gallery doorman, and by the time she was fifteen, she had seen, from the heights of the gallery, Booth and Barrett, Jefferson and Wallack, Maggie Mitchell and Lotta Crabtree, and Lucille Western. Lucille Western became Katharine's ideal actress in her teens, and she hated the handsome villain, Mr. Herne, who was so cruel to the lovely Miss Western and always made her cry.

Suddenly, when Katharine was sixteen, the fortunes of the family took a turn for the better. An uncle, who had emigrated to America, and formed political connections in New York, obtained a soldier's widow's pension for Mary, together with a substantial amount of back pay. Deciding to go to California, he took his sister's family with him. They settled in San Francisco in a small comfortable house with a garden and were to know no more poverty. A photograph of Katharine taken at this time shows a slender graceful girl of seventeen, with large dark eyes and a sensitive face, her delicate features surrounded by a wealth of dark hair.

Katharine was now able to indulge her fondness for the theatre, and she took full advantage of the exceptional variety and quality of theatrical entertainment in the city. It was boom-time in San Francisco, and two large new theatres, the last word in red-plush magnificence, had just opened their doors — Wade's Opera House at Mission and Third, and Baldwin's on Market near Powell. Barry Sullivan, the Irish tragedian, opened the new Baldwin with *Richard III,* and another Irishman, the handsome and romantic James O'Neill, soon starred there. And James A. Herne, another Irishman, was starring in *Rip Van Winkle.* It was a great day for the Irish in the San Francisco theatre. Katharine had a school girl crush on James O'Neill, but she remained cold to James A. Herne, remembering his stage cruelty to Lucille Western.

With teen-age impulsiveness Katharine plunged into various of the arts — languages, music, and painting — each undertaken with all the enthusiasm of youth, and each dropped in disgust a few months later. Finally, she decided she wanted to be an actress. She enrolled as a pupil of Mrs. Julia Melville, mother of the then famous Emilie Melville who was a shining light on the American stage for over 60 years. Mrs. Melville, who had made such a success of her daughter, saw promising material in Katharine Corcoran. True, she did not have the gorgeous beauty of Emilie, but she had a lovely voice, her enunciation was clear and distinct, she had a quick mind, and she had charm. Mrs. Melville set to work with enthusiasm.

Mrs. Melville's own training had been rigorous and thorough, and in the classic tradition of the old school. She was a merciless perfectionist, and she had the unflagging energy and drive of a drill sergeant. She began with the fundamentals — standing, sitting, walking. Then came lessons in dancing — and fencing! Voice followed, diction and enunciation, and how to manage the voice through all the graduations of human emotion. Then she put her promising pupil through the entire repertory of classic drama, from Juliet to Lady Teazle. She soon discovered that she had an apt, interested, and enthusiastic student, for Katharine, somewhat to her own astonishment, had also made a discovery, and knew that she had found her career. This was not work. It was interesting and exciting — it was fun!

At the end of two years, Julia Melville gazed upon her masterpiece with satisfaction, and felt that it was finished. She went to her old friend, James A. Herne, manager of the Baldwin, and asked if he would give Miss Corcoran a hearing. Fresh in Julia Melville's memory was Herne's casting of little Katie Mayhew as Ophelia to the Hamlet of Barry Sullivan over the protests of the management and the leading lady, and the big hit the young and inexperienced Miss Mayhew had made in a part usually assigned to more mature actresses. She knew that Herne was a good judge of talent, that he was open-minded and free from the usual cynicism of managers about amateurs. Herne hesitated when he learned that Miss Corcoran had never actually appeared on the stage, but he respected Julia Melville's judgment, and consented.

Mrs. Melville had a shrewd knowledge of human psychology, so she did not tell her protege that a stage manager would be watching her that morning at the Baldwin after the regular rehearsal was over. She merely told Katharine that she wanted her to go through a scene at the Baldwin to find out how her voice would carry in a theatre.

The scene Mrs. Melville had selected was the one in Sheridan Knowles' *The Love Chase* in which Constance, the heroine, describes an exciting hunt. The choice of that scene, which was considered at the time a test of the powers of any actress, and one which even the great stars considered a challenge, was proof of Mrs. Melville's complete confidence in her pupil.

In the darkened and apparently deserted theatre, Mrs. Melville seated herself in a chair at one side of the empty stage. She knew, but Katharine did not, that Herne was standing at the prompt entrance, concealed by the proscenium arch. Katharine sailed into the scene with the assurance of the born actress, achieving the effect of spontaneity and naturalness which comes only as a result of native ability backed by thorough training and study. Shortly before she finished, Herne strolled quietly away, leaving Mrs. Melville in an agony of apprehension.

She soon learned, however, for a few days later Herne called at Katharine's home and offered her the part of Peg Woffington in a benefit performance of *Masks and Faces* which was to take place ten days later.[12] It was to be a benefit for Herne himself, and his asking her, a girl who had never appeared in a play, to take the part of the heroine in Reade's famous drama, a part made famous by Mrs. Scott-Siddons, by Matilda Heron, and by Laura Keene, took her breath away. The most she had hoped for at the beginning was some small part. But she dared not protest — the opportunity was too dazzling. In her excitement, she did not notice Herne's intense and serious gaze, and she did not realize that he had fallen in love with her.

The news that Jim Herne was starring a novice, who had never spoken a line on the stage, in the part of Peg Woffington soon spread around the theatre. Only one inference could be drawn, and Herne was the butt of the usual guying. But at the first rehearsal the novice astonished the company by being letter-perfect in her lines, by never fumbling an entrance or a cue, and by her general poise and authority. She was not a great beauty, but she had a voice that was exquisitely sweet, and she had intelligence and charm. Whether or not Jim was in love with her, he had, they all agreed, made a dramatic discovery, and they welcomed her into their ranks. Herne himself was as much astonished as is possible for one in his condition. He told his children years afterwards that he had never before seen a beginner who took to the stage so quickly, who possessed so much instinctive sense of the right thing to do and the right time to do it.

On the night of her debut, although Herne was playing the popular role of the poor young artist James Triplet, and although he was well liked in San Francisco, it was Katharine who received the most applause. Public, critics, and fellow players were impressed by her poise and grace, her dramatic instinct and ability, her power of emotional expression, and her melodious voice. She appeared to be completely without self-consciousness, and her emotional maturity seemed amazing to those who did not know that they were seeing a young girl who had fought for her existence on the streets of New York, who had known want, sorrow, and death at an age when most children are listening to fairy tales.

Shortly after the performance of *Masks and Faces,* Herne went on a tour of the Coast cities with Katharine as his leading lady, their repertory consisting of those plays in which he had been successful, *David Copperfield, Dombey and Son,* and *Oliver Twist.* At the start of the tour, on the steamer going to Portland, Herne asked Katharine to marry him. She refused, saying that she was interested only in her career, but Herne was not discouraged. On their return to San Francisco, Herne became seriously ill. It was the first time in his life that he had ever had a serious illness, and it was to be the last until the fatal illness of his old age. His sickness affected Katharine deeply. She became more and more devoted to him as she thought she was about to lose him. Then one day standing by his bedside as he was convalescing, she promised to marry him. It was April, 1878, when they were married.

It was a marriage that was to endure through many trials and crises and one that was to be singularly happy. Herne was to write all the leading feminine parts in his plays for his wife, and she was to create all but two of them. For some years they trouped across the country together, and later, when the children came and they had established a home, first at Boston, and then in New York, Herne, out on the road, would write to Katharine and the children every night after the performance.[13] Whatever his problems, whether personal or professional, they were discussed with Katharine, and she in turn brought hers to him. There were no closed doors between them, and their marriage was a working partnership all their lives.

One of the best pictures we have of Herne in his home comes

from the pen of his daughter Chrystal, in her unpublished autobiography: "How I loved him — so gentle, so patient and so much fun. He was our beloved playmate, sharing with us his rare sense of fun, his joy in life and sunshine. He loved assuming different characters for our amusement. He would be a Frenchman, swearing with fine fire in perfect French, a German with deep gutturals and Prussian pomposity, a Cockney with crafty wit, or a Scotchman, canny and dour. But of this cast of characters our dearest delight was the Little Old Man in the Cellar. We would be clinging round my father in the precious moments before bedtime. Suddenly from the depths would come the voice of the Little Old Man. He was salty and humorous, but very stiff with us—we must mend our ways and be good little girls. We would shiver in exquisite terror, half believing this alien presence in the dark cellar. We were completely baffled, for my father was an expert ventriloquist. . . . My father rarely punished us. . . . When I was particularly bad, my father would take me into his study and talk to me, and with such gentleness and understanding point out my faults, that I would shrivel up with shame and remorse and vow to be a better child. Once my exasperated mother told him that I was really an impossibly bad little girl. We went once more to his study; his eyes had a hurt look, for he loved me very much. He picked up a new photograph of me that stood on his desk; his fingers caressed my pictured face and he said softly: 'A little girl with those wide-set honest eyes, that delicate pointed chin, can never be really bad — you must try to live up to them and not make your mother so much trouble.' His voice twisted my heart, and I like to think that I was a better child from then on."

4

HEARTS OF OAK

David Belasco was stage manager of Maguire's New Theatre in San Francisco when Herne took over the job of manager on his arrival in California in November, 1874. Belasco was only twenty, but he had already had extensive theatrical experience. The son of English Jewish parents who kept a fruit store in San Francisco, young David had early manifested an ardent theatrical interest and had been a circus performer, a tavern entertainer, and a strolling player in the small companies that toured the mining camps. Now he was a fledgling playwright and stage manager at Maguire's. His father, who had been a harlequin on the English stage, was not an especially good business man, and David had overcome almost incredible obstacles in making his way upward in his chosen vocation. But his motto was: "I have often been beaten — but I never give in." Blessed with a superabundant vitality, a tremendous capacity for work, a keen mind, and a passionate ambition to excel, he was inevitably destined for success. At twenty he was slender and handsome, with a shock of coal black hair and sensitive brown eyes. He had a mobile and expressive face, and his mercurial emotions found an uninhibited outlet in his countenance and in his quick gestures.[14]

At Maguire's, Belasco was a kind of general factotum; in addition to his duties as stage manager, he acted small parts, served as Maguire's secretary (Maguire's education had been so limited that he could scarcely write his name), reworked old plays, and adapted popular novels for the stage. As hack playwright he was extremely adept. He had met Dion Boucicault at Piper's Opera House in Virginia City, Nevada, in the winter of 1873, and he had studied the methods of that prolific genius. He had made prompt books of every successful play produced in California, and his retentive memory was teeming with plots and situations that had proved effective on the stage. He worked with amazing rapidity and could work up an actable play in less than a week. He had an innate dramatic sense, and he was highly inventive, constantly thinking up new and sensational effects. His great ability, then and later, lay in the creation of stage effects that had a tremendous emotional impact upon audiences.

Herne early encountered an instance of his young stage manager's flair for the theatrical. When the company presented Herne's version of *Oliver Twist,* Belasco was cast as Fagin. On the opening night, Belasco told Herne that he had thought up a new effect in the prison scene in which Fagin goes mad. Herne was already aware of the vast amount of effort the young Belasco expended in creating his parts, even visiting the lunatic asylum in order to study madness at first hand. But he was unprepared for what he saw when, standing in the prompt entrance, he beheld Fagin, at the climax of his ravings, tear great bunches of red hair out of his scalp. Herne, along with the audience, gasped with horror. Belasco had had a special wig made, with the hair only lightly fastened, and the fact that it had to be remade after each performance was no deterrent to this indefatigable craftsman. This was Herne's first introduction to the Belasco who was never to spare any expense or trouble to create an impressive stage effect, who was later to secure strange and marvellous effects with stage lighting by such expedients as putting tin pans and colored silks before locomotive headlights, and who was to produce a battle scene which *The San Francisco Bulletin* was to call "the most realistic ever produced on the stage."

When Herne became stage manager of Maguire's new Baldwin Theatre in 1876, Belasco became the assistant stage manager, and the two manager-actor-playwrights became more closely associated than before.[15] The company at the Baldwin was one of the last of the great stock companies, and it contained such famous players as James O'Neill, Rose Coghlan, Lewis Morrison, F. F. Mackey, and Little Maude Adams; and to both Herne and Belasco the opportunity it presented for the playwright seemed a golden one. Each had produced a number of dramatizations of popular novels, but they did not undertake a major collaboration until in 1879 they worked together on a dramatization of Gaboriau's *La Corde Au Cou,* which they called *Within An Inch of His Life.* The plot was complex and filled with the stock devices of melodrama. The hero was saved from the guillotine at the last moment by the confession of an idiot boy, and a chateau burned down in full view of the audience. But despite the best efforts of Belasco on the stage effects, the play failed to draw. Their next effort was another heavily plotted piece, an adaptation of a melodrama by Watts-Phillips called *Camilla's Husband.* The Belasco-Herne version was called *Marriage by Moonlight.* It related the sad story of a beautiful girl who, to save her fortune and the ancestral estate, is being forced into marriage with a cousin whom she hates. To escape this fate, she weds a wandering artist; the ceremony takes place in a moonlit garden, and the bride and groom part immediately without having seen each other's faces. When they meet some years later the artist has become famous, and they fall in love. After a series of contretemps and misunderstandings the two are finally reunited. This fabrication, like the previous play, lacked plausible and sympathetic characters, a defect which seems not to have been apparent to Belasco at the time, though it was to the audiences.

Belasco was never to lose faith in the potency of melodrama to fill a theatre; in fact, the great successes of his later career were nearly all melodramas — *The Girl I Left Behind Me, Rose of the Rancho, Under Two Flags, The Darling of the Gods, Zaza, Andrea, DuBarry,* and *The Heart of Maryland.* But before he achieved this later success he learned a vital lesson — that action is meaningful and suspenseful only when it happens to believable and interesting people. Herne had not been satisfied with either play, though Katharine, who had played in both, thought highly enough of *Marriage by Moonlight* to take the script to New York to try to interest Lester Wallack in it. She returned defeated, however, for Wallack rejected it politely but firmly.

Belasco was with the Hernes a great deal at this time. He usually had supper with them after the performance and would walk home with them; then the three would often talk until the small hours of the morning. Herne liked the younger man as a person, and had a good deal of respect for his energy, ability, and industry; but Herne, in his slowly growing disillusionment with melodrama, had already moved on ahead of him. Thus, even at the time they had agreed to collaborate, there was a fundamental disagreement between them. Herne, although he was scarcely aware of the fact at the time, had absorbed some of the atmosphere of the new movement, realism, which had already gained a foothold in the American novel.

There is no record that in 1880 Herne had ever read Howells or James, or that he had read any of the novels of Balzac or Flaubert, the great initiators of the new movement in Europe, though later both he and Katharine were to read most of the novels of these great realists. He was unaware, as were most

Americans in 1880, that the first American novel embodying the principles of the new movement, J. W. DeForest's *Miss Ravenel's Conversion from Secession to Loyalty,* had been published in 1867. Howells, as the editor of the influential *Atlantic Monthly,* had been an active champion of realism for the past ten years and had already exemplified it in a few novels, although the first one in which he was to have the courage to embrace more or less fully the principles of the new movement (*A Modern Instance*) was not to appear until 1881. And by 1880, Henry James had published *Roderick Hudson, The American, The Europeans,* and the sensational *Daisy Miller.* Likewise, in the field of the short story, the American local color movement, started perhaps by Bret Harte with his *The Luck of Roaring Camp* in 1869, was in full swing by 1880. Although there was a large element of the melodramatic and the sentimental in the works of the local colorists, there was nonetheless a marked tendency towards authenticity of setting, speech, and character portrayal. In short, the new climate of realism was setting in, with its emphasis on character rather than plot, its ideals of objectivity and truth, and its serious concern with social conditions and with the problems of contemporary life, although as yet there was little evidence that it had invaded the American theatre.

All through the decade between 1870 and 1880, the new movement had been slowly creeping into the popular fiction read by the general American public. The popular novels of Edward Eggleston are an example. His *Hoosier Schoolmaster,* published in 1871, was almost as melodramatic in plot as the general run of the popular novels of the time, but it did have an authenticity of setting and contemporary American dialect that set it apart from the works of the domestic sentimentalists, such as *St. Elmo,* which had preceded it. Eight years later, Eggleston's *Roxy* showed an appreciable advance in realism, adding to authentic speech and setting a more serious interest in the psychology of individual character. Yet as firmly fixed in Eggleston's mind as in that of any novelist of the previous age was the concept of a plot as a complicated fabrication of melodramatic incident, and so the plots in these two novels were both alike with respect to this basic assumption. In brief, in the popular novel there had been some advance in realism during the decade, but this advance had not yet affected plot. As far as plot was concerned, the popular novelist had not changed since Cooper, however much he might reflect the influence of the new literary climate in other respects.

Another instance is Mark Twain. Probably one of the principal reasons for the enormous popular success of *Tom Sawyer* in 1876 was the story's highly melodramatic plot, the single element in the story that today we regard as a major flaw. In 1884 appeared Twain's great masterpiece, *Huckleberry Finn,* with its inimitable realism of setting, its characters who leave the printed page and live forever in the imagination. But the plot was essentially the old romantic flight-pursuit pattern of Cooper, whom Twain, ironically, so much derided. Whether the book would have attained its immediate popular success without its conformation to the taste of the public with respect to plot is doubtful. Howells at this time was widely condemned by the American critics for his plotless stories, and his novels were not popular with the general public because "nothing happened" in them.

It was inevitable that the drama, as the art form most directly dependent upon immediate popular acceptance for its success, should reflect the influence of new literary movements more slowly than the novel. Even in the novel, the new realism made its way slowly — a period of twenty years had elapsed between *Madame Bovary* and *Daisy Miller.* And then the public had not accepted James's story, and the newspaper critics had condemned it. If Herne, in 1880, had moved beyond Belasco and the old melodrama, as we have said, yet it must be kept in mind that he was a practicing playwright with his finger held quite close to the pulse of public sentiment. In 1880 the new realism had scarcely touched the American drama. In all his life Herne had seen no play by a contemporary which did not have a complex, melodramatic, or sentimental plot. That a drama must have such a plot was a convention that one accepted if he were an American playwright in the year 1880. Steele Mackaye, a contemporary American dramatist who, like Herne, had long been an advocate of realism in acting, and an opponent of the cruder and grosser devices of the old melodrama, wrote in 1880 what was to prove his most famous play, *Hazel Kirke,* which ran for years to crowded houses. Dr. Arthur H. Quinn, historian of our American drama, tells us in his preface in *Representative American Plays* that Hazel Kirke, "represents the transition from the older theatrical tradition to the newer realism," and remarks upon the naturalness with which the incidents develop and the absence of the stage villain. Yet the plot seems to us today so melodramatic that a modern audience could accept it only as pure farce.

When *Marriage By Moonlight* failed, the prolific Belasco had the rough draft of another play ready. He had titled it *Chums,* and it was based on an English melodrama, *The Mariner's Compass.* Belasco did not inform Herne of this bit of literary piracy, probably thinking it unnecessary, since the practice was so common. Herne thought the play had possibilities and rewrote it entirely, aiming for greater naturalness of character and dialogue in the individual scenes.[16] He did not substantially alter the original melodramatic plot, except with respect to the ending, a change which Quinn notes in his comparison of the two plays in his *History of the American Drama.* In the original, the ending was violent melodrama: The old man whom the heroine had married out of a sense of duty returns unexpectedly after an absence of years and finds his wife married to the young man she had been in love with. A highly emotional scene ends with the heroine's attempted suicide in the mill race and her rescue by her young husband, who drowns. At the dropping of the curtain the old man is holding his wife in his arms. Herne eliminated the melodramatic rescue from drowning, the death of the young husband, and, in a scene much closer to the original Enoch Arden inspiration for the play, had the old man quietly but pathetically refuse to stop the wedding of the heroine and her young lover, which is taking place in the church that forms the backdrop for the scene. Quinn also notes other changes which Herne made in the original, such as his substitution of a scene of quiet dialogue for the one in which the heroine dramatically flings her wedding ring into the sea.

Substantially, however, Herne used the old plot, including the shipwreck in Act I. What principally sets the play apart from the average melodrama of the time is the pains Herne took to establish character. In an almost leisurely manner, seemingly indifferent to the demand of the plot for action, and at the apparent risk of boring his audience with a static scene, he painted his characters in scenes of quiet dialogue. His characters are not complex, but they are rounded, human, and convincing, and their speech is natural. One cannot read this old play today without being impressed by the way it crudely and tentatively, yet unmistakably, illustrates Herne's growing conviction that audiences are more interested in people than in

Hearts of Oak

action for itself. This was the lesson that Herne taught Belasco. The grand old master of melodrama never forgot it, for even the most breath-taking productions of his later years had believable characters. But Herne also learned something from Belasco during this brief period of collaboration — the importance of realistic setting and stage effects. The old play shows abundant evidence of Belasco's hand in the multiplicity of stage directions for the shipwreck scene, the mill scene with a real mill wheel and real running water, the winter scene with snow landscape backing both windows, snow falling heavily, and a real log fire in the fireplace. The later plays of both men were noted for such effects, and it may be assumed that Herne, who later carried realistic stage effects to the extreme of having a real roast turkey in a dinner scene, was influenced by Belasco in this respect.[17]

Chums, which was later re-named *Hearts of Oak,* was the first really successful play of the two partners, and it was likewise the cause of the permanent break between them. At first, it seemed as if they had another failure on their hands. It opened at the Baldwin on September 9, 1879, with Herne as Terry Dennison, Katharine Herne as Chrystal, and little Maude Adams as the child, but it lasted only two weeks. Both partners were discouraged, but Katharine, believing that a play about the New England sea coast might be more successful in the East, urged that they try it there. The partners got together a few thousand dollars, engaged a company, and, making Katharine treasurer, set out for the East. Their first destination was Chicago, but they stopped at Salt Lake City for four performances, which netted $1800.

In Chicago they soon discovered that neither of the two big managers, Healey and McVicker, was interested in the play. The only manager they could interest was John A. Hamlin, the proprietor of an old and dirty variety theatre. The two partners agreed to clean and renovate the theatre, to replace the broken gas globes, and to share the net profits with Hamlin. The place was cleaned and painted, and as a final touch Belasco had the whole interior perfumed. He also decorated the lobby with potted plants. His flair for advertising and promotion resulted in a crowded house on the opening night, November 17, 1879. The play was a pronounced success, and Herne was to play it steadily all over the country for seven years, and later to revive it, always with success.[18]

What happened, once the play set out on tour, is a curious page from the history of the American theatre. Someone discovered the indebtedness of the play to *The Mariner's Compass,* which had been performed in New York in 1865 and for one matinee in 1872 with indifferent success. John A. Hamlin, after the Herne-Belasco company had left his theatre and were on tour, got hold of a copy of *The Mariner's Compass,* and assembling a company of actors put on the play under the title *Hearts of Oak.* Herne and Belasco filed suit and won the right to the exclusive use of the title *Hearts of Oak.* Then a manager named Lingard began touring through the midwest during the season of 1879-80 in a play called *Oaken Hearts,* a composite of *The Mariner's Compass* and *Hearts of Oak.* Herne and Belasco brought suit against Lingard, and secured a decision which prevented Lingard from using any of the material from *Hearts of Oak.* That Herne's play impressed his contemporaries as being superior to *The Mariner's Compass* is evidenced by the comment of the dramatic critic of the St. Louis Republican on January 8, 1881. Having seen both plays, he wrote: "Herne took *'The Mariner's Compass'* which had been played, printed and shelved as a failure and made *'Hearts of Oak'* out of it. He not only remodeled the play the better to suit stage purposes, but he cut, revised, transposed and rewrote the old scenes and wrote in new ones. By this work of adaptation and authorship he made a valuable play out of the materials and suggestions of *'The Mariner's Compass,'* which was worthless as a dramatic attraction in its original form, and he clearly deserves the benefits that may accrue from it. The Dickie Lingard company of last season were enjoined from using any of Herne's work, and hence the heaviness and flatness and failure of that performance, which would not have taken in so many people as it did if the title, 'The Mariner's Compass' had been used instead of 'Oaken Hearts'. This explanation is given in justice to Mr. Herne and the genuine 'Hearts of Oak.' "

Exactly who was to blame for the quarrel which now separated the two partners in a successful enterprise is impossible to determine. The final break came in Philadelphia, when Belasco sold his rights in the play to Herne. But further difficulties arose over rights in the play, and Belasco sued Herne and Herne then sued Belasco. The cases were finally settled with Herne in undisputed possession of the play.

With the passage of time, and after both partners had attained fame and fortune, the two became friends again. Whenever Herne produced a new play in New York Belasco would visit him backstage and be enthusiastic in his praise. Herne himself was a man who, although quick-tempered, could never hold a grudge for any length of time. In later years he always laughed about the old trouble and was quick to give his own sincerely admiring estimate of the younger man's outstanding ability as a producer and stage director.

Both recognized in their later years that a break would have been inevitable, sooner or later, because the two men represented two irreconcilable points of view. Belasco was a romanticist who believed in the exotic, the bizarre, the sensational, the unusual; Herne was a realist who believed in painting life as it actually is. Belasco was to continue to collaborate with others all his life, but his later collaborators were all men who shared his beliefs. His view of the theatre was that of his biographer, William Winter, as stated in his *Life of David Belasco,* "The home of that magic art which cheers the loneliness of life and opens the portal into an ideal world." This was, and still largely is, the view of the great masses of the public; those who view the drama as a serious criticism of life will always be in the minority. The road Herne had to follow was the loneliner and more difficult one, as later events were to show.

Belasco's admiring biographer, William Winter, the acknowledged dean of the New York dramatic critics at the time and a thorough-going romanticist, was conspicuously unfair in his criticism of Herne, apparently for no other reason than that Herne represented the new realism, which Winter detested. Winter's bias in favor of romanticism was such that he could write of Belasco's inferior melodrama, *The Girl I Left Behind Me,* that it was among "the best plays that have been contributed to American dramatic literature. Its superiority to all the problematic, polemic, didactic, sociological disquisitions pretending to be plays which of late years so cluttered our stage is very great." (*Life of David Belasco* I, 406).

Winter was one of the leading members of a closely-knit group of writers and critics who had determined to stem the rising tide of realism by every means in their power. The other leading members of the group were Richard Henry Stoddard, Bayard Taylor, George H. Baker, Richard Watson Gilder, and Thomas Buchanan Read. Because of their close association with the leading newspapers and magazines of the day, and the fact that they represented the bias towards romanticism of the public of the time, they exercised considerable influence, especially in New York. These "defenders of ideality" had the additional advantage of being very closely connected, thus always presenting a united front. Willard Thorp says of them in *The Literary History of the United States* (II, 809): "They reviewed one another, dedicated books to one another, and cajoled editors to help along their common cause. Surrounding them were a dozen writers, obedient to the same canons of criticism and allied to them through friendship."

Faced with this alliance, Herne and his *Hearts of Oak* did not have a chance in New York.[19] The play opened there at the Fifth Avenue Theatre on March 29, 1880, and lasted just two weeks, having received a very poor press. Not until many years later, with his *Shore Acres,* was Herne to achieve a New York success.

But Belasco, who had exactly gauged the taste of the critics and public of the time, scored a big popular success with his sensational melodrama, *La Belle Russe,* at Wallack's in 1882, and with William Winter and his cohorts solidly behind him, advanced victoriously to still more spectacular successes.

Hearts of Oak might well be described as a typical example of the local color school: it was a mixture of romanticism and realism, with the former predominating. The public — outside New York — loved it.[20]

5

BOSTON

The Hernes ended their first season of *Hearts of Oak* in Boston. Boston liked the play, and Herne was charmed with Boston — so much so that he decided to make his home there. Katharine was expecting a child, and on October 31, 1880, the Hernes' first child, a girl, was born in the Adams House in Boston. She was named Julie Adrienne. From the time Katharine's baby was born, the theatre assumed a place of lesser importance in her life.[21]

A visitor to the Herne home at 3 Beale Street, in Ashmont, a suburb of Boston, during any summer in the early eighties would have found a square white house set back among the maples and evergreens, not greatly different from the other houses on the middle class street. Behind the house was an orchard, a vegetable garden, and a strawberry bed, and here Herne would be found working with hoe and rake in the afternoon. Unlike most actors, he was always an early riser. In the summers he was up at daybreak, and even on the road, no matter how late the performance the night before, he was up early for a spin on his bicycle. At Ashmont, in the summer, after an excellent breakfast which Katharine had cooked, Herne would cross the hall to his study, whose windows overlooked the rose garden. Much of his time in the study was spent in mapping out his route for the coming season, and this necessitated the writing of many letters to the owners and managers of the various theatres across the country. He did not have to use a railroad map, for he was familiar with every "jump" in the country. Selecting and engaging a company presented no difficulties, since he kept practically the same cast during all the years he toured with *Hearts of Oak*. The advertising — largely lithographs and posters — was done by a Welsh lithographer in Cincinnati, Thomas Morgan. He did all Herne's work of this kind. Herne was a methodical worker and, after finishing his chores as business manager, usually found time to work on a new play before the noon meal. He was always working on a new play, and during his ten years at Ashmont he wrote six.

These ten years were undoubtedly the happiest of his life. His family was increased by the birth of two other children, Chrystal and Dorothy. Katharine was a devoted mother and a fine wife, completely unselfish, whose every thought was for the happiness of her husband and children. When he was on tour during the winter months she missed him terribly and wrote him daily about the children, the home, and her reading. There is space for only a few extracts from her letters, but these are typical: "We will read the book all over again some winter night by the roaring fire in your room. How I look forward to those promised times when we shall be together, *never, never,* to be parted again. Will it ever be?" "I wish you were home, our life would be fuller, better. I can only wait and hope, and so I begin this New Year with much hope that it will soon see us together. God bless you my Jim and keep you well and happy until I see you." When Herne had a minor illness on the road, from which he soon recovered, she wrote: "Dear Heart, A great weight has been taken from my mind now that you are yourself once more, yet I cannot help marveling at the good fortune that you have had in your recovery. . . . Good night, God bless you and make you happy. Love and kisses from all." And again she wrote: "All I want now to make me perfectly happy is My Gardener. I have been thinking and dreaming of you all day, darling. Oh dear, those two long weeks more! Will they ever pass? I'm getting so impatient to see you. Your little chum wife, Katie."

To his children he was always a beloved companion. Invariably, on fine days during the summer, at four o'clock he would set out with them on the horse cars for Harrison Square, a quaint old place on Dorchester Bay where there was a bathing beach that was safe for children. He was a born entertainer, and his admiring audience of three little girls was completely captivated by his seemingly endless fund of songs, stories, tricks and games. They thought "Papa" the most wonderful person in the whole world. His study desk was often cluttered with their dolls or toys undergoing repair, and when he was on tour his flying visits home were interludes of delight to them, anticipated eagerly and regarded with wistful longing after they had passed. Most of the outdoor photographs that have survived show Herne playing with his children.

Undoubtedly his life would have been happier if he had been willing to go on year after year playing in *Hearts of Oak,* as Joseph Jefferson was doing in *Rip Van Winkle,* or James O'Neill in *The Count of Monte Cristo.* But there was too much enterprise and ambition in his nature to make him content with a moderate success, even when it represented, as *Hearts of Oak* did, security. In his ambition to climb higher he was constantly aided and abetted by Katharine, whose estimate of her husband's ability was extremely high. In her adoring eyes he was nothing less than a genius, and a versatile one, too. It was because of her urging to try something different, that he made the mistake of writing an historical drama of the American Revolution. He had little ability for romantic historical plays in which his contemporary Bronson Howard had already attained a measurable success, culminating in the popular *Shenandoah* in 1888. Had Belasco been with him still, it is probable that one of the "gorgeous spectacles" that Winter so greatly admired might have been made of Herne's play. But as it was, *The Minute Men of 1774-5* was little better than an average romantic historical play, without the intense suspense that is a requisite for an outstanding success in the form.[22] The plot was highly complex, and Herne lacked the cleverness necessary to make this kind of machinery work. The story is loaded with the stock devices of the old romantic melodrama: Dorothy Foxglove, apparently the daughter of Reuben Foxglove, a frontiersman, is really the daughter of a British nobleman; Roanoke the noble Indian is really a white man, stolen in infancy and given to the Indians by the villain, who has the double aim of simultaneously depriving the good old father of his property and of his daughter. There are three romances progressing during the course of the action, with two rivals for the hands of the two young women, and there are numerous captures, escapes, and fights, both major and minor. The battle of Lexington takes place on the stage, and General Washington himself appears in the final grand tableau. The extras — Indians, Minute Men, British soldiers — and the amount of ammunition expended were both considerable. But all this is clumsily handled. Belasco or Howard or Gillette might have taken the same material and made a successful play of it, but Herne could not; he did not have that kind of talent.

The play had a successful opening night wherever it was performed — then business dropped off rapidly. It was obvious that the play had no drawing power; but Herne, encouraged by its opening nights, and hoping that it might click, continued to play it across the country in the season following its opening in Philadelphia on April

6, 1886. It was a costly production and he poured all his savings into it, finally losing all the money he had made on *Hearts of Oak,* and running into debt.²³ For years these debts were to hang like a millstone around his neck. He tried everything — popular prices, school children's matinees, professional matinees — but the public was not interested. Nothing makes a stronger appeal to the fighting spirit of the Irishman than a lost cause; so, long after it was apparent to others that the play was a failure, Herne stubbornly continued to present it to half-empty houses. The complete exhaustion of his capital and his credit finally forced him to stop.

The Minute Men of 1774-5 can only be regarded as a relapse into the old romantic melodrama, a step backward on the road towards the new realism. The two principal characters, Dorothy and Reuben Foxglove, are really alive, but the demands of the complex plot prevent the dramatist from developing them fully and establishing them as centers of interest. The audience is confused by the necessity of constantly switching its interest from the main plot to the sub-plot. In fact, there is no clearer example in American drama of the way heavy plotting can ruin a play which has at least two potentially interesting characters. Herne's acting in the part of Reuben and Katharine's in that of Dorothy were highly praised, but the obstacle of the plot was too great to be overcome by good acting. The marriage of the heroine, Dorothy, to the supposed Indian, Roanoke, also weighed heavily against the creation of suspense in the play. Roanoke, it is true, is discovered to be a white man, but still he looked, spoke, and acted like an Indian, and Dorothy's love for this strange creature could not have been sympathetically regarded by an American audience. In one respect, however, the play has considerable historical importance. In his *America Takes The Stage,* Professor Richard Moody states: "This was the first attempt to study realistically the effects of civilizing influences on the character of the Indian" (p. 109).

Herne never again attempted to portray noble savages, frontiersmen, British officers, and historical events, and he never wrote another romantic melodrama. *The Minute Men of 1774-5* taught him, at considerable cost, what he could not do. The next season (1887-8) he set out on tour with his old stand-by, *Hearts of Oak,* which never failed to make money. During the winter he wrote the first part of his next play, *Drifting Apart.*²⁴ As the various parts were completed he sent them home to Katharine for advice and criticism. The leading part, Mary Miller, was written for her, and Katharine took her usual keen interest in her husband's work. She sent him long letters about her reactions to every scene and character, and wrote: "Oh, God grant that this play will be a success! I am very anxious, too, dear. I share your feelings. I know too well the tumult that is in your poor heart, and all for us! I will work as hard as I can with you, dear, and if this play fails, well, we'll go to California and work hard together to retrieve what is lost. I shall begin at once preparations for Mary. Send me the part or bring it to me that I may study it at my leisure." And again: "My own darling: I am perfectly *wild* over this part. Oh, if I can only act it as I feel it should be acted! I have not yet begun to study the *words* of the Fourth Act, but the spirit of it is upon me strong. It is great for acting. I am positively ill I cried so over it this morning. I am going out for a walk and when I return I will give a few hours more to Mary. You see, I do not — cannot — study the lines. I read them and do a great deal of thinking. Oh, Jim, *if* I can only play the part. There are so many exquisite things in it."

The first performance of *Drifting Apart* took place at the People's Theatre, New York, on May 7, 1888, with Herne and Katharine in the leading parts of Jack Hepburne and Mary Miller. Herne's choice of New York for the play's opening was unfortunate, since *Drifting Apart* was precisely the "problematic, polemic, didactic, sociologic disquisition" so much despised by William Winter, who, as we have seen, dominated New York dramatic criticism. The bad press that ensued was only to be expected. Actually, Herne is admirably objective in this sociological tragedy whose theme is the evils of the drink habit, and there is no explicit preaching in the play. The plot is one of simplicity, and both setting and characters are drawn from the plain and rugged life of the New England fishing village. Historically, the play would have been of great significance as probably the earliest American realistic tragedy on a sociological theme had Herne not forced a happy ending by making Acts III and IV, in which the logical consequences of Jack Miller's slavery to drink are portrayed with telling realism, into dream scenes. This is an early use of the dream device in the history of American drama, and is thus historically interesting in itself, but it destroys the status of the play as a tragedy. Such was the compelling verisimilitude of the dream scenes, however, that the audiences refused to accept them as such and regarded the play as a gloomy and depressing tragedy. The theatre-going public of the day had not been trained to accept realistic tragedy, and the sop Herne had thrown them in making his sombre story a dream was ineffective. On tour, Herne stubbornly managed to keep the play going for 250 performances, but it was another financial loss.

The play was highly regarded by theatre managers, but they correctly estimated that it would not be popular with the public. Hamlin Garland in "On the Road with James A. Herne" (*Century*, August, 1914) quotes Herne as saying: "The managers all admit the good points of my play," he explained to me. "In fact, they say it is too good. 'The public doesn't want a good play,' they say. 'It wants bad plays. Write a bad play, Jim. Not too bad, but just bad enough' is their advice. Meanwhile I must play in theatres which are not suited to my way of doing things, and I am obliged to insert into my play tricks and turns which I despise."

It was an extremely humiliating experience to have the first class theatres closed to him and to be forced to accept bookings in the popular-priced houses, where he was given time only because of the former drawing power of his name. The popular-priced houses were usually located in the poorest sections of the cities and were frequently dirty and run-down. Some were operated in conjunction with bars. The only audience to which Herne could hope to appeal with his serious play did not attend these second-rate houses, which played mostly lurid melodramas, farce comedies, and burlesque. The rowdy audiences of these places, accustomed to "tank plays" (melodramas which featured a tank of water into which the villain threw the hero or heroine) were utterly unable to appreciate Herne's play and manifested their boredom by noisy and disconcerting remarks. In the midst of all this misery, Katharine's health broke, and three times during the tour she was forced to go home to recover. Meanwhile Herne's money was dwindling away. Sometimes the company played to only $50 a night. At the Bon Ton theatre on Chicago's West Side, the total receipts for ten performances were less than $1500. Herne's share was a little over $700, hardly enough to pay his company and the railroad fares. The Hernes had to sell their few bonds and Katharine's jewelry, and finally they mortgaged their Ashmont home. Katharine had told the little girls at Ashmont to pray

God to make Papa's play a success, and every night they dutifully knelt and prayed, "Please God, make Papa's play an excess." The children knew something was wrong, for when Mother and Father made a flying visit home, Papa seemed quieter, less given to entertaining them, and spent long hours going over accounts and papers at his desk. When Mama came out of the study she looked as if she had been crying. Sometimes as they fell asleep at night they heard him pacing back and forth in the study below. One day little Julie, who was sitting on the floor by the bookcase reading, was startled to hear her father utter what seemed like an involuntary cry, wrung out of his worry and despair. "Julie," he said suddenly, "I wish I had a hundred dollars." She never forgot the deep misery in her father's voice.

One bleak January afternoon in 1889 an obscure and impecunious teacher at a small school of oratory in Boston was given a couple of tickets to see a play called *Drifting Apart* which was running at a cheap, second-rate house in the South End. The teacher was Hamlin Garland, and that night he was profoundly impressed. The next day he wrote: "The second act in this play, for tenderness and truth has not been surpassed in any American play. A daring thing exquisitely done was that holiest of confidences between husband and wife." Apparently the audience in the cheap South Boston theatre differed from the audiences Herne had encountered in similar theatres in other cities, for Garland continued, "The audience sat hushed as death before that touching, almost sacred scene, as they do when sitting before some great tragedy. What does this mean if not that our dramatists have been too distrustful of the public? They have gone round the earth in search of material for plays, not knowing that the most moving of all life is that which lies closest to hand, after all." Later, in *The Arena* of October, 1891, Garland further commented: "Mrs. Herne's acting of Mary Miller was my first realization of the compelling power of truth. It was so utterly opposed to the 'tragedy of the legitimate.' Here was tragedy that appalled and fascinated like the great fact of living. No noise, no contortions of face or limbs, yet somehow I was made to feel the dumb, inarticulate, interior agony of a mother. Never before had such acting faced me across the footlights. The fourth act was like one of Millet's paintings, with that mysterious quality of reserve — the quality of life again."[25]

All actors attract their own little special groups of admirers, and the Hernes acquired loyal friends in various cities. But the happiest thing that came to the Hernes through *Drifting Apart* was meeting with Hamlin Garland.

6

HAMLIN GARLAND

When Hamlin Garland saw *Drifting Apart* in January, 1889, he was a teacher in Brown's School of Oratory in Boston, at a salary of $12 a week. He had been in Boston for less than five years, where he had come in the hope of entering Harvard University; but, because of his extreme poverty, he had been forced instead to resort to a course of extensive reading at the public library. He had almost starved to death during his first year in the city, but had been rescued by kindly friends, and now through his lectures and articles he had acquired a number of literary friends, among them Charles Hurd, the editor of the *Transcript;* E. B. Chamberlin, who conducted *The Listener* column in the *Transcript;* and, most important of all, William Dean Howells, the great American novelist whom he described as "the most vital literary man in America."

Garland as a young man of thirty had already arrived at complete agreement with the literary doctrines of Howells, the great master of American realism, even before he met him. Darwin and Spencer had formed the bulk of the young man's reading during his lonely first year in the city.[26] "I became an evolutionist in the fullest sense, accepting Spencer as the greatest living thinker," he says in *A Son of the Middle Border*. The basic principle of the new literary movement — the objective portrayal of truth — had become an abstract conviction through his study of science several years before he wrote his first short story. Born of this conviction in the mind of the intensely serious and somewhat humorless young man was a changed conception of the function of the literary artist in society: no longer tenable was the older romantic conception of the artist as an entertainer. No, the literary artist was now a scientist — a sociologist, a psychologist — as well as an artist. Again he tells us, "Obscurely forming in my mind were two great literary concepts — that truth was a higher quality than beauty, and that to spread the reign of justice should everywhere be the design and intent of the artist."

When he saw Herne's *Drifting Apart* in 1889, the ideas that were to find expression two years later in *Crumbling Idols* were already bubbling in his mind. "While the new realism is reinvigorating art in every nation of Europe, shall we sit down and copy the last epics of feudalism and repeat the dying echoes of Romance?" he asked indignantly.[27] His *Crumbling Idols* excoriated the New York "defenders of ideality" and the American reading public who "devour some millions of tons of romantic love stories, or stories of detectives and Indians." He attacked the college English departments which were "dominated by conservative criticism," where "sneering allusions to modern writers" were made daily, where the student was taught to worship the past and "kept blind to the mighty literary movements of his own time."[28]

Specifically, how little literature, he said, that was true and real had been produced by the great Western middle states — Wisconsin, Illinois, and Iowa. Yet a great drama had been going on there for forty years, a drama "as thrilling, as full of heart and hope and battle as any that ever surrounded any man." Why, he demanded, had this great story not been told? Because the young American writer had been taught to imitate the stale romanticism of the past rather than to write truthfully about the life that lay everywhere about him.

Garland was not only a rebel in the field of literature, but also in the realm of economics and politics. A boyhood filled with hardship on farms in Wisconsin, Iowa, and on the Dakota prairies had stamped indelibly on his sensitive nature the hard lot of the farmer in those days. He could never forget the time he had almost frozen to death in a blizzard, nor the blistering, back-breaking toil in the harvest fields under the merciless August sun; nor could he forget the ceaseless drudgery of the farmer's wife that was to age and break his mother prematurely. He had seen at first hand the results of the terrible drought of 1887 with its burned-out crops, its dust storms, and its starving farmers fleeing west, leaving the work of a lifetime in the hands of the mortgage companies. He hated the mortgage companies, financed by the capitalists of the East, with a farmer's hatred, and he eagerly embraced the revolutionary doctrine of Henry George and his Single Tax, a panacea for all the evils of capitalism. Later he was to take an active part in the campaigns of the Populist Party.

Garland's admiration of Henry George was little short of worship. He had already read *Progress and Poverty* when he first heard George speak in Faneuil Hall and had become convinced that the

Single Tax would eliminate monopoly and speculation and restore economic equality in all classes of society. He came away from the meeting a devoted disciple, for the "Bayard of the Poor" had a personal magnetism that turned followers into disciples. The formation of a Boston Anti-Poverty Society followed the meeting, and he became one of its most eloquent speakers. Throughout his long life Garland was in demand as a speaker. He had learned many of the secrets of the art of public speaking from Robert Ingersoll — the importance of colloquial, unaffected directness, of the confidential, friendly, yet authoritative tone, of ease and naturalness, of humor, of clear enunciation, of not reading from a manuscript.

The year 1889 was a memorable one in Hamlin Garland's life, for it saw the publication of his first realistic short story, *A Prairie Heroine*. Knowing that the story was too grim to find a place in any of the established periodicals, he sent it to the *Arena,* a new and radical magazine edited by B. O. Flower. Not only was the story immediately accepted, but Flower urged Garland to restore certain passages that he had cut out in the belief that they were too strongly realistic. "My magazine is not one that is afraid of strong opinions," Flower said. In fact, radical dissent was the policy of the publication, and it featured articles on evolution, liberalism in religion, psychical research, political corruption, and land reform. The leading article, on some such subject as *"The Menace of Plutocracy,"* was likely to be written by Flower himself, and the other articles had such arresting titles as "Communism of Capital — The Real Issue Before the People." *The Arena Publishing Company* also published books, which were liberally advertised in its issues, such books as *A Call to Action* by James Baird Weaver, who later became the Populist candidate for President; *The Irrepressible Conflict Between Two World Theories,* by the Reverend Minot J. Savage, author of *The Morals of Evolution; Is This Your Son, My Lord?* by Helen H. Gardener, advertised as "The most powerful realistic novel of the day;" *Bond Holders and Bread Winners,* by E. S. King, Esq.; and dollar editions of *Origin of Species, The Descent of Man,* and *First Principles.* Later, most of Garland's early books such as *Main Travelled Roads, A Spoil of Office,* and *Jason Edwards, An Average Man,* were to be published by Flower.

Flower and Garland had much in common — both were young, both came from the Middle West, both were radical "social reformers, and both had literary aspirations. They became close friends, and Garland was a frequent visitor at the Arena office, which he described as "a center of civil zeal." When more conservative friends remonstrated that association with "cranks" like Henry George and Flower was likely to do a budding author harm rather than good, Garland at first indignantly spurned their advice; but later he came to see that such associations might have a detrimental influence upon an artist — that propaganda is not art, and that it is far too easy for a reformer who is also an artist to let his stories degenerate into tracts. Howells proved to be the moderating influence, and although in 1889 the radical reformer was dominant in the young man, that there was actually a deep internal conflict in Garland between the opposing claims of art and reform is shown by the seriousness with which he took Howells' criticism of his tendency to preach.

That the young Garland was no narrow doctrinaire was shown by his later almost equal enthusiasm for Shakespeare and Ibsen. When Edwin Booth was playing in Boston, Garland would go to the old *Museum* night after night, even when he could afford only standing room. Edwin Booth, he said, taught him the greatness of Shakespeare and the glory of English speech. There he saw "in wondrous procession," the plays of Shakespeare, and he says, "These were my purple, splendid hours. From the light of this glorious mimic world I stumbled down the stairs out into the night, careless of wind or snow, my brain in a tumult of revolt, my soul surging with resolves." But Ibsen had an equal appeal. No sooner had he read *A Doll's House* than he began to talk and write on Ibsenism, to such an extent, in fact, that a contemporary critic later called him "the Ibsen of the New World." Dr. Lars Ahnebrink, in his *The Beginning of Naturalism in American Fiction* (1950) declared that "Many of his early works bear the stamp of Ibsen; some books contain ideas found in Ibsen's plays; others present similarities in plot, characters, and incidents. . . . Garland applied Ibsen's message of revolt, of freedom and independence to the overworked, subjugated Western woman." (p. 407). That the young Garland should feel an immediate kinship with Ibsen was inevitable; the two, differing widely in genius, were similar in temperament; both were rebels against previously accepted literary and social conventions, and both were unsparing social critics.

Garland as a young man was keenly interested in the theatre, for he had aspirations of becoming a playwright as well as a writer of fiction. Later, probably inspired by Ibsen and Herne, he was to write a play, *A Member of the Third House*. Then, too, he was in intimate contact with the world of the theatre through his brother Franklin, who was an actor and who lived with him in Boston. When Garland saw Herne's *Drifting Apart* on that stormy night in January, 1889, and was so profoundly impressed, he could not rest until he had met the author. He wrote a letter to Herne telling him how significant he thought his play was in the history of the American drama and asked to meet him. He received an immediate reply from Herne, expressing a desire to meet him. But since Herne was closing in Boston to open at the Bon Ton in Chicago and then embarking on a road tour, the meeting would have to be postponed until spring. Actually, it was early summer before the meeting took place. The Hernes asked Garland to Sunday dinner.

Garland, who tells of that first meeting in *A Son of the Middle Border* and in *Roadside Meetings,* found the Hernes delightful. It was a meeting of minds and hearts. "No one understood more clearly than the Hernes the principles I stood for," he tells us, and "No other household meant as much to me. . . . They were true Celts, swift to laughter and quick with tears; they inspired me to bolder flights. They met me on every plane of my intellectual interests, and our discussions of Herbert Spencer, Henry George, and William Dean Howells often lasted deep into the night. In all matters concerning the American Drama we were in accord."[29]

The Hernes, whom Garland called "these rare and inspiring souls," were equally impressed. Little Julie could never forget that first visit. To her, he seemed to sweep into the quiet household like a cyclone from his own prairies. He was a picture of rugged masculinity — strong and broad-shouldered. Though of medium height, he seemed to fill her father's study. He was very handsome, with his dark beard, finely-cut features, and his deepset, flashing eyes. He threw himself into the armchair beside Herne's desk and began to talk — magnificently — while the family listened spell-bound as the words poured out, vivid, polished, perfectly phrased. The whole family liked him at once. Five minutes after they met, Herne, Katharine, and Garland were talking together as if they had known one another all their lives. Before that first visit was over — and it lasted long into the night — they found that they were in general agreement about drama, literature, religion, and politics.

"The Dean," as they soon began to call Garland, was utterly unlike anyone they had ever met before. He scorned tact, diplomacy, and small-talk. When the conversation did not interest him, he would get up abruptly and walk away. His manner was harsh, brusque, and forthright, his attitude defiant and bellicose; he was always attacking or defending someone or something, and always to the last ditch. Sometimes the discussions were heated, as when Katharine, who shared most women's dislike of Whitman, found herself the object of the combined barrage of her husband and Garland. Or Garland would launch an all-out attack on what he called "effectism" in the theatre, and here Herne, himself a rebel against the traditions of the old melodrama, yet a child of the theatre, would object that Garland did not know the conditions of his medium. When Garland came to write his own play, *A Member of the Third House,* he found that Herne was right.

Garland soon became an established visitor at the Ashmont home, and on many summer afternoons he would pedal his bicycle out Dorchester Avenue to Beale Street.[30] Arriving at the garden gate, he would ring the little bell on the handlebar of his "safety," and the children would run out to greet him. Inside the house, Garland and Herne would immediately plunge into some discussion, and Katharine would leave her work in the kitchen to join them. On very warm days they would adjourn to the garden; on cool afternoons they would wander over the lovely Dorchester hills, the children gambolling about them. They talked mostly about their work. Herne read a play he had been working on, which he called *The Hawthornes* (the genesis of the later *Shore Acres*) and listened intently to Garland's criticism. Inspired by the younger man's enthusiastic praise and discerning criticism, Herne began to revise *Drifting Apart*. Garland, in turn, read to Herne some of the short stories which were soon to be published as *Main Travelled Roads.* Herne was deeply moved by these grim, harsh stories of the farm men and women of the prairies. Of course he did not know that they were the finest things Garland was ever to do, the most genuine, and the most typical of his true talent as a writer, and that Garland was never in his long life to equal them in artistry. He knew only that they were masterpieces of realism, and since Garland was only a young writer and these were his first stories, Herne naturally supposed that he would go on to far greater heights. He had liked "The Dean" as a person, but after hearing "The Return of a Private," "Under the Lion's Paw," and "Among the Corn Rows," he looked upon him with the admiration and awe that is accorded to a genius. To Herne these stories showed the complete comprehension and realization of a subject, as well as the spontaneity and naturalness of expression which characterizes the highest art. And these were the first stories that the young man had written! It is small wonder that Herne exaggerated the literary importance of his new-found friend, and that "The Dean's" advice and criticism acquired a new and enlarged significance. Garland did not have to convert him to realism — he had already embarked upon that road — but he easily converted him to the Single Tax — and to Ibsen.

Garland had seen his first performance of Ibsen at a special matinee given in Boston in the fall of 1889, with Beatrice Cameron (Mrs. Richard Mansfield) playing the part of Nora in *A Doll's House*. This performance made him an enthusiastic Ibsenite, and he was in at the beginning of the Ibsen controversy that was to develop rapidly during the next few years. Herne did not see the play, since he was on tour at the time, but he was the recipient of a series of impassioned lectures on the subject by Garland as soon as he returned. Five years later, when Garland's *Crumbling Idols* was published, Herne and Katharine both declared that there was scarcely a single idea in the book that was new to them, for Garland had previously delivered all these lectures at their home in Ashmont. We are safe in assuming, therefore, that the "series of suggestions," as Garland insisted on calling the essays in *Crumbling Idols*, were in essence what Herne heard from "The Dean."

In his "suggestions" on Ibsen, Garland praised him for dealing realistically with modern life — but this moderate statement of course fails to reproduce the muscular vigor of the young Garland's style. "See how great a part pure intellect plays!" he exclaims. "We are done with machinery, fustian, and clap-trap as we enter his dramatic world. . . . His words come to us at times like the thrust of naked fists." In this style, Garland treats the great innovations of Ibsen: the simplicity of his plots ("hardly anything approaching a plot, the interest depending entirely upon the characterization and the thought"); the new natural dramatic technique with its elimination of the old devices such as soliloquies and asides; the new woman, no longer "characterless, colorless, and passive, no longer a passive dramatic bone of contention, but an *active agent.*" But for all his enthusiasm, Garland has reservations. Ibsen's women are sometimes too daring, too unconventional, and "there is a strain of morbid psychology in many of his characters which I do not value." Garland also misses "the *kindly* humor" that one finds in Howells. "Ibsen is a great herald, his dramas lead to the future," but American dramatists must not imitate him. "Ibsen has helped us in our war against conventionalisms, but he must not dominate us. His plays are not to be models. Our drama must be more human, more wholesome, and more humorous."

These lines might have been written by Howells, and they accurately depict the gulf that lay between continental realism and the American realism of the Post-Civil War period. Behind the American novelist or dramatist was a different tradition — Puritanism, Anglo-Saxon reticence and restraint and humor, optimism born of America's unexampled opportunity and prosperity. In ringing tones he might proclaim his devotion to the new realism, his devotion to the truth, but there were limits beyond which he could not go. The young literary radical of Boston insisted that "the American realist should stand for a liberated art," but in the same breath he warned against "French sexualism" and Scandinavian morbidity. Ibsen might be a powerful ally in the fight for American realism, but he was still a foreigner, and some of his ideals were foreign to the American tradition. The leaders of the American realistic movement were strong nationalists; they might praise an Ibsen or a Zola, but they insisted that the new American literature must be "true to our conditions." And, Garland declared, "the surest way to write for other lands is to be true to our own land and true to the scenes and people we love. . . . To imitate is fatal."

Thus Herne was introduced to Ibsen, and Ibsen's plays were read and discussed, with "The Dean" as mentor. It was practically impossible for Herne actually to see one on the stage, for during these years Ibsen performances were rare in the United States, and when they were given Herne was acting in his own plays. What might have been the influence of Ibsen upon him if he had discovered the great Master Builder for himself, it is impossible to say. Perhaps the impact of Ibsen would have been similar to what it was on another impulsive Irishman in England, and America would have been shocked by a play in the vein of *Widowers' Houses* or *Mrs. Warren's Pro-*

fession. Actually Garland and Howells, whom Herne was later to meet through Garland, were stronger influences upon him than Ibsen. Deep introspective probing into states of soul must be avoided because that way lay morbidity. Real life, yes, but the American drama must be wholesome.

Yet the influence of Ibsen upon Herne was profound. Like Ibsen, he was a practical playwright who had grown up in the old Scribe-Sardou romantic dramaturgy; like Ibsen, he knew all the tricks of the old trade — and despised them. In *Drifting Apart* he had already made progress towards a simpler and more natural technique, but had retained some of the old devices because he thought they were necessary. And by a trick — the dream device — he had brought about a happy ending to a play that was logically a tragedy, because he feared the effect of a tragedy on the box office. Herne's practiced eye saw at once that Ibsen had revolutionized the old dramaturgy, and he was fascinated by the obviously successful results. Not only had Ibsen eliminated the soliloquy and the aside, as Garland had noted, but had made other changes and eliminations so drastic as to change the whole structure of the play. He had achieved, in fact, an almost complete dramatic objectivity in which the characters lived and spoke their story as in life itself. He had eliminated the old cumbersome exposition, with its talkative servants, and had begun his action in the midst of a crisis, relying upon retrospective exposition, expressed in natural allusions or inadvertent remarks, to illuminate the past. He had eliminated the old sub-plot; he had reduced the number of acts and characters; he had shortened the time interval. He had swept away most of the old romantic devices such as the complex intrigue, the misunderstanding, the coincidence, and the lost letter and document and ring. All superfluous dialogue had been dropped; the speech of his people was clipped and realistic. The way he would create suspense by breaking off a question, and not answering it until the next act; the marvellous dialogue, in which each speech was interlocked by implication to the total structure of the play and in which every phrase was important in the total effect; the skillful way in which the drama of the past and the drama of the present are interwoven — all these interested Herne much more than they did Garland, who inevitably, in these days, was principally concerned with Ibsen as a great moral teacher and reformer.

Herne too could appreciate Ibsen's courage as a social critic. Herne had lost all his money, and was even then perilously approaching bankruptcy for having treated realistically rather than melodramatically an unpleasant social problem — drunkenness — in *Drifting Apart*. He thrilled to the battle cry of the new morality at the close of the *Pillars of Society:* "The spirits of Truth and Freedom — they are the pillars of society." But how far, Herne asked himself, did one dare to go in that pursuit? Even though he had compromised with his ideals in *Drifting Apart*, the audiences had registered their disapproval by staying away in droves. Already Herne and Garland had heard rumors that the plays of Ibsen would be banned in England, and the English had seen only *A Doll's House*. What would happen when J. T. Grein tried to put on Archer's translation of *Ghosts*? In New York William Winter was already thundering about the theatre's presenting "sociological views which would disrupt society. . . . and are offensive to the general sense of decency, refinement, and good taste," and had declared that Ibsen had "a disordered brain." The whole problem set up an inner conflict in Herne comparable to that in some of Ibsen's tragic protagonists.

In addition to introducing him to Ibsen's plays, Garland converted Herne to the Single Tax crusade of Henry George. Henry George, Jr., in an article in the *Single Tax Review* for July, 1901, describes the conversion: "He had become an ardent Single Taxer, largely through the intelligent propaganda work of a struggling young writer in Boston . . . Hamlin Garland. The poet and novelist found ready listeners in Mr. and Mrs. Herne, and he was a constant visitor and constant expounder of his single-tax religion, until the great tender-hearted actor felt the conviction of the new faith, and its hope and enthusiasm. Mr. Herne was in the happiest mood when he came to the *Standard* office that day to meet my father. That sweet kindness was in his smile and shining light in his eyes which beamed from the face of his Uncle Nat in *Shore Acres* soon afterwards. He said that this philosophy explained what before was to him inexplicable, and that he would hereafter do all in his power to preach it. To that vow he was true to the last. He gave much time and effort and was liberal with his purse for the new anti-slavery cause, and there are probably few large cities in the United States where on some Sunday afternoon or evening, in church or theatre, he has not discoursed on the great theme with that exquisite blending of the actor's art and propagandist's intensity which gave a singular fascination to his eloquence. . . . I never knew a man who, displaying so much genius in his profession, at the same time gave so much thought to the great social problems."

In spite of the protests of theatre owners and managers that it was bad for business, Herne kept up his public speaking for the Single Tax to the end of his life. It was the reason he was not invited to join the Players' Club, and it cost him money at the box office, but he persisted. His first speech was in a small hall in Dorchester, on the same platform with Garland. Herne made a strong plea for the Single Tax and finished by reading Garland's *Under the Lion's Paw*. While Garland's oratory was impassioned, Herne's was earnest, quiet, and natural. In his Prince Albert coat and white linen tie and with his naturally benign countenance, he made an almost clerical impression, not inappropriate to the Single Tax crusade, which resembled in many respects a religious revival.

Herne was on tour when Henry George ran for the office of mayor of New York in the fall of 1897. On Sunday night, October 31, there was to be a big political rally in New York and Herne had been asked to speak. He was playing Buffalo that week and planned to leave on the midnight train on Saturday. On Friday morning when Herne and his daughter Julie went down to breakfast at their hotel, Herne stopped at the newsstand and bought a morning paper. On the front page was the news of Henry George's death. After sending a telegram to Mrs. George and one to Katharine, he walked about the streets for hours with Julie, never uttering a word. The depth of a grief that could find expression only in silence, as well as the personal sacrifices he had made for almost a decade, testify to the sincerity of Herne's devotion to social justice.

Henry George had likewise had a similarly profound effect upon a young Irish music critic and novelist in London named Bernard Shaw. When Shaw first heard Henry George in the Memorial Hall in London, the young writer left with a copy of *Progress and Poverty* under his arm, and it was this book, he says, that sent him off to the British Museum to read. It was Henry George's "extraordinary eloquence" that made him give up the writing of novels at the age of twenty-six and directed his attention to "economic science." That lecture was the turning point in Shaw's life, for from his study of "economic science" he went on to socialism, and from socialism to the drama.

It is doubtful if either Shaw or Herne ever fully understood all the economic implications of George's now discredited panacea. To both he was a powerfully persuasive symbol of social justice, and with George came Ibsen, Shaw declaring that he himself became "one of Ibsen's ghosts."

Herne owed his introduction to both George and Ibsen to the intense and shabby young man who had come to dinner on that summer Sunday in Ashmont in 1889.[31] Hamlin Garland was the exciting force that was to lead to the next act in the developing drama of Herne's life — an act in which Herne was to make American stage history and incidentally to bring himself and his family to the brink of financial disaster.[32]

7

MARGARET FLEMING

William Dean Howells, in the light of later dramatic criticism, was prophetic when he declared that *Margaret Fleming* was "epoch making." One of the most important historians of the American theatre of our day, Arthur Hobson Quinn, has called it "unequalled in realism by any other known American drama of its century." (*The Literature of the American People,* 1951, p. 805). And Sculley Bradley in *The Literary History of the United States* states that Herne "obviously ahead of his time . . . had brought realism to the theatre" (p. 1005).

It has been said that there are two strains in American realism — there is the native American, which, stemming from American folk lore and folk humor, found expression in the local color school; and there is the foreign, the imported continental realism stemming from Flaubert, Ibsen, and their disciples. The two strains are separate and distinct, but sometimes they fuse, as in some of the early stories of Garland in which the motif of the quaint and the picturesque suffused with sentiment, characteristic of local-color fiction, is combined with unsparing sociological analysis. In 1890 there had been few examples of the extreme realism of Flaubert by an American author in the field of fiction, and no American dramas which fully exemplified the principles and practices of Ibsen.

Herne in 1890 gave the American drama its first example of Ibsenesque realism in *Margaret Fleming,* an unflinching objective, unsentimental analysis of a contemporary social problem.[33] He could not have chosen a worse time for his bold venture into advanced realism. He must have known what the theatre-going public were paying to see in that year. The popular plays were sentimental melodramas such as *East Lynne, The Octoroon, Ten Nights in a Bar Room* or romantic adventure dramas such as *Held By The Enemy, Beau Brummel, Shenandoah, The Rajah,* and *Don Juan.* The most successful plays at the Boston Theatre that year were *Ben My Chree,* a dramatization of Hall Caine's *The Deemster;* Hoyt's *A Midnight Bell;* the same author's farce comedy, *The Brass Monkey,* featuring "The Razzle Dazzle Trio"; and Richard Mansfield in *Dr. Jekyll and*

Mr. Hyde. An unprecedented run of twenty-one weeks was enjoyed by *The Soudan,* which returned for another run of four weeks, and at the last performance, its 169th in Boston, a silver loving cup was presented to Henry Neville, leading man of the company, together with an address and an autograph album signed by the Governor, the Mayor, and many prominent citizens. It was a bad time to try to put on such advanced realism as that of *Margaret Fleming.* Moreover, as a result of the failure of *Drifting Apart,* Herne's finances were at a low ebb.

Margaret Fleming resembled no other play Herne ever wrote.[34] It was grim, bleak tragedy, pitiless and uncompromising in its portrayal of the emotional and ethical conflict between an unthinking sensualist and his high-minded wife. Except for Margaret's "light" scenes in the early part of the play and some of the lines of Joe Fletcher, the peddler, the sombre story was unrelieved by any of the warm humor of Herne's earlier plays. Act I opens in the office of Philip Fleming, the young president of a large mill in Canton, Massachusetts. The opening scene between him and his employees is remarkable for its realism, its absence of theatricalism, and the skill with which Herne presents Philip Fleming, whose character is established by his own unconscious definition of himself. The audience easily infers that Philip is the likable, socially popular and somewhat spoiled son, on whose shoulders the succession to the presidency of the company has fallen after the death of his father, whose business ability the son does not possess. Philip has all the conventional virtues of his class, and only a modicum of imagination is required of the audience to see him as a member of the best clubs at his university, correct in all his attitudes as well as in dress, but mediocre in character and in ability. Joe Fletcher, an old foreman of his father's who had grown up with the mill and whom Philip had known since childhood, drops in. Joe has become a victim of drink and is now in his old age an itinerant peddler. He is penniless most of the time and tells Philip that his wife has left him. Philip is kind to the old man, gives him money and a drink, and as the two reminisce about old times, Philip tells of his own happy marriage and of his baby daughter. Unconsciously, in his restrained speech, he reveals how deeply dependent he is upon his wife, Margaret.[35]

To the reader familiar with the typical American plays of the period, the absence of the usual obtrusive exposition is a notable feature of the play, as well as the absence of the aside and the soliloquy. The dramatic technique seems entirely natural and modern.

Dr. Larkin, the Fleming's family physician, enters the office and with him the exciting force that starts the rising action of the play. Dr. Larkin has been called into consultation in a childbirth case. The mother, a girl named Lena Schmidt, is in serious condition. At the mention of the girl's name, Philip's smooth complacency is upset, and he becomes increasingly agitated as Dr. Larkin reveals that he knows all about Philip's treatment of the girl. In the dialogue that follows, Philip's essential selfishness and lack of character are revealed.

> Philip: I tried to get her away months ago, but she wouldn't do it. She was as stubborn as a mule.
> Doctor: Strange that she would want to remain near the father of her child, isn't it?
> Philip: If she'd done as I told her to, this thing would never have happened.

Philip's callous indifference to the risk involved in abortion arouses the doctor's indignation. Philip's only thought is for himself; if his wife hears of this his home will be ruined. The scene ends with Dr. Larkin ordering him to go to see the girl. Philip objects strenuously, but there is an implied threat in the doctor's manner that forces him to obey.

The second scene of Act I opens in the living room of the Fleming home. Margaret and the German nursemaid, Mrs. Maria Bindley, are preparing little Lucy for bed. This scene of maternal tenderness shows such a sensitive knowledge of woman's nature that William Winter, ever anxious to seize upon anything that might discredit Herne, decided that only a woman could have written it, and he thereupon jumped to the amazing conclusion that Mrs. Herne, and not Herne himself, had written the play. Without any other foundation than the known fact that Katharine Herne with her knowledge of the theatre was of great help to her husband in his work, Winter proceeded to publish this charge. The facts are that Katharine was the inspiration for the character of Margaret Fleming, and this scene, as well as other scenes in which Margaret appears, is dominated by Katharine's deeply emotional femininity as Herne had seen it over the years. A legitimate criticism that Winter might have made is that Herne stretches the long arm of coincidence in making Mrs. Bindley the sister of Lena Schmidt. When Mrs. Bindley tells Margaret that her sister is desperately ill, Margaret sends her off to care for her. Philip enters, tired and dispirited, and Margaret's tender devotion comforts him. His remorse and contrition take the form of an outburst of generosity, and he makes over to her a large sum of money, the deed to the house, and $20,000 worth of government bonds to be kept in trust for Lucy, an action which he explains by alleging the uncertainty of his business situation.

Act II opens in the Fleming home. Dr. Larkin has been treating Margaret for an infection of the eyes, which, he secretly warns Philip, may result in blindness should she be subjected to any great shock. He advises Philip to take her away for several weeks. Mrs. Bindley returns with word that her sister is dying, and Margaret, her heart touched with pity, determines to go to see her. She does not tell Philip where she is going.

At the beginning of Act III Dr. Larkin is at the cottage where Lena Schmidt has died that morning. The landlady tells him that nothing will agree with the baby; it must have mother's milk. Margaret enters. Dr. Larkin tries to persuade her to leave, but when she sees the baby she declares that it must be taken care of. From Maria she learns that the baby's father is her husband, and she breaks down and sobs hysterically. Disregarding Dr. Larkin's plea that she leave, she sends a note to Philip telling him to come. Then followed the much-criticized ending to the scene. The baby cries with hunger. Margaret, taking it into her arms, "unbuttons her dress to give nourishment to the child, when the picture fades away into darkness."[36]

The curtain rises for Act IV at the Fleming home seven days later. Margaret has gone blind, but is able to walk about the garden. Dr. Larkin and Maria are with her and the two babies are in the nursery. Philip, who has not been at home for a week, returns. He begs for forgiveness and Margaret forgives him. But when he tries to take her into his arms, she refuses.

> Margaret: The wife-heart has gone out of me.
> Philip: Don't — don't say that, Margaret.
> Margaret: I must. Ah, Philip how I worshipped you. You were my idol. Is it my fault that you lie broken at my feet?
> Philip: You say you want to forget — that you forgive! Will you—?
> Margaret: Can't you understand? It is not a question of forgetting,

Margaret Fleming

or of forgiving — (For an instant she is at a loss how to convince him) Can't you understand, Philip! Suppose — I — had been unfaithful to you?
Philip: (With a cry of repugnance) Oh, Margaret!
Margaret: (In a broken voice) There! You see! You are a man, and you have your ideals of the sanctity — of — the thing you love. Well, I am a woman — and perhaps I, too, have the same ideals. I don't know. But I, too, cry "pollution."

It was Herne's attack upon the double standard of morality that chiefly vexed the critics. Even as advanced a thinker as Henry George told Katharine that it was a wife's duty to forgive. The managers who read the play turned it down emphatically. Herne completed the play in the spring of 1890, and finally did three performances at Lynn, Massachusetts, beginning July 4. But the Boston managers avoided it like the plague. The praise of such a distinguished man of letters as Thomas Sargent Perry, who was among the handful of Boston people who saw it at Lynn, had no effect upon the managers. Perry later wrote to Herne: "I was pleased with your play, very much indeed. In general I hate the ordinary play of the period, but yours does not belong to that sort. Your third act was admirable, with its abandonment of the conventional methods, its truthfulness, and its pathos. Everyone was moved by it. It is a magnificent task you have set yourself, to paint life and not to copy sun-dried models."

Failing to get a hearing with the Boston managers, Herne tried New York. The only manager there who showed any interest was Herne's old friend, Abraham Lincoln Erlanger, who had just entered into his famous partnership with Marc Klaw, a combine which was later to come close to dominating the American theatre. But the negotiations with Erlanger came to nothing, and Herne came back to Boston with his money almost gone. At this juncture he fell back on his old stand-by, *Hearts of Oak,* which never failed him in a pinch. He assembled a company, and embarked in the fall of 1890 on a nation-wide tour which took him to the Pacific coast. The tour was arduous, for most of the popular-priced houses at which he played gave two performances every day. Herne returned to the East in time to appear in Wilson Barrett's *A Four-Legged Fortune,* which opened in New York on February 23, 1891, and managed to get as far as Boston during its short run. After its failure, he was engaged to direct *A Fair Rebel* by Harry P. Mawson.

It was at this time that Herne awoke to the fact that New York was now the theatrical center of the country and that he must live in or near it if he wanted to stay in the theatre. The old local stock companies were dead or dying, forced out of business by their successful competitors, the "combination" houses, playing stars who travelled with their own companies. With the growth of the combinations under Klaw and Erlanger, theatrical business had become concentrated in New York. The letterhead of Klaw and Erlanger already bore the legend: "Representing the Principal Theatres and Attractions of America." It was in New York that plans were made for the production of new plays and for flooding the country with road companies, sometimes four or five at once, playing Broadway successes. Here a group of bright young men — keen, quick-witted, realistic businessmen like Klaw and Erlanger, the Frohmans, and the Haymans — were superseding the older men. A small Broadway clique, they decided the fate of every new play and made and unmade stars. Their power was growing rapidly, and theater after theatre all over the country was falling under their control. They were promotors, speculators and gamblers, but they gambled only on what their shrewd instincts of what the public would buy told them would be a sure-fire money success.

Obviously this group was not interested in *Margaret Fleming,* which, as far as the American public of the period was concerned, was almost an entire generation ahead of its time. Nor were they interested in starring Herne in any of their plays, for he was not a fashionable star, a matinee idol, or a society favorite. But no man in America had a better knowledge of the theatre than Herne, and they knew it. So one day when he was talking to Erlanger in his office, the keen, dark little man turned to him suddenly and said, "Jim, how would you like to come in with us as our stage manager? We'll fit you up an office here and you can direct all our plays." The salary, Erlanger went on to say, would be $100 a week. Herne accepted this offer with the eagerness of a drowning man grasping a life-line. It meant steady employment for thirty or forty weeks a year and a measure of security for his wife and children.

It also meant selling the Ashmont house and moving to New York. The Hernes' house-hunting finally ended far up-town on Washington Heights, at Convent Avenue and 145th Street, where John D. Rockefeller had built a group of houses to sell. Number 79 was vacant and was a bargain, the agent said, at $25,000. Herne was staggered at the price asked, but Katharine loved the house. It had a magnificent view of the East River and the Bronx from the dining room windows, it would be cool in summer, and the children would have fresh air and a place to play, Katharine said. As a final argument, she declared that the house was an excellent investment, for they could sell it for more than they paid for it. Herne was always easily convinced by Katharine, and his offer of $18,000 was promptly accepted. With the money received from the sale of the Ashmont house, and by taking a mortgage, he was able to make the purchase.

Washington Heights in the nineties was almost an hour's ride on the "El" from Broadway and Thirty-Third Street, then the theatrical center of New York. It was still somewhat rural, with open fields stretching to the Hudson River, heavily wooded vacant lots, and rocky promontories where a few goats could occasionally be seen grazing. Some of the old mansions of the previous era, when all this region consisted of country estates, were still standing. But now St. Nicholas Avenue was lined with handsome residences of brick and stone, and there were shops and even apartment houses on the avenues and side streets. Number 79 was one of a row of five houses, all as new and smart and modern as pressed brick and the liberal use of limestone in the best late Victorian tradition could make them. Inside, the decor was both substantial and ornate, with a quantity of heavily carved mahogany and golden oak, open fireplaces with elaborate mantels, large gas chandeliers, and in the bathroom a shining nickel tub. Later, the Hernes were to discover that the hot air furnace was inadequate to heat the house and that the fireplaces smoked, that the house was not only cold in winter, but hot in summer, that it was hard to reach, hard to take care of, full of inconveniences, and that it was expensive to run. But it was Katharine's pride and joy for many years.

Herne's new job with Klaw and Erlanger did not begin until the fall. He had the greater part of the spring and the entire summer for his own, and he determined to use this time to get a hearing for *Margaret Fleming,* for his faith in the play was invincible. He and Katharine returned to Boston, and there Garland volunteered his services as unofficial press agent. Garland scurried about Boston and its environs and obtained the signatures of fifty-five prominent men, chiefly writers, artists and journalists, who agreed to attend a performance of the play if it could be produced. Among the signers were Governor Russell, William Dean Howells, B. O. Flower, John J. Enneking, J. E. Chamberlin and E. H. Clement of *The Transcript,* Mary E. Wilkins, and Philip Hale. Armed with this letter, Garland applied to five Boston managers and was rebuffed by all of them.

In *Roadside Meetings* Garland describes a discussion between Howells and Herne at this time. Howells advised the discouraged dramatist to follow the example of Sudermann and his associates, who, when they could not get a hearing in the Berlin theatres, hired a hall on a side street, and brought out their productions there. Howells suggested that Herne should "hire a hall or stable and produce your play in the simplest fashion. The people will come to see it if it is new and vital."

Later events were to show that Howells was endowing the theatre-going public with his own enthusiasm for the new realism. Herne was impressed by Howells' suggestion and went to New York to try to make some money to carry it out. While he was away Katharine tried to get J. B. Schoeffel of Abbey, Schoeffel, and Graw, owners of the Tremont Theatre, interested in the play. Schoeffel, however, would consider it, he informed her, only if radical changes were made. "Not one line of this play will be changed, Mr. Schoeffel," she said, and went home and wrote a long letter to her husband, full of high resolve and deep faith, which closed with the words: "We will do the play ourselves, Jim."

A few days later Herne returned from New York, arriving early one morning before the family had had breakfast. He found his wife in the nursery, helping the children to dress, and they greeted him with cries of joy. He stood very still, looking at them with an impassive face. "Any luck, Jim?" Katharine asked anxiously. With great solemnity Herne took a paper from his pocket and handing it to her, asked her to read it aloud. Katharine looked at it wonderingly, and read. It was a contract in which Herne agreed to write a comedy to be called *My Colleen* for one Tony Farrell for the sum of $2000. As Katharine was reading, Herne pulled from his pocket a roll of bills which he threw at his wife's feet with a fine, careless gesture; from other pockets he drew more bills, until the floor was covered with money. The children applauded and shrieked with delight, but Herne just stood there with a dead-pan expression on his face. The children rushed about excitedly, gathering up the money and giving it to their mother. Katharine counted it. It amounted to $300, the advance payment on *My Colleen*. "Now we can do *Margaret Fleming!*" she exclaimed happily.

The Hernes were determined to follow Howells' suggestion, though such a procedure was almost unheard of in America at the time. They found that Chickering Hall, a small concert hall above the Chickering Piano showrooms, seating about five hundred people, could be rented. It had no theatrical equipment whatever, and to the Hernes, accustomed to the large theatres of the day, it seemed like a doll house. Herne, however, was permitted to make some alterations at his own expense, and he engaged a carpenter to raise the stage and an electrician to install proper lighting.

Herne and Garland conferred for hours in Herne's study at Ashmont (for the house had not yet been sold) discussing ways and means. Herne was to cast and direct the play and to play the part of Joe Fletcher, the peddler; Katharine was to play the part of Margaret and to supervise the stage settings and costumes; Garland (without pay) was business manager and press agent. Katharine bought a quantity of heavy repp of a soft old-rose shade, and had it made into draw curtains and a proscenium arch. She designed and made her own dresses. Furniture and properties were lent by the friendly proprietors of Boston shops, and some came from the Herne home. But the project proved much more expensive than they had supposed. Herne soon spent all his available cash and borrowed what he could. Still there was not enough, and it is believed that Howells and Flower underwrote the remainder.

Actors were always eager to work for Herne, and those he selected for the cast in this instance, realizing what a risk he was taking, made their salaries as low as possible. David Murray, a young actor with a sympathetic personality, was chosen to play Philip Fleming. Although he was not ideal for this difficult part, he gave a creditable performance. Herne never really liked anyone in it except Charles Richman, who played it in New York some years later. For the part of Dr. Larkin, Herne chose the veteran character actor, C. P. Flocton, a member of the Boston Museum Stock Company. He was a charming, cultured Englishman, whose hobby was playing the zither. Tall and gaunt, with smoldering dark eyes and aquiline nose, he looked like a Savonarola. His rendition of the part was a blend of gentleness and sterness that was most effective. The character was a favorite with Herne and he thought no one ever equalled Flockton in it. Maria Bindley was played by Miss Jakoban Prom, a young Norwegian musician with no stage experience, but Herne trained her in every line, and his patience was rewarded by a remarkably fine performance.

While the rehearsals were in progress, Garland was working indefatigably to create interest in the production. He talked to the critics and other members of the press; he called upon or wrote to important people exhorting them in his characteristically vehement manner to be sure to see this important play. There was no money for posters or billing, but small placards were printed, and Herne's little daughters Julie and Chrystal went proudly about Ashmont, Milton, Grove Hall, and Field's Corner asking the permission of storekeepers to put the cards in their windows. Circulars were sent through the mails containing the open letter to James A. Herne signed by many prominent people of Boston: "We have heard," it read, "of the strength and seriousness of your new play, 'Margaret Fleming,' and earnestly hope it may soon be brought out on the Boston stage. We shall be very glad to attend its representation by yourself and wife." It was signed by W. D. Howells, T. S. Perry, Mary E. Wilkins, Wm. Lloyd Garrison, Mildred Aldrich, Louise Chandler Moulton, John J. Enneking, Barrett Wendell, and many others. The circular also contained Herne's reply, in which he declared that "I unhesitatingly seize the chance to state the *truth* in drama without restriction or compromise, so firm is my faith in its ultimate success." This was followed by a paragraph written by Garland: "Mr. Herne is thus strengthened, and with reason, in the belief that there is a public ready to support a drama that depicts the life seriously. . . . Chickering Hall is to be our *theatre libre* for a week at least. There is a very great general interest in the performance and the radicals in literature are likely to have a play after their most advanced ideas."

A second circular featured a statement signed jointly by Garland and Flower and a letter to Herne from Howells. The statement is as follows:

In the Interests of American Drama

It is generally admitted that the American drama is immeasurably below the work of American painters and novelists, and a

Margaret Fleming

despondent tone runs through much that is written upon the subject. We do not share this despondency. We believe with Mr. Howells, Mr. Perry and other of critics in the comparative school, that literary ideals are relative, and that literature, and especially the drama, follows intimately the changes in social life.

Without taking space to detail our reasons, we state our belief that we are on the eve of a great change in the drama commensurate with that already begun in the novel, that is, the change from the drama of plot and style to the drama of character and purpose.

The American public is large, and we believe there is a growing number of people to whom melodrama no longer appeals, and to whom farce comedy is a weariness, with its heartless as well as thoughtless caricature. This public is ready to welcome serious studies of American life.

We are convinced that this movement toward a higher dramatic art should be made — at least in its inception — along independent lines somewhat as in Paris and Berlin, maintaining, however, the same distinction as to choice of subjects that now exists between the French and American schools of novelists.

As a first modest trial of the independent art theatre we take genuine pleasure in calling attention to Mr. and Mrs. Herne's coming production of their latest play, "Margaret Fleming," at Chickering Hall, beginning May 4th. We do this the more readily because these thorough artists have been working alone and (in a literary way) unrecognized in the attempt to bring the accent of life upon the stage.

"Margaret Fleming" is not a perfect play; it could not reasonably be expected to be, but it has qualities which fit it to stand for the new idea, as Ibsen's "Young Men's Union" stood for the innovation in Norway in 1869. It is absorbingly interesting, legitimately dramatic, has comedy as well as pathos, and mounts in the last act into an intellectual atmosphere unreached, so far as we know, in any other American play, and Mrs. Herne plays it with that marvellous art which conceals art, leaving the embodied character standing in place of the actress.

We thus publicly endorse Mr. and Mrs. Herne and their purposeful play, because they entirely merit our support, and also because we wish to oppose the pessimistic cry of "the decay of the drama." The drama changes, but it never decays. There are scores of plays in America waiting the establishment of a theatre freed from the necessity of compromise and whose production would be an honor and an inspiration, as we believe "Margaret Fleming will prove to our stage.

B. O. Flower
Hamlin Garland

Then followed the letter from Howells to Herne:

My dear Mr. Herne:—
I am glad there is a prospect of our seeing "Margaret Fleming" on the Boston stage. I told you when I read the play how highly I thought of it, and I feel it is a great loss not to have been at its production in Lynn. It has qualities which I believe will make a stronger appeal than those of any other American play.

While it is wholly and perfectly true in our conditions, it has the same searching moral vitality as Ibsen's best work, and it is most powerfully dramatic. I have no doubt of its success with a fair chance, and with Mrs. Herne and yourself in it, I predict an epoch-making effect for it. Your fidelity to the ideal of truth, the only ideal worth having, is witnessed in every part of it, and it will be recognized by everyone who can feel and think, as a piece of nature and a great work of art.

I do hope you may get it into one of our theatres.[37]

Yours sincerely,
W. D. Howells

The opening on May 4, 1891, was a memorable first night. Garland's vigorous press campaign and his tireless personal proselyting were rewarded by an audience composed of the most discriminating minds in Boston.[38] They were an eager, curious, and even excited crowd, a remarkable thing in Boston. The play and the acting aroused them to a pitch of enthusiasm extremely gratifying to the three people who had planned this perilous adventure. As Margaret, Katharine made the greatest success of her career. The play became the talk of the artistic world of Boston, and the engagement was extended for a second week. Groups of Boston notables crowded the small space backstage after every performance to congratulate the Hernes, some of them even journeying out to Ashmont, among these being Mr. and Mrs. Thomas Bailey Aldrich.

But even in Boston in 1891 the intelligentsia was limited in numbers. During the second week the attendance dropped off sharply, and the ugly fact had to be faced that the play was not even paying expenses; in fact, it had not repaid its initial cost. Never was there a better demonstration of the fact that new developments in the theatre must await the general development of public taste, for the theatre must depend upon the general public for its support. Herne was forced to close the play at the end of the second week.[39] The case was somewhat brutally stated by a New York manager whom Herne tried to interest. He wrote: "Your venture has not tested the financial worth of the play in the slightest degree. . . . The opening night must have demonstrated to you that the enthusiasm of a handful of admiring friends could not be relied upon to pay rent or salaries. Plays are generally written for theatres and theatres are generally built for plays. I have never heard of a successful departure from the regular order of things, especially where public support was necessary, and I never expect to hear of one."

It is strange, under the circumstances, that the hard-headed Erlanger should have agreed to underwrite a second trial for the play in October. But such was actually the case. If successful, it was to tour New England and then appear in New York. The second engagement opened at Chickering Hall on October 5. Again there was the same enthusiastic handful of intellectuals present — and again the Boston public remained indifferent. Klaw and Erlanger were ready to close the play two days after the opening. Herne bore the result stoically, but he wrote to Garland: "Of course they look only at the money loss. I look at the failure of my life." At a professional matinee attended by all the stars and their companies then playing in Boston the enthusiasm was tremendous. William Gillette made a special trip to Ashmont to congratulate Katharine. Only the public remained unimpressed. Klaw and Erlanger withdrew their support after two weeks; Flower underwrote it for an additional week; then it closed.

After the Hernes had moved to New York, Katharine tried to persuade A. M. Palmer, one of the most important of the New York managers, to put on a New York production. But Augustus Thomas' *Alabama* had started what was an indubitably long run at Palmer's Theatre at the corner of Broadway and Thirtieth Street. Finally Palmer agreed to put it on at a special matinee. Herne was in Chicago superintending the opening of Klaw and Erlanger's *The Country Circus* and his guiding hand at the rehearsals was sadly missed, although the cast was excellent. The matinee took place on December 9, 1891, and was an unequivocal failure. The audience was cold, and the critics, led by William Winter, excoriated the play.

Dithmar of the *New York Times* was urbane and condescending. He wrote, in the issue of December 10: "Some interest is attached to the piece because it was acted in Boston, in a hall, under the auspices of a few enthusiastic persons who contemplate the establishment in that city of an Independent Theatre; because it has been regarded by a select few as an example of what the drama that aims to depict contemporary life should be, and because that eminent and authoritative writer, William Dean Howells, has spoken very kindly, in print, of Mr. Herne as a playwright."

Howells' kind words had appeared in the August number of *Harper's*. Howells had said, after telling the story of the play: "The power of this story, as presented in Mr. Herne's every-day phrase, and in the naked simplicity of Mrs. Herne's acting of the wife's part, was terrific. It clutched the heart. It was common; it was pitilessly plain; it was ugly; but it was true, and it was irresistible. At times the wife preached, and that was bad; there were passages of the grossest romanticism in the piece, and yet it was a piece of great realism in its whole effect. This effect, in Boston, where it was produced, was most extraordinary. Probably no other new play ever drew such audiences there, in the concert hall where it took refuge after being denied a chance at all the theatres. Literature, fashion, religion, delegated their representatives to see it, and none saw it without profound impression, so that it became the talk of the whole city wherever cultivated people met. It would be rash to prophesy its future, but not Mr. Herne's. It is evident that in him we have not only an actor of the most advanced type (he did a refuse Yankee in the play deliciously) but a dramatist of remarkable and almost unequalled performance. We have spoken of his work in both kinds before. We could not now speak of it too hopefully."

Two months after the New York failure Herne was offered a chance to put on *Margaret Fleming* at McVicker's Theatre in Chicago, along with his new play *Shore Acres*. James H. McVicker was universally admired and respected in the world of the theatre. He had made a large fortune from his magnificent theatre, but more important, he had a genuine love of the drama and was always eager to give a new play an opening if he thought it had merit. He had no illusions about *Margaret Fleming* as a popular success, for he wrote to Herne: "I doubt if the play will ever be a money maker for the reason that it treats of an unpleasant *truth*." McVicker suggested some changes "to soften the play," such as restoring Margaret's sight. Many people who had seen the play, including Henry George, had expressed the wish that there could be at least the hope of a reconciliation between the husband and wife at the end — so many, in fact, that Katharine was now in favor of this change. Herne had the greatest esteem for McVicker, and with all this pressure upon him he set about making changes that would "soften" his play, including the rewriting of the last act.

Margaret Fleming was produced on July 7, 1892, with Mrs. Herne as Margaret, Herne as Joe Fletcher, Forrest Robinson as Philip Fleming, George Fawcett as Dr. Larkin, and Maude Banks as Maria Bindley. It was an especially good performance, but the critics viewed it with mixed feelings. Elwyn Barron of the *Inter-Ocean* noted the new naturalistic technique, which he attributed to the influence of Ibsen, and called the play "simple and natural in treatment, with commonplace incidents, an entire disregard of situation and climax, its characters distinctly defined and interestingly sustained, its story consistently developed from a given basis to a logical conclusion." But he added that "as a play *Margaret Fleming* is no more viable in the atmosphere of the stage or in the sympathies of the general theatre-going public than are the futile plays of Ibsen." *The Chicago Tribune* declared: "Those who reject an Ibsen will not readily be reconciled to the comparative crudities of his American disciple," but added that it was "a brave, strong play — one to make people think, though they may not agree with the author."

The Chicago critics, in strong contrast to the critics of New York, were appreciative of the merits of the play, even if they were not enthusiastic. But again *Margaret Fleming* failed to attract the general public. It closed on July 16.

The play was later produced in New York at the Fifth Avenue Theatre under the management of Carl and Theodore Rosenfeld, two German producers who had made a great deal of money with The Lilliputians, a group of clever German midgets, and who had obtained the American rights to Gerhart Hauptmann's *Hannelse Himmelfahrt*. The Rosenfeld brothers, familiar as they were with continental realism, but not with the taste of the American public at the time, were enthusiasic about *Margaret Fleming,* and it was produced on April 9, 1894, with a splendid cast, Katharine as Margaret, Charles Richman as Philip, F. F. Mackey as Dr. Larkin, and Maude Banks as Maria. But the changes made in Chicago to soften the play did nothing to appease the New York critics, who pounced upon the play and its author with fury, led as usual by William Winter. That ex-bohemian, now in his old age turned stern moralist, occasionally had softer moments when he wrote sentimental poetry or when a new romanticist such as "Ian Maclaren" (Dr. John Watson) swam into his ken. He said that Dr. John Watson was "the finest literary artist in the art of mingled humor and pathos that has come into literature since Sir Walter Scott." But when he wrote of Ibsen or Herne his pen was always dipped in acid.

Many of Herne's friends regretted the changes he had made to please McVicker, especially the new ending, and felt that the earlier tragic ending was the stronger, the more logical, and more dramatic of the two. And the public still disliked the play, which this time ran for a little over two weeks. The Rosenfelds had such faith in it, however, that they offered Katharine a contract to star in it on the road the following season. But she declined, and told them that she had decided to give up the stage for good and devote herself to her husband and children. She never played Margaret again, and the play was never produced again during Herne's lifetime.

Margaret Fleming lay neglected and forgotten for nearly thirteen years. During those years great changes occurred in American taste. Realism had advanced slowly but steadily in all the arts. Ibsen came to be regarded as the great master builder of the modern drama, and the plays of his English disciple Shaw, who described himself as "one of Ibsen's ghosts," were familiar to all theatre goers. The star of the 1907 production in Chicago was Chrystal Herne, who in the six years since her father's death had developed into one of the country's most respected young actresses. At the time of the Chicago engagement she had starred with Arnold Daly in a number of plays by George Bernard Shaw in the leading American theatres, and had already signed a three-year starring contract with the famous Charles Dillingham. Now for a limited time during the winter of 1906-1907, until her engagement with Dillingham should open, she was the leading lady of the New Theatre in Chicago, an artistic repertory theatre subsidized by a group of wealthy drama lovers such as H. C. Chatfield-Taylor, Medill McCormick, and Arthur Bissel. After plays by Hauptmann, Sudermann, and other European dramatists had been presented, the last two weeks of the season were assigned to *Margaret Fleming*.

This time, sixteen years after it had first been produced in Boston, the play was a popular success and a money success. A new generation of critics hailed it as a great play. The review by W. L. Hubbard in *The Chicago Tribune* on January 30 was typical: "It is

Margaret Fleming

entirely reasonable to expect that now this greatest of Herne's dramas will find wide recognition at the American public's hands, and that it will be accepted for what it is — one of the strongest, best plays yet written by any American. It is a creation to which we as a literary and a stage-possessing nation may point with justifiable pride, for none of the modern dramatists of Norway, Russia, Germany, Spain, France, Belgium or Italy have produced a better. And it was written over fifteen years ago and in this country when conditions and matters theatrical were far different from what they are today. . . . It is a drama so true to life in the conditions depicted, so human in the emotions expressed, so real in the people involved, and so finely and strongly dramatic in the problem worked out, that it easily takes rank as one of the few really notable and powerful dramas yet created by any native dramatist."

In *The Record Herald* of January 30, James O'Donnell Bennet wrote: "In this play Mr. Herne drew a simple, veracious, sincere picture of life, a picture that was realistic without being sordid or savage, that was human without being commonplace. . . . The ethics of the play are right and strong, the craftsmanship simple and good, the characterization definite and natural. . . . The passing of fifteen years has made the American public less squeamish if not more honest, and today brave old James Herne's brave play will move nobody to feverish declamation."

The house was crowded nightly, and the directors of the New Theatre, finding themselves unexpectedly with a success on their hands, were ready to engage a downtown theatre and put the piece on for a run. They even planned taking it to New York. But Chrystal Herne was committed to her contract with Dillingham, and their plans had to be abandoned. Plays, like people, have their moments of opportunity and fulfillment. *Margaret Fleming* was, at its first presentation in Boston in 1891, years ahead of its time. In Chicago, in 1907, its great moment came, and there was no one to grasp it. The moment passed, and the opportunity never came again. *Margaret Fleming* dropped out of sight, to be rediscovered by scholars and historians of literature many years later.

8

WILLIAM DEAN HOWELLS

When Herne, through Garland, met William Dean Howells, in 1889, Howells was the most prominent and most highly respected American novelist. Both at home and abroad he was regarded as the Father of American Realism, and he was soon to be acknowledged the Dean of American Letters. Garland was to declare later in *Roadside Meetings:* "That he was the chief figure in American literature was indisputable even by those who disliked his fiction." At the age of fifty-two he had already written more fine novels than any other first-rate American novelist, and among them were some that were undoubtedly masterpieces — *A Modern Instance, Indian Summer,* and *The Rise of Silas Lapham.* His exceptionally graceful style, marked by an artist's feeling for words, was a delight to thousands of readers. As Mark Twain had said, other men, including himself, *sometimes* found the right word, but Howells *always* found it. His insight into human nature was so fine, so sensitive, and his creativity so powerful that his characters left the printed page and lived in the imaginations of his readers. Wherever intelligent people gathered, his novels were discussed, and his readers were as diverse as Mark Twain and Mr. and Mrs. Henry Adams.

Not only was Howells one of the leading novelists of the country in 1889, but he was also one of its most prominent literary critics. As editor of *The Atlantic* during the period of its greatest prestige, he encouraged such writers as Mark Twain, Henry James, Sarah Orne Jewett, George W. Cable, and Joel Chandler Harris and published their work. And now for the last three years in The Editor's Study of *Harper's,* he had championed the cause of realism so vigorously that a nation-wide critical controversy had been started, a controversy which had developed into a battle between the romanticists and the realists, a battle which, as Howells himself was to say later, became "sulphurous" in its intensity. In the heat of the conflict, Howells unduly depreciated the work of great romanticists such as Scott, Thackeray, and Dickens, and perhaps overpraised such realists as Flaubert, Zola, Bjornson, and the Goncourts, but he championed the men who were to become the great names of the future

— Hardy, Ibsen, Henry James, Turgenev, Dostoevsky, and Tolstoy — and he emerged as the champion of the great principle that was to dominate the American literature of the future: Literature was not an escape from reality, but a truthful study of life. In 1889 he was already the Sainte-Beuve of the United States, as well as one of its most important novelists.

Howells' personality was one that from his earliest appearance in Boston had won all hearts. Genial, modest, generous, sincere, he was esteemed from the first not only by the blue-blooded Brahmins, but by people in far humbler walks of life. To all he was the amiable, self-effacing, amusing gentleman who bore his great wisdom lightly and masked his genius in a broad humanity and kindliness. He had achieved an almost perfect balance between the cool, austere aloofness of the great writers of the New England school, who had made Boston the Athens of America, and the open-hearted robustious democracy of the West. The friend of the Adamses and the Lowells was also the friend of the struggling young German impressionist painter, Enneking, who had arrived in Boston from the little German settlement of Munster, Ohio, by way of the Paris studios; he was likewise the friend of the intense, indignant and seedy young radical, Hamlin Garland, and of Garland's friend, Jim Herne, the unsuccessful Irish playwright who lived in Ashmont.

Even before he met Howells, Herne's admiration for him was great, for he had read his novels. When Howells about 1887 began his great espousal of the cause of American social justice with the publication of *The Minister's Charge,* Herne's admiration for him grew. On June 12, 1889, Herne wrote to Garland from Rochester, "We bought *Annie Kilburn."* Earlier in the year he had been anxiuos to meet Howells, but Winifred, Howells' daughter, had died in March, and as Herne wrote to Garland, "His grief was too sacred— I did not wish to intrude upon it." Later they met, and their lifelong friendship began. Howells' efforts in behalf of *Margaret Fleming* inspired a passionate loyalty on Herne's part that none of the difficulties connected with their association in later years could ever shake. Herne always said that his debt to Howells was very great.

The difficulties arose in connection with Howells' attempt to become a dramatist.[40] Early in his career, he had written a number of delightful parlor comedies, short plays designed to be read rather than acted, though some of them had had a brief appearance on the stage, and he continued to write them occasionally for years, since they were popular with magazine readers both here and in England. Kirk and Kirk, in the Howells volume of the American Writers Series, record the enthusiasm of such English readers as Sir Edmund Gosse for these "middle forms between drama and narrative," as Howells called them. Clarence Gohdes in *The Literature of the American People* comments upon the popularity of Howells' one-act farces with the readers of *Harper's*, as does Arthur Hobson Quinn in his *History of the American Drama*.

But Howells was not content to confine himself to his "middle form" and aspired to write full length dramas for the professional stage.[41] One of these, *A Counterfeit Presentment*, was purchased by the actor, Lawrence Barrett, who appeared in it for the first time in Cincinnati in October, 1877, but Barrett refused to play it for more than a night or two in any one place, and it never reached the New York stage. A somewhat similar fate attended Howells' other attempts to become a dramatist. Walter J. Meserve, in his *Complete Plays of William Dean Howells* (1960), points out that the only plays by Howells which enjoyed even a moderate degree of success on the stage (and it was never a financial success) were a translation from the Spanish which was given the title, *Yorick's Love,* and a translation from the Italian called *Samson.* While Barrett played *A Counterfeit Presentment* some thirty times, Meserve states, he seemed to share the opinion of Joseph Jefferson and William Gillette that it lacked dramatic action.[42]

Since both Howells and Herne moved to New York at about the same time, they were in fairly close touch with one another. Herne called on Howells at the Navarro Apartments on West 59th Street, occasionally, and they kept up their correspondence, as people did in the days before visiting by telephone became the custom. Julie Herne recalls the Christmas Day in 1892 when she as a little girl carried a box of flowers, and a letter from her father to Howells, since Herne, who had to be at the theatre, could not go. Awed by the presence of the great writer, some of whose books she had read, overwhelmed by his distinguished graciousness and by the beauty of his daughter Mildred, Julie gave him the flowers but forgot to deliver the letter in her pocket. When she reached home, Katherine said that she must return and apologize to Mr. Howells for her carelessness. But Julie refused. It would be a stupid, silly anti-climax to her beautiful visit. So it was agreed that she should write a note of explanation and leave it with the letter at Mr. Howells' door. It took her an hour to compose her note of apology and another hour to make the long journey downtown to the Navarro Apartments and back. But she was rewarded a few days later when Mr. Howells wrote a charming letter of thanks to her father, and mentioned his pleasure in Julie's little note.

On March 5, 1894, Herne produced a one-act tragedy by Howells called *Bride Roses,* which had been written the previous year and had appeared in *Harper's.*[43] Herne put it on as a curtain raiser at a special matinee of *Shore Acres* given for the unemployed actors of the city. The audience at Daly's either failed to grasp the implications of the little play or simply were not interested.[44] But Howells, who attended the matinee, was delighted with the performance, which, with its outstanding actors, was excellent, and he went behind the scenes and congratulated Herne.[45] On this occasion Herne renewed the invitation he had first extended to Howells two years earlier — to spend some time behind the scenes and study play production from the practical standpoint of the actor and producer.[46] Herne always felt that Howells' desire to write for the professional stage was far more serious than Howells pretended and that if Howells could be induced to familiarize himself with stage conditions and requirements he could write successful plays. But Howells always refused. Herne attributed it to shyness, but the real reason lay deeper.

In Howells, as all readers of his novels know, there was a large element of almost feminine delicacy and refinement. As a young man he had recoiled in horror from the scenes a night editor on a Cincinnati paper was forced to come in contact with and had fled back to the "cleanly respectabilities" of Columbus. Later, in *Years of My Youth* he spoke of "the necessity of my morbid nerves to save themselves from abhorrent contacts." There can be little doubt that the scenes backstage were too rough and crude for him to face, and in *The Story of a Play* he speaks of the "bareness and roughness which seems the first characteristic of the theatre behind the scenes." The dramatist, Maxwell, in this novel has an instinctive distaste for the theatre and the things connected with it, and it is difficult to believe that Howells has not introduced some of his own sensitiveness into Maxwell. "But he hated to be mixed up with all that, and he perceived that he must be mixed up with it more and more, if he wrote for the theatre. Whether he liked it or not, he was part of the thing which in its entirety meant high-kicking and toe-practice, as well as the expression of the most mystical passions of the heart. There was an austerity in him which the fact offended, and he did what he could to appease this austerity by reflecting that it was the drama and never the theatre that he loved; but for the time this was useless. He saw that if he wrote dramas he could not hold aloof from the theatre, nor from actors and actresses — heavies and juveniles, and emotionals and soubrettes. . . . He reminded himself that Shakespeare even must have undergone all that. But this did not console him. He was himself, and what another, the greatest, had suffered would not save him." From the well-ordered security and respectability of the Editor's Study Howells could write that of course the dramatist must know the theatre, and in the July, 1889, issue of *Harper's* he had stated that "Shakespeare, Goethe, Schiller, Goldoni, Moliere, Lope, to mention only the greatest of their kind, wrote their plays in the theatre or in constant rapport with it, and from their intimacy with actors and acting learned how to make their words, 'speak to the eye,' as Mr. Harrigan has fortunately phrased it; and so far as we yet have a drama, it has been produced on the same terms, and on these terms only." This was all very well in theory, but the actuality, if we may believe that *The Story of a Play* was based upon Howells' own experience, was quite different. Not only was the atmosphere of the physical theatre repulsive — "Women in long aprons were sweeping the floors and pounding the seats, and a smell of dust from their labors [was] mixed with the smell of paint and glue and escaping gas which pervaded the atmosphere of the stage" — but the actors and actresses were repulsive too — eogtistical, unreliable, and scarcely respectable. Speaking of the actor-producer who had taken his play, and had promised to present it regularly on his tour, but who instead gave it only occasionally, Maxwell says bitterly, "Well, I might have known it! Why did I ever trust one of that race? They have no idea of what good faith is, except as something that brings down the house when they register a noble vow." The character of the actor-producer, Godolphin, might have been based on that of Lawrence Barrett, who similarly put on Howells' *A Counterfeit Presentment* for a night or two in smaller towns, and finally in Boston, but who never gave it an extended run, or put it on in New York, as he may have promised to. Maxwell's attitude toward the whole race of actors is thoroughly cynical. Not only have they little moral integrity — Maxwell marvels that Godolphin has been married to his leading lady for a whole year and yet there has been no rumor of a divorce — but they likewise have no artistic integrity. Godolphin, to Maxwell's horror, was constantly suggesting senseless changes in the play to "fatten" his part, and he refused to go on with the play unless the really talented Yolande Havisham was dismissed from the cast — because Yolande was stealing his scenes. We know that Lawrence Barrett was constantly making changes in *A Counterfeit Presentment* and in *Yorick's Love*.

Howells actually had the greatest contempt for the stagecraft which Herne innocently kept urging him to learn, for there is little doubt that Howells is speaking through Maxwell when the latter says: "They talk about a knowledge of the stage as if the stage were a difficult science, instead of a very simple piece of mechanism whose limitations and possibilities any one can seize at a glance. All that their knowledge of it comes to is clap-trap, pure and simple." With this condescending and cavalier attitude towards the art of the drama, it is not surprising that the great novelist never could write a really successful play for the professional stage, though he tried more than once.

In this novel Howells undoubtedly describes the kind of play he would have liked to write: one that dealt with "facts of American life — simply, vigorously, and honestly. . . . It was not mawkish and it was not romantic. In its highest reaches it made you think, by its stern and unflinching fidelity to the implications, of Ibsen; but it was not too much to say that it had a charm often wanting to that master. It was full of the real American humor; it made its jokes, as Americans did, in the very face of the most disastrous possibilities; and in the love-passages it was delicious. The whole episode of the love between Haxard's daughter, Salome, and Atland was simply the sweetest and freshest bit of nature in the modern drama." This was the sort of thing that Howells had done more than once in the novel, but he could never do it in a play because he blindly refused to recognize that the techniques of the two arts are different.

Herne early recognized that Howells had a great play in his novel, *The Rise of Silas Lapham,* and in 1889 he wrote to Garland: "Should you and Mrs. Howells conclude to write a play or plays, particularly should you induce Mr. Howells to work with you on a dramatization of Silas Lapham — and put it before the public — will you give me the stage management of it? I know I can do grand work for you in that line, and at the same time benefit myself through winning the endorsement of — and perhaps the acknowledgement of being worthy to be enrolled in — in a measure — in the army of the realistic workers of the day." Nothing came of Herne's suggestion.

But that Howells shared Garland's esteem for Herne's ability as a dramatist even before he had seen *Margaret Fleming* is revealed by Howells' endeavor in January of 1890 to get Herne to produce *The American Claimant,* a revision of a play, *Colonel Sellers as a Scientist,* which Clemens and Howells had written in 1883. Herne wanted to make substantial changes, which apparently neither Howells nor Clemens was willing to accept, and Clemens in 1892 published the work in story form. The exchange of letters between Howells and Clemens is printed in *Mark Twain - Howells Letters,* (1960), edited by Henry Nash Smith and William M. Gibson.

Howells, influenced by his reading of Tolstoy, had embarked upon his series of novels of social protest, beginning with a *Hazard of New Fortunes* in 1890 and including *The Quality of Mercy* (1892), and *A Traveler From Altruria* (1894). Howells did a few of the short parlor pieces for *Harper's* during these years when he was a social reformer in fiction, but as far as is known, no serious full-length drama.

Then in the *New York Mirror* on February 22, 1896, there appeared a brief item stating that Howells and Paul Kester were dramatizing *The Rise of Silas Lapham* for the actor-producer, William Henry Crane. Howells could hardly have made a more unsuitable choice of actor and collaborator. Crane was primarily a comedian, and although he had made a great success in Bronson Howard's *The Henrietta,* he was entirely unsuited for the part of Silas Lapham, since he was a very small, wiry little man with a comical face. Paul Kester represented all that Howells had been preaching against in the American novel and drama, for Kester wrote wholly in the "cloak and dagger" tradition. In 1893 he had had a stage success in a romantic play, *Zamar,* and later he was to write *Sweet Nell of Old Drury* and to dramatize *When Knighthood Was in Flower.* One reason for Howells' choice of Kester was that they were relatives — Kester's mother and Howells were cousins — and

William Dean Howells

Howells and his wife and children always had a great affection for Paul Kester and his brother Vaughan. Letters show that Howells had helped the young man with encouragement, advice, and loans of money which he would never let Kester repay.

After the scenario was written, Crane lost interest, and Herne, hearing of the work, wrote to Howells asking to see it. Howells, who was living at the Westminster Hotel, dispatched a note to Kester, who lived at the corner of 101st and Riverside Drive, asking him to bring the manuscript to the hotel. Herne at this time was playing *Shore Acres* in Jersey City, Newark, and Brooklyn, opening in Brooklyn on November 29, 1897. During Herne's engagement at the Fifth Avenue Theatre in January of 1898, Howells conferred with Herne about the play, and as a result of these conferences, Kester went ahead with the writing, Howells stating in a letter to Henry James that "Paul gets it together, and then I revise it." In the same letter (*Life in Letters*, II, 8) he tells James that there "is a good prospect" of Herne's taking the play. Herne meanwhile had embarked on a long tour through the South and to the Pacific Coast, not returning until May, 1898.

Herne's letter to Howells, written on June 8, 1898, is worth quoting.

> Dear Mr. Howells:
> We have gone over the play very carefully. You have in Acts 1 and 4 the theme — the story — for a very great play; but, as a whole, the work in its present form is not a play — it is a transcript of the book. Silas Lapham as a book is very great — a marvelous piece of art. The characterizations perfect and all that, as of course you know. But while there is a great play in the book, the book is not a play.
> Since reading your manuscript, I am more than ever convinced that my theory of the impossibility of dramatizing a great book is correct. What one must do in order to make a play of a great book is freely *adapt it*. Fill himself with the strength and beauty of the book, the story, the characterizations and all that, then close the book and write his play, retaining all the strength of the book, and contributing to it stagecraft, introducing fresh characters, new talk, and departing from the book when necessary.
> Your play is not clearly set forth for theatre audiences. There are many beauties in it, but . . . ."

Herne then proceeds to go into considerable detail about the deficiencies of the Kester - Howells manuscript as a stage play. He concludes by inviting Howells and Mildred to come down to Herne Oaks for a few days and "go over the whole thing."[47]

Howells wrote at once declining Herne's offer and his invitation and then wrote to Paul Kester on June 10, enclosing Herne's letter.

> My Dear Paul:
> The enclosed letter will explain itself. I am writing to Mr. Herne that I cannot undertake the radical reconstruction he looks to, with the uncertainty of succeeding at last. I do not know whether to suggest that you would do the work; perhaps this letter will seem more encouraging to you than it does to me. I feel that so far as he is concerned it ends the matter.
> Yours ever,
> W. D. Howells

Herne, accustomed to the rough give and take of the world of the stage, had spoken frankly and bluntly, and perhaps with too little appreciation of the more delicate sensitivity of the literary artist he was addressing. It is not difficult for us to imagine the dismay with which the sensitive Howells read his letter, especially the unfortunate phrases about "introducing fresh characters and new talk." In his detailed analysis of the play, Herne had stated that the love story must have "a different treatment." We can imagine how this must have shocked Howells; yet we know today that the love story is the great weakness of the novel — a farcical mix-up out of harmony with the fine realism of the main story. Herne was right, but he was not tactful. Had Herne read *The Story of a Play* which was to appear later that year, he would have had a clearer comprehension of Howells' whole attitude towards the stage, which was that of a fastidious person forced against his will to handle some very dirty tools. "It won't do to despise any public, even the theatre-going public." Maxwell added the last words with a faint sigh. "It's always second-rate," said his wife passionately. "Third-rate, fourth-rate!" When Mrs. Maxwell uses the phrases of the theatrical world they "make her flesh creep," and whenever Maxwell comes into contact with this world we can feel him wince. And when Godolphin, the actor-manager, talks of making changes in his play, Maxwell's aversion mounts to horror. "I was just thinking how everything he ever got me to do to it," he looked down at the manuscript, "was false and wrong." When Maxwell and his wife learn that Godolphin plans to make basic changes in the play, "The thought of this was so petrifying that even Louise could not at once find words for it, and they were both silent, as people sometimes are, when a calamity has befallen them, in the hope that if they do not speak it will turn out a miserable dream." Neither had dreamt of "anything so high-handed as his undertaking to work it over himself," and Maxwell paces the floor in "mute anguish."

Howells had a high esteem for Herne and his work, as we have seen, and this regard was as high as ever in January of 1898 when in reply to an invitation from Herne to see *Shore Acres* at the Fifth Avenue Theatre, he replied: "Thank you for the box. I shall be delighted to come, not only to see the dear Little Julie, but the sweet and gentle play again." But when Herne proposed changes in *Silas Lapham* he committed sacrilege, and it is doubtful if Howells' feelings towards him were ever really cordial again. Howells wrote to Henry James on July 31, 1898: "I have been fool enough to dramatize *Silas Lapham* for an actor who wanted it, and now does *not* want it. What a race! Their obligations are chains of flowers." And on August 2 he wrote to Clemens in almost identical words. (*Life in Letters,* II, 94, 96).

As a matter of fact, Herne had found only one scene in the Kester-Howells play that was stageworthy as written — the dinner scene at the Corey's in which Lapham gets drunk and disgraces himself. Herne's judgment was confirmed by the subsequent history of the play. Howells offered it to one manager after another, and all rejected it. It was offered to Crane again, and finally in 1903 to Daniel Frohman, who rejected it and wrote: "If the play should be desired by anyone, for stage purposes, it would have to be put in more effective theatric condition, as the dialogue is somewhat extensive." Many years later, in 1919, Howells permitted Lillian Sabine to dramatize the play. Dr. Quinn, who saw this version, found it very satisfactory, but it was not a popular play.

Herne deeply regretted the break in his friendship with Howells, and he viewed the great novelist's attitude towards the stage as one of those unaccountable limitations or blind spots that are found in even the greatest of men. During the summer of 1898 Herne read aloud to his family *The Landlord at Lion's Head.* He considered the book one of Howells' greatest achievements and wrote the author a letter of praise and congratulations.[48] He received a courteous note in reply, but their old footing was never resumed. When *Griffith Davenport* was produced in New York early in 1899, Herne invited

Howells to see it, but his invitation was declined. Even Herne's death, two years later, failed to heal the wound, for Howells' note of condolence to Katharine was so brief and distant that it hurt her deeply. She said, "He had better not have written me at all."[49]

The injustice in Howells' attitude towards Herne, and "that race," and the illogicality of his attitude towards the theatre constitute a curious lapse in imaginative sympathy in the great novelist. Howells would have been the first to insist upon the importance of craftsmanship in his own profession of novelist, and that the novelist must undergo a long apprenticeship in his craft before he could claim to be a professional. Nonetheless he declared that this did not hold true of the theatre — it was "a very simple piece of mechanism whose limitations and possibilities any one can seize at a glance." But, if it was so simple as all this, why did all managers reject his play? And it was a direct contradiction of what he had written ten years earlier in the Editor's Study; then he had stated that all the great dramatists, including Shakespeare, "wrote their plays in the theatre or in constant rapport with it."

Like the rest of us, Howells could rationalize at times, and he could be as irrational about the theatre as his friend Mark Twain was about business. For up to the time of his great disaster, Clemens believed that in business anyone could succeed if he were lucky enough to find an invention and patent it and if he had sufficient enterprise to promote it. Of course, in his own field it was quite different — there, as Clemens often told aspiring writers, only a thorough knowledge based on a long apprenticeship, plus native talent, could bring success. In the end, Clemens was snatched from certain disaster by a professional businessman, H. H. Rogers. Ironically enough, a professional also stood ready to help Howells, to help him learn in the theatre the many things that go into the making of a play, or to make his play for him. But Howells could not bring himself to face either alternative.

9

SHORE ACRES

The story of the writing and production of *Shore Acres*, Herne's most popular play, is a story of success achieved in the face of apparently insuperable obstacles. In the early summer of 1888 at Ashmont, after he had made plans for the coming season's tour in *Drifting Apart,* Herne had begun work on a new play which he tentatively titled *The Hawthornes.* One day the children, playing in the garden, heard their father reading aloud, through the open window of his study. They crept closer and listened attentively to the first act, in which an old farmer called Uncle Nat was pleading with his brother not to sell the land where their mother lay buried. The sadness of their father's voice moved the children to tears, but the second act in the farmhouse kitchen, with the family bustling about preparing a turkey dinner for a silver wedding anniversary, went more cheerfully, and they were delighted when the youngsters in the play got off some of their own family jokes.

But many discouraging years were to pass before the new play finally emerged as the highly successful *Shore Acres,* and many, many changes in the script — those "changes" that so horrified Howells in the world of the theatre. That the dramatic scene in the lighthouse in Act III was suggested by a similar scene in an old play which Herne had adapted and acted in his youth, Murdoch's *The Keeper of the Lighthouse Cliff,* is probably true, but that Act III was "taken" from the old play as Winter states in his *Life of David Belasco* is as inaccurate as many of Winter's other statements about Herne.[50] The locale was the New England sea coast. Herne did not decide definitely on the coast of Maine until after Katharine and the children had visited Lamoine that July. She and the children went by steamer to Bar Harbor early in July, and from Bar Harbor took a small steamboat to the little fishing village of Lamoine across the bay from Mt. Desert Island. For the first few days after their arrival, the Hernes boarded with the skipper of the small steamer, Captain Cousins, and his wife, and Katharine learned at first hand the engaging qualities of the true Down East Yankee. Later they joined some Ashmont friends at the Galt House, a rambling old farmhouse converted into a summer hotel, which overlooked the bay. Directly across the expanse of blue water was the rapidly blossoming magnificence of Bar Harbor with its splendid big houses and its New York millionaires, but Katharine preferred the simplicity and kindliness of Lamoine, with its clover fields stretching gently down to the sea from its fragrant forests of pine.

But, unfortunately for the peaceful simplicity of Lamoine, a wealthy real estate dealer from New York conceived the idea that summer of making a second Bar Harbor out of Lamoine and began taking options on all the shore front farms. The minds of the simple farmers and fishermen were soon inflamed with dreams of wealth, and a tremendous land boom, still remembered by some of the oldest inhabitants, was started. Never was there a truer illustration of the old adage that the love of money is the root of all evil. Families were rent asunder by heated arguments as to whether to sell now or to hold on for a higher price. One venerable patriarch, according to a story still recalled, rose from his deathbed to pronounce a curse on his children if they sold the land. The stories reached the Galt House, of course, and the "summer people" were transformed from a group of city people seeking rest and relaxation into a crowd of excited gamblers. Like the rest, Katharine was soon discussing shore rights, options, and mortgages like an expert, and she quickly grabbed up a choice site, a rolling meadow overlooking the bay, from James Berry, and with the mortgage safely in her hands, wrote to her husband of their good fortune.

When Katharine returned home, she gave her husband a vivid description of Lamoine, its people, and the boom; and if Herne remained somewhat skeptical about the value of the land, he was convinced that Lamoine must be the setting for his play and its land boom the background of his story. He began to rewrite the script. But the summer was almost over, and he soon had to set out on tour. Most of the work on the new play had to wait for next summer's "leisure."

Katharine kept urging her husband to go to Lamoine himself next summer to get local color at first hand for the play, but when the next summer came Herne felt that he could not afford it, for the season had not been financially successful. It was the year of *Drifting Apart* and the *Minute Men,* both financial failures, and although he had recouped his losses and accumulated a little surplus late in the season with his old standby, *Hearts of Oak,* he still did not think he could afford a trip to Maine.

Early that summer, Hamlin Garland and his brother Frank, the latter now an actor in Herne's company, had been persuaded by Katharine to take a trip along the Maine coast to Lamoine. It was a short trip, for neither of the two brothers had much money, but when they returned they were enthusiastic about Maine. Hamlin Garland arrived at the Hernes' one Sunday, as usual in time for the big midday dinner, shouting at the top of his voice about the wonderful beauty of Maine, and he described with his habitual gusto the old salty characters he had encountered.

"I tell you, Herne," he boomed (he always prefaced his statement with this phrase), "that's the country for you. There's where you should finish your play. You should see those people, the old fishermen with beards under their chins, looking as though they had sprouted from their chests."

The words of "The Dean" always carried great weight with Herne, and a few minutes later he announced to his delighted family that he was going to Maine with them this year. Incidentally, when he played Uncle Nat, he wore just such a beard as Garland described, and this make-up became traditional with all the actors who played the part.

The Galt House, where the Hernes stayed, is still standing, though now closed, its front porch overlooking the bay to Mt. Desert Island in the distance, and likewise the general store on the main road where Herne talked with the fishermen, farmers, and lobstermen who congregated there. An old man is still living, as this is being written, who remembers driving Herne along the single road that borders the shore and cuts through the pine forest. He recalls that he thought Herne looked more like a senator than an actor and that he seemed to have the politician's interest in stopping to talk with people whenever he saw an opportunity. One day on Captain Cousin's little steamer, the *Minnehaha,* the Hernes went to visit a lighthouse. Herne plied the keeper with questions as he was being shown the interior, and later made notes of all he had seen and heard. The mornings he devoted to working on the play, and on August 5, 1889, he wrote to Garland: "I've finished *The Hawthornes* — 'rough finished' — and you'll like some of it." Herne had absorbed much of the local color of Lamoine and much of the character of its people during the summer, and he had familiarized himself with the details of the land boom.[51]

The boom, incidentally, soon collapsed, and the New York promoter was never heard of again in Lamoine. Bar Harbor, across the bay, had, in fact, reached its peak as a fashionable resort, and was to undergo a gradual decline. Lamoine today is still beautiful, but almost deserted, only the foundations of a few of the hastily built summer hotels remaining as mute witnesses of its former dreams of grandeur. The Galt House has been preserved only because it was in the area later included in the present Lamoine State Park. Katharine's venture into real estate promotion was, however, highly successful in that indirectly it gave Herne the background material for his most successful play.

The Hawthornes was laid aside, as we have seen, for the great adventure of Margaret Fleming, and for some pot-boilers that Herne had to write as a result of the financial failure of that play. One of the pot-boilers was the Irish play, My Colleen, written on commission for the actor Tony Farrell and his wife. My Colleen was in the sentimental tradition established by Dion Boucicault's The Shaughraun, and Tony Farrell was a lesser Chauncey Olcott — good-looking, clever, with a pleasing light tenor voice. Edith Wharton in The Age of Innocence tells of the popularity of The Shaughraun in the seventies: "The Shaughraun always packed the house. In the galleries the enthusiasm was unreserved; in the stalls and boxes people smiled a little at the hackneyed sentiments and clap-trap situations, and enjoyed the play as much as the galleries did." Twenty years later this type of play was still very much alive, for the Farrells played several years in My Colleen, for which Herne received $2000. Even Garland was amused by the humor which Herne had sprinkled liberally through the play. Herne wrote the play rapidly in May and June of 1891, and as he finished each act he would read it to his wife and Garland, who would give his own peculiar laugh, a high, raucous "Ha!" when Herne read a witty line.

Then followed Herne's time-consuming duties as stage manager for Klaw and Erlanger, and the removal to New York. Neither during the rehearsals nor the tours of such huge spectacles as The Soudan and The Country Circus did Herne have much time to devote to The Hawthornes. Another play that he wrote during the winter of 1891 was a comedy of Negro life which had been commissioned by Klaw and Erlanger. This play, which Erlanger had stipulated should be a mixture of comedy, melodrama, songs, and dances, was entitled *Coon Hollow*, but was never produced. During the New York run of *The Country Circus*, however, he found some time to work on *The Hawthornes*, whose title he had now changed to *Shore Acres*.

Unlike most actors, Herne was an early riser, and he would write all day on *Shore Acres* and leave for the theatre about seven o'clock after an early dinner. After *The Country Circus* had been running for several weeks, Katharine noticed that he had changed his schedule and was leaving at half-past six instead of seven, and returning much later at night. She could not understand why he had to get to the theatre so early, and when she questioned him he replied evasively. Finally, when she insisted on an explanation, he told her that one of the actors playing a small part was seriously ill, and that he had taken his place in order to save the man's job and salary for him, for in those days, actors received no pay when illness forced them out of the cast. Actors of standing might endanger their prestige by pinch-hitting for "bit" players, and Katharine was concerned about the injury Herne might do to his reputation. She begged him to stop this folly and let Klaw and Erlanger get an understudy. But Herne said quietly, "The man is sick, he has a family, and he needs the money," and he continued to fill in for him until the actor was well enough to return to the cast.

In January of 1892, almost four years after he had written the first rough draft of *The Hawthornes,* Herne finally completed *Shore Acres*. It was quite a different play from the early version of 1888. The setting is "Shore Acres Farm on Frenchman's Bay, with a view of Mount Desert Island and Cadillac Mountain. "To the right," the stage directions continue, "are the stately Schoodic Mountains, veiled in mist. On the right of the stage, at the back, on a rocky bluff dotted with dwarf pines, and overlooking the bay is Berry Light. It is separated from the farmhouse by a shady road, which runs across the stage from left to right. The farmhouse, on the right is barely visible, being hidden in a profusion of shrubs and flowers. Trees overhang the roof; a whitewashed fence divides the dooryard from the road. To the left of the stage is an old barn, its doors open, its littered yard enclosed by a rail fence. A dove cote is built into the peak of its gabled roof, and doves come and go leisurely. Outside the fence, at the upper end, is a pump, beneath which is a trough filled with water. Against the lower end of the fence lies a plough. Trees overhang the roof of the barn, and join those overhanging the house from the other side. At right center is a gnarled old tree, and beneath it is a bench. At the rise of the curtain, and until the act is well in progress, the wind gently sways the foliage with a slight rustling sound. Birds sing, and flit to and fro. The sound of multitudinous insects is the one distinct note of the scene. The bay is calm, and in the distance a catboat is occasionally seen sailing lazily, appearing and disappearing among the islands. A tiny steam launch appears once, about the middle of the set, and is seen no more. A mowing machine is heard at work in the distance off left."

At the rise of the curtain there is a short scene in which the country mail carrier arrives. There is a short colloquy between him and a little girl. Then Helen Berry, "a girl of seventeen, with a frank yet thoughtful manner," enters. She has golden-red hair and brown eyes, and carries a small pail full of berries. She is followed by Uncle Nat, "a man of sixty, whose large, sturdy frame shows signs of toil. His eyes, of a faded blue-gray, have the farseeing look common to sailors. He wears his yellow-white hair rather long, and he is clean shaven save for the tippet of straw-white beard that seems to grow up from his chest, and to form a sort of frame for his benevolent, weather-beaten old face. Uncle Nat is of the soil, yet there is an inherent poise and dignity about him that is typical of men who have mastered their environment. He has great cheer, and much sly, quiet humor. He wears overalls of a faded blue, a blue-checked jumper, beneath which one glimpses a red flannel shirt, and on his head is a farmer's much-battered, wide straw hat. His sleeves are rolled back, and he carries a pitchfork in his hand."

No resumé can give an idea of the complete naturalness, spontaneity, and simplicity with which Herne endows these two characters in his opening scene. They speak from the heart and to the heart in language that seems to have nothing of the theatre about it. They have spoken for only a few minutes before they have established themselves permanently in the affections of the audience. Helen, a girl of intelligence who has made the most of her somewhat limited educational opportunities, is in love with Dr. Sam Warren, a young physician of advanced ideas. Her father, Martin Berry, the owner of Shore Acres and the keeper of Berry Light, is opposed to the

James A. Herne

"One of the best pictures ... of Herne ... comes from the pen of his daughter Chrystal ... 'How I loved him—so gentle, so patient and so much fun. He was our beloved playmate, sharing with us his rare sense of fun, his joy in life and sunshine ... (he) rarely punished us ... my father would take me into his study and talk to me, with such gentleness and understanding ... that I would vow to be a better child."

"...photograph taken years later, when he was middle-aged, shows him standing in a sm[a]ll boat...at Sayville. Herne...looks more like a prize-fighter...his chest is broad and dee[p] ...arms and legs muscular...features are regular, but...not handsome...gives an i[m]pression of strength and masculinity."

With Herne in the photograph are Julie (center) and Dorothy at Herne Oaks.

y darling Chrystal,

All that I have achieved and more, it possible for you to achieve—Have confi- ce in yourself—assert that indomitable 'I' d success will surely come to you.
With deep love
Jas. A.

ville, L.I., 1846"

trait by C. F. Conly, Boston

Julie Herne

"Most of the information about Herne's early life is derived from Julie Herne's biography and was related to her by her father.... From about the time when she made her first appearance in Shore Acres she began to plan her biography of her father and made extensive notes of his conversations with her."

The portrait of Julie Herne was taken from the printed program of *Richter's Wife*, written by Julie and presented in 1905 by Katharine Herne with Julie and Chrystal in the cast.

"As in the book, his Griffith Davenport is an idealist and a mystic, but he makes him more real and human by giving him a sense of humor. The manuscript...was lost in a fire...but the copy of Act III found...by Julie...clearly reveals this quality in Herne's recreation of the character of Griffith Davenport."

The Herne family in 1899, the year he produced Israel Zangwill's *Children of the Ghetto* and opened his own play *Sag Harbor*. The strain was too great.

"He was in high good spirits... but they were shocked to see how worn and thin he was; the rehearsals and the grilling heat had taken something out of him that he was never to regain, and he seemed to have aged in a few weeks."

From left to right, Dorothy, Katharine, James A. Herne with Jack, Chrystal and Julie.

"Suddenly, when Katharine was sixteen, the fortunes of the family took a turn for the better. An uncle...deciding to go to California...took his sister's family with him ...a photograph of Katharine...shows a slender, graceful girl of seventeen, with large dark eyes and a sensitive face, her delicate features surrounded by a wealth of dark hair."

Portrait by Jones, Robertson & Calverley, Elite Photographic Studio, San Francisco.

James A. Herne as Nathaniel Berry in *Shore Acres*.

"... Uncle Nat, 'a man of sixty, whose large, sturdy frame shows signs of toil. His eyes, of a faded blue-gray, have the far-seeing look common to sailors ... he is clean shaven save for the tippet of straw-white beard that seems to grow up from his chest.'"

Portrait by J. K. Stevens & Son Co., Chicago.

Katharine Corcoran Herne

"Public, critics and fellow players were impressed by her poise and grace, her dramatic instinct and ability, her power of emotional expression, and her melodious voice...her emotional maturity (at her debut) seemed amazing to those who did not know they were seeing a young girl who had fought for her existence on the streets...at an age when most children are listening to fairy tales."

Portrait by Apeda Studio. Inc., New York.

Julie as Helen Berry and James A. Herne as Nathaniel Berry in *Shore Acres*.

"Then Helen Berry, 'a girl of seventeen, with frank yet thoughtful manner' enters. She has golden-red hair and brown eyes and carries a small pail full of berries. She is followed by Uncle Nat,...No resume can give an idea of the complete naturalness, spontaniety and simplicity with which Herne endows these two characters...they have spoken only a few minutes before they have established themselves permanently in the affections of the audience."

Portrait authographed "To K. C. (Katharine Corcoran) from Julie A. & Jas. A."

Katharine Corcoran Herne with Julie (left) and Chrystal.

"It was a marriage that was to endure through many trials and crises and one that was to be singularly happy. Herne was to write all the leading feminine parts ... for his wife and she was to create all but two of them. ... later when the children came ... Herne would write to Katharine and the children every night after the performance."

Portrait taken about 1888 by Conly, Boston.

Chrystal Herne

"*Tyler's offer meant that Herne's best-loved child was... to try her wings for herself... he knew her to be more sensitive and more highly emotional than his other children, but with a great capacity for suffering.... Chrystal developed an inner strength and spiritual power that sustained her through many bitter ordeals.*"

Herne Oaks

"It was the conventional 'Queen Anne summer cottage' of the nineties, complete with gabl[e] and dormer windows,... its best feature being a wide verandah which commanded a love[ly] view of the bay framed in tall trees.... Herne soon installed ... a semi-circular room on t[he] second floor whose six windows overlooked the woods and the bay. It was his summer wo[rk] room for the rest of his life."

Shore Acres

match because of his detestation for Dr. Sam's ideas. Helen is bitter and depressed, but Uncle Nat, who loves her as if she were his own daughter, cheers her and counsels patience. Martin Berry wants Helen to marry an older but wealthy man, Josiah Blake, the postmaster and storekeeper, who is a persistent though frequently rebuffed suitor. The scene which follows, in which a neighbor, Joel Gates, comes to borrow Uncle Nat's shotgun to kill a fox, is a remarkably realistic bit of genre painting, showing how thoroughly Herne had grasped the nature of the Down East Yankee. Herne introduces the Lamoine land boom in a scene between Josiah Blake and Martin Berry. Josiah urges Martin to sell him the farm, for which he is willing to pay a high price, but Martin hesitates because he had promised his mother never to sell the land. Blake's proposals are most attractive. As he says, land in Bar Harbor is so high you can't touch a foot of it, not by covering it with gold dollars, and Lamoine is bound to be next in the line of development. He shows Martin how quickly he can become rich, so rich he can live in Bangor, and can move his mother's remains from the little family burial space on the farm to the fine cemetery in Bangor. But Martin still hesitates because of the promise he had given his mother, and says he will talk to his wife Ann, and to Nat, about it. Concerning Josiah's wish to marry Helen, he is, however, in full agreement and has little doubt that Helen will obey his wishes. Dr. Sam Warren is despised by Martin for his "free-thinking," his open advocacy of the doctrines of Darwin, and by Josiah for his lack of wealth.

Herne's sense of the stage, based upon the experience of a lifetime, is evidenced by his understanding of the dramatic importance of contrast — a serious scene is almost invariably followed by a light scene of genre painting and humor. Instinctively he seems to know just when to break the tension. The scene between Helen and her fourteen-year-old brother, which occurs at this point in the play, is an example. Incidentally, it reveals a knowledge of adolescent psychology worthy of a Mark Twain. Herne's boys are always real boys.

The next scene, between Helen and Dr. Sam, is tragic in its implications, and much of its intensity undoubtedly derives from Herne's own experience of the tragedy of the man who is a generation ahead of his contemporaries in his thinking. Dr. Sam, with his love of truth and his devotion to it, is far more religious than the rural traditionalists who scorn him because "he doesn't believe in Hell." He is discouraged because he is an object of suspicion among the simple folk of the countryside, and has few patients. By implication, Herne in his portrayal of Dr. Sam and his situation raises the question of punishing a man for his beliefs. He presents the situation with simple realism, without preaching, and without propaganda. Sam and Helen are both "advanced" social thinkers; Sam gives her Howells' *A Hazard of New Fortunes,* and she is delighted with it and eagerly scans the pages.

Martin Berry comes upon the two lovers, and there is a bitter argument between the two men over Sam's "infidelity," which ends with Martin ordering Sam off the farm. Sam, who plans to go West, make some money, and come back to get Helen, says goodbye to her in a scene of great tenderness. Act I ends with a scene between Martin and Uncle Nat in which Nat quietly pleads with his brother not to sell the land on which their mother is buried.

Act II opens with the famous silver-wedding dinner in the Berry's farm house kitchen. This was probably the most realistic dinner scene ever presented on the American stage. It was a real Down East farm kitchen authentic to the last detail. Not only was there a real fire in the big wood-burning range, but the potatoes and cranberry sauce were cooked on it, and a real turkey was taken out of the oven, golden brown and savory. And the people on the stage actually ate the food — not merely pretended to. The scene must have brought back nostalgic memories to thousands of city dwellers who saw it at the turn of the century for many of them had come from the farm. All the neighbors from the nearby farms are invited, and Herne has caught the hearty spirit of the country festival admirably. Blake finds an opportunity to renew his proposal to Helen, and he is again rejected. Dr. Sam, who is outside the house, manages to get a final farewell with Helen. But all the men at the table are soon talking about the land boom, how many rods of shore front each has and how much the New York millionaires might be willing to pay. Suddenly Martin announces that he has decided to sell his land. His wife Ann is shocked and declares that she will never leave her home. The happy celebration is soon turned into an ugly quarrel as the husband and wife hurl recriminations at each other. All the guests have got up from the table. Then a boy comes in with the news that a sum of money is missing from Blake's till at the store.

Blake at once accuses Dr. Sam of the theft, since Sam had tried to borrow money from him that morning and had been refused. Helen, indignant, calls Blake a liar. This starts a violent quarrel between Helen and her father. The guests leave, and Ann bursts into tears. Helen declares that she is going away with Sam, and Uncle Nat arranges for the two to go down the coast on Captain Ben's boat.

Act III opens in the interior of the Berry Light. It is a stormy night. Uncle Nat is in charge of the light. Martin rushes in and shouts that Helen is gone. Uncle Nat tells him that she and Sam have gone with Captain Ben in the *Liddy Ann*. Martin is filled with anger towards his daughter and Sam, and says vindictively that he hopes their boat sinks. There is a distant sound of a ship's gun, and Nat with horror notes that the light has gone dim. He rushes towards the stairs leading up to the light, but Martin bars his way. Again the ship's gun sounds, louder and nearer shore than before. There is a fight between the two men. Uncle Nat wins, and makes his way, exhausted and falling, up the stairs. The scene shifts to the stormy seas outside with the *Liddy Ann,* her gun booming, storm tossed, off her course, and perilously near the rocks. Then the light shines from the lighthouse, and the *Liddy Ann* makes her way safely past the rocks.

This melodramatic scene is in strong contrast to the realistic genre painting of the rest of the play. William Archer felt that the contrast was so strong that it destroyed the general tone of the play, and other critics shared his opinion. He says in *Playmaking* (p. 20) ". . . . the late James A. Herne inserted into a charming idyllic picture of rural life, entitled *Shore Acres,* a melodramatic scene in a lighthouse, which was hopelessly out of key with the rest of the play." Of course, the theatre-going public of the day loved this scene, and one might conclude that it represented a deliberate concession by Herne to the public taste of the time. Herne's reply to the critics was that the scene was necessary for the sake of contrast.

In Act IV, laid in the Berry farm house on Christmas Eve fifteen months later, Herne returns to the mood of realistic genre painting. Martin is grieving over the absence of his daughter, Ann is mending stockings, and Uncle Nat is playing with the children. Outside, the east wind moans and the snow is blown against the windowpanes. The children are sent off to bed, and Nat and Ann fill their Christmas stockings and put their presents around the tree. Blake arrives with the depressing news that the bottom has dropped out of the land boom. Then Helen and Dr. Sam arrive. Helen has a baby in her arms. Martin throws his arms about his daughter and kisses her, and takes Sam's outstretched hand. He takes his grandson in his arms proudly. Blake apologizes for having accused Dr. Sam of the theft, and shakes hands with Sam and Helen. There is a suspense element involving the land boom and Martin's possible loss of his farm, which is resolved by Uncle Nat near the end of the act, but the principal element of interest is the deep emotional appeal of the reconciliation of the family on Christmas Eve, which Herne develops with a naturalness beyond praise. And this is the general impression of the play — one of quiet realism. For William Dean Howells it was always, as he said, "that sweet and gentle play." And William Archer was to write later in the London *Morning Leader* (Dec. 22, 1900): "In three of its acts it is a faithful, uneventful, quietly humorous picture of rural life in New England. One act, the third, is a sort of melodramatic interlude, thrown in to conciliate the groundlings, but even in this there is a certain imaginative merit. The play, as a whole, is a very original and artistic production."

Herne's struggle to get the play produced is a little drama in itself. *Margaret Fleming* had so damaged his reputation as a playwright with public appeal that the managers to whom he submitted *Shore Acres* all rejected it offhand. All of Herne's plays had been failures; Herne was over fifty and had never yet written a successful play; Herne as a playwright was hopeless — this was their attitude. Finally he took it to Erlanger, who actually read it, and who saw in it the possibilities of a big hit — if he could star Joseph Jefferson, then starring under his management, in the role of Uncle Nat. Erlanger said he would produce the play under no other conditions. But Herne had written the part of Uncle Nat for himself, he had put all that life had taught him into that character, and he felt that only he could interpret Uncle Nat with full sympathy. He tried to persuade Erlanger to see his viewpoint. But Erlanger could never brook opposition. He called Herne a pig-headed, stubborn fool, and fell into one of his frightful rages. Herne, too, had a temper, and a stormy scene ensued which ended with Erlanger firing Herne (when his contract terminated at the end of the season) and shouting as Herne left his office, "And you're the last damned anarchist that ever steps foot in this office!"

It was on February 1, 1892, that Herne lost his job and incurred the enmity of the most powerful man in the American theatrical world. The play on which he had labored for four years had been rejected by the man who controlled most of the theatres in the country. He was fifty-three years old, and in debt. What must have been his feelings as he made his way home to his wife and children can well be imagined.

The next scene in the drama of Herne's life could never be used in any play, story, or novel — it would be regarded as too gross a violation of the law of probability. A few days later Herne received a letter from James H. McVicker, owner of one of the largest and best theatres in Chicago.[52] It read: "Will you please give me an idea of the cost of production, cast, staging, etc. of *Margaret Fleming* — stating if it would suit your purpose to do the play here this coming spring, and what other material you could have in the way of plays to fill two or three weeks? Chicago is always good from June out, and this year I expect it will be extra good." McVicker was one of the most successful managers of his generation and a man for whom Herne had the greatest respect and admiration.[53] His letter lifted Herne from the depths of despair to the mountain tops of hope. He answered at once and sent the manuscripts of both *Margaret Fleming* and *Shore Acres*.

McVicker's reply with respect to *Margaret Fleming* we know. Of *Shore Acres* he said: "I have read *Shore Acres* and like it with all its faults for the reason that I think they will be easily wiped out. I would advise omitting the 1st scene of the 2nd act, for the reason that it would be almost impossible to give it the effect you intend. It requires character horses, character vehicles, and character actors, and with my experience I fear this combination of characters in bits is almost an impossibility and quite so for road purposes. This scene would make a good sketch in the Garland style for a magazine, but I doubt if it can be made valuable on the stage. The 3rd act will be effective when you make the change suggested as to the storm scene, during which talk is unnecessary, and in my opinion the act had better end with the audience in doubt as to the safety of Sam and Helen.[54] This point is debatable, however, and I may be wrong, having only read and not studied it. Now the last act is the weak one for the reason that the interest is centered in Sam and Helen, and you have too much after the audience is satisfied that they are all right, and yet they have nothing to do to hold the interest felt for them. In some way you should settle all difficulties between Blake, Martin, and the farm, and have Sam, Helen, and the baby a surprise party just at the end, and not twenty pages or more after their fate is known. You have got so good a play in *Shore Acres* that you should amend all its faults before you launch it. While the title is good in its way, a better one, I think, for money would be 'Booming' — that is better for the entire country."

The difference in point of view between a critic such as Archer and a theatre owner and manager is interesting. Archer would have changed entirely or eliminated the melodramatic third act; McVicker, although one of the most enlightened managers of his day, would eliminate one of "the sketches in the Garland style," and retain Act III in its entirety except for the dialogue in the last scene. Herne, as we have seen in the case of *Margaret Fleming,* was always anxious to please McVicker — perhaps too anxious — and he eliminated the first scene of Act II and cut out the dialogue from the second scene of Act III. He did not agree with McVicker, however, that Act III should end with the audience in doubt as to the safety of Sam and Helen, and it always ended with the light streaming out from the lighthouse, and the ship once again safely on her course. He likewise clung to his original title. McVicker never liked the title and later wanted a second title added, *Or Town Lots,* and later still, *Shore Acres Subdivision.* When Herne arrived in Chicago early in May, he found that McVicker wanted the ending of *Shore Acres* changed. As Herne had written it, Uncle Nat, left alone in the old kitchen after the family had gone to bed, putters around for several minutes, locking doors, shaking down the stove and making all safe for the night. Herne intended the scene to be played in absolute silence, with only the smiling face of the old man conveying his thoughts to the audience. Such a thing had never been done before and McVicker feared its effect on the audience. He wanted a "comedy finish," and wished the act to end on the scene in which Uncle Nat with the entire cast on stage, is going through the manual of arms with his old army gun, and it goes off accidentally. Although Herne's artistic conscience rebelled at this incongruous ending, he finally consented, though with great reluctance. He likewise agreed to the title *Shore Acres Subdivision* although he felt that it sounded like a real estate advertisement.[55]

Shore Acres, under the title *Shore Acres Subdivision,* had its first production on any stage at McVicker's Theatre in Chicago on May 23, 1892, with Herne as Uncle Nat, Mrs. Herne as Helen Berry, George Fawcett as Martin, William Courtleigh as Sam Warren, and C. Leslie Allen as Blake. It was a good cast and a good production. The reviews were favorable, the audiences apparently pleased, but — the play failed to draw. In fact, it barely paid expenses. *Shore Acres* was a play of atmosphere and character and depended for its effect upon the perfect co-ordination of all its elements — acting, scenery, lighting, and stage effects. Herne said that his aim in the production was to create the harmonious effect of a symphony orchestra. Perhaps this quality was missing in Chicago, because the play had not had time to mellow. But undoubtedly McVicker's "comedy ending" and his unfortunate change in the title, contributed to the play's failure.[56]

But although the play failed to draw, Herne made a personal success as Uncle Nat, and this gave McVicker another inspiration. During the first week of its run he decided that the play must be re-titled *Uncle Nat.* The Chicago drama critics approved of the change, and one of them wrote: "*Shore Acres Subdivision* is as misleading a title as could have been tacked onto Mr. Herne's vital and poetic homely play, which is a folk drama of strong emotions and purposeful characters, with delicate humor and joyous mirth to sweeten its pathos and relieve its passions." The play ran two weeks longer under its new name, but business did not improve; in fact, the change in title seemed to confuse the public and hurt the play. *Uncle Nat* closed on June 11, having run for three weeks to disappointing audiences.[57]

The critics had been favorable, and Amy Leslie's verdict was typical: "The very favorable impression made by this interesting, human folk-drama, the delight of audiences in its droll humor, bright mirth, and quaint pictures, and their sympathies with the deeper emotions of the characters, show how easily this play might have run through most, or all, of the summer season. . . . It has all the elements of popularity that gave *The Old Homestead* a place in the affections of the public, and is a more vital, purposeful drama, with the story of profounder interest, and might be sure of increasing patronage from the great number of those who enjoy these pictures of homely life given in natural colors and truthful simplicity."[58]

Katharine noted how, as the other actors worked into their parts and the cares of directing became lighter for her husband, he enriched his portrayal of Uncle Nat, adding a bit of business here, a better reading there, illumining the character of the old man, making him more human, touching, and endearing so that at the end of the run he was giving the perfect performance he should have given on the opening night. Katharine felt this might have made all the difference in the success of the play. She said nothing then, but in her heart hope was high.

Hamlin Garland, who was now living in Chicago, was on hand, as usual, in his capacity of unofficial press agent. A few nights after the opening of *Margaret Fleming* the Papyrus Club gave a reception for the Hernes and Garland. To Katharine, one of the most touching experiences of the summer was her meeting with Garland's mother. He had described his mother's bleak, lonely existence on the desolate farms of the West, without books, music or recreation, numbed by toil and starved for beauty. Now, old and partly paralyzed, Mrs. Garland was making her first visit to the city. Garland took her to see *Shore Acres* and afterwards behind the scenes to meet the Hernes. Her wistful face, her pathetic pleasure when Katharine gave her a bunch of flowers, and Garland's joy in being able to bring a little brightness and color into her life made an unforgettable impression on the Hernes.

The season in Chicago had been a financial failure and the Hernes returned to New York with only a few hundred dollars to show for their summer's work. Before leaving Chicago at the end of July, Herne wrote a farewell letter to McVicker expressing his appreciation of all the manager had done for his play and voicing his regret that the season had not been the success they had hoped for. McVicker replied: "The very pleasant words contained in yours of yesterday, I assure you are fully appreciated. The financial results will soon be forgotten by me, while the pleasant thoughts created by yourself and wife will linger while memory holds a seat."

No one, save Katharine and Herne himself, had any faith in *Shore Acres* after its Chicago failure. The Hernes had enough money to live on, for the payments on *My Colleen* were coming in, and in October Herne received $600 as a down payment for rewriting an unsuccessful play called *The Volunteer*. Much of his time he devoted to revising and rewriting *Shore Acres* in the light of the Chicago production, and in vainly trying to interest managers in the play, one of them Field of the Boston Museum. One day early in December, as Herne was walking down Broadway, he met two men whom he had known in California — the actor, Joseph Grismer, and William A. Brady, the manager of the new heavyweight champion, James J. Corbett. "Jim Herne!" they said. "You're just the man we want to see. We want you for the part of a Negro in our new play, and we'll pay you a hundred and fifty dollars a week."

The play was *The New South,* by Clay M. Greene. Brady was the producer, and Grismer and his wife Phoebe were to have the leading roles. The part they wanted Herne for was only a bit, but it was of great importance to the play, and no actor of importance could be found willing to appear as a Negro. At that time, Negro actors, except in variety or minstrel shows were practically nonexistent. Vanity, the besetting sin of actors, was notably absent in Herne, and he accepted the part. After he read it, he found that it was, indeed, only a bit. He was on the stage hardly fifteen minutes during the entire play. But it had always been his conviction that a good actor did not need a star role in order to make a hit. All he needed was a chance to act. "Give me one moment of real acting in any part," he often said, "and I'll hold my own with any star on earth." He saw that the part of Sampson had such a moment. He signed the contract to play it for the four weeks of the New York run.

A few days after Herne signed the contract he got a letter from Field in Boston stating that an English play called *Agatha,* which had been a success in London and which Field had booked for the Boston Museum with the expectation that it would finish out the season, had proved a failure on its out-of-town tryout, and in consequence he had two weeks' open time in February. He proposed to fill it with a tryout of *Shore Acres,* and he was sending his stage director, Edward E. Rose, to New York to hear the play read. Herne did not have much hope of the result. Field had never been sympathetic towards him, and while he knew him to be a cultured, courteous gentleman of the old school, he also knew that he was very conservative, old fashioned, and fearful of theatrical innovations. If Rose, whom Herne did not know, resembled him, it boded ill for Herne's play, for on Rose's approval hung the fate of *Shore Acres.*

Rose appeared. He was the exact opposite of Field. He was young, progressive, modern and open-minded, as well as an extremely shrewd man of the theatre. He and Herne understood each other at once, despite a great disparity in age and background. Rose was hardly more than thirty, a dark, handsome man with a charming voice and the keenly intelligent face of the Boston intellectual. Rose liked the play, and when he left for Boston he assured Herne he would throw all his weight in favor of its production. A few days later, the contracts were signed. Field had shown himself typically conservative in the matter of compensation. Herne's salary was to be $100 a week, and he was to receive no royalty for his play beyond a very small percentage of the profits when they reached a certain figure.

Herne wrote to McVicker that the play was to have a Boston tryout, and received in reply a letter of congratulation, suggesting as usual, certain changes, among them "a gay party in a boat of some kind — singing." But Herne had learned his lesson. He was determined that this time *Shore Acres* should be produced just as he had written it. Herne also wrote to Howells, and Howells wrote a very gracious letter of praise to Field, a letter later printed in the program.[59]

Herne made his usual careful preparations for playing the part of Sampson, the Negro politician and murderer in *The New South*. In those days, actors playing Negro parts, blacked up as minstrels did with burnt cork. But Herne, who had observed that Negro faces are rarely dead black, decided to use several shades of dark grease paint. With the help of Charles Meyer, the wig-maker, whom Herne considered the greatest expert of his day, he achieved a make-up that was a marvel of realism. The cast was excellent. It included Charles Mackey, son of the noted actor F. F. Mackey; the lovely and talented Marie Rene, the first wife of William A. Brady and the mother of Alice Brady; and a promising young actor named Holbrook Blinn. In the first act, Herne was the flashily dressed, insolent, over-bearing ward politician to the life, but there was also the subtle overtone of the childlike Negro of the plantation suddenly raised to a position of power and influence. Later on, in his convict's rags, he was a wretched, hunted animal. In the last act, when Sampson had to stand silently on stage for several minutes, near the summerhouse where he had committed the murder, his face was a study in guilty fear. His mouth became dry, he tried to swallow, but could not. At that moment the audience actually pitied the murderer. In the end, when he was confronted with the proof of his crime, he sprang at his accuser's throat with a cry that had in it all the primitive rage and terror of a jungle savage. On his exit, Herne received an ovation from the audience, who would not be satisfied until he had taken a scene call.

Grismer witnessed Herne's triumph with consternation. Soon it became more than he could bear to stand on the stage in the presence of the entire cast while Herne took a scene call every night. Grismer conferred with his friend Brady. On the night before a professional matinee, to which all the actors playing on Broadway were invited, Grismer called a rehearsal after the performance and announced that he was making some slight changes in the last act of the play. It soon transpired that all the changes were in Herne's scene and were obviously designed to kill it. Herne waited until Grismer had finished talking, and then, very quietly, he announced that he refused to allow any changes to be made in his scene. He had signed a contract to play Sampson in a certain way, and he would hold Brady and Grismer to that contract. If they wished, he would leave the cast on Saturday night, but meanwhile he would continue to play the part of Sampson as he had been playing it, at least until after the professional matinee, for he set a high value on the respect of his fellow actors. Grismer and Brady were forced to back down and drop the changes. Afterwards all the actors in the cast congratulated Herne upon his courageous stand; much to Brady's chagrin, his wife Marie Rene was among them. At the professional matinee the house was packed to the doors, and when Herne had finished his big scene the audience of actors shouted, stamped, and cheered while Herne appeared again and again in response to their calls.

Herne and Katharine went to Boston on the first of February. Katharine insisted that she and Mr. Rose should relieve Herne of the direction of the play so that he could devote all his attention to the part of Uncle Nat. Herne followed her advice, and found Rose a highly competent director. The rest of the cast were members of the stock company at the Museum. The day before the opening Herne shut himself in his room at the Adams House, and while his wife gave him his cues, he went over every line, every facial expression, every bit of the stage business of Uncle Nat, repeating every reading again and again until he got the right inflection, making himself complete master of the character.

The opening night, February 20, 1893, was the coldest night of the winter, but Bostonians are noted for their hardihood, and there was a large audience. Many of Herne's friends were there — Hamlin Garland, the Flowers, the Ennekings, Chamberlin of *The Transcript,* Mildred Aldrich, and Mary E. Wilkins. The play, in Garland's words, was "an instantaneous success." From the rise of the first curtain, the audience was enchanted by what Howells called "its fine poetry." At the end of the third act Herne was called before the curtain to make a speech. At the end of the play, as old Uncle Nat, candle in hand, clumped up the stairs to bed and as the curtain fell, the audience remained perfectly silent, so completely under the spell of the play were they. Then they broke forth in a tremendous burst of applause.

It was the happiest moment of Herne's life. After years of poverty and toil, of heartbreaking struggle, disappointment and defeat, he had at last, when he was well past fifty years of age, achieved a triumph. He had achieved artistic successes before — and one of them, *Margaret Fleming,* had, unknown to him, made history in the American theatre — but this was his first monetary success. Naturally, for a man with a wife and family who had existed for so many years on the brink of financial disaster, he thought of the money, and wrote to his daughter Julie: "We think we have a money success in *Shore Acres,* but of course, it's too soon to tell yet. The house last night was only a few dollars less than that of Monday which is a good indication. Mama is busy cutting out 'notices.' I have made the greatest personal hit in Nathaniel Berry that I've made since I played Rip Van Winkle years ago. I ought to make a lot of money out of this character. Ah, well! Who can tell? The papers have treated me nobly. *The Transcript* of last night had a column — great. We'll send you one tomorrow."

The press, almost without exception, liked the play. *The Transcript* (Feb. 21, 1893) said that it was "above the level of the best stage pictures of New England life our generation has seen . . . . its merits are sterling and vital; its faults remediable and superficial . . . . Mr. Herne's Uncle Nat is a portrait worthy to hang forever in the Museum gallery of great traditions." *The Daily Globe* (Feb. 21, 1893): "The character of Uncle Nat is charming in its conception and above criticism in its delineation." *The Journal* (Feb. 21, 1893): "The most charming bit of dramatic realism witnessed in a long period. . . . Mr. Herne has woven into this homely fabric some beautiful threads of poetry, pathos and humor." *The Commonwealth* (Feb. 25, 1893): "A strong, consistent, interesting play, rich in homely detail." *The Courier* (Feb. 24, 1893): "Mr. Herne has done his best work, and made a play and people such as ought to be taken at once to the heart of the public." *The Times* (Feb. 26, 1893): "Shore Acres is one of the sweetest, homeliest, most truthful representations of New England life and character that has ever been presented. It is full of poetic realism."

There were some critics who dissented, the chief of whom was Henry A. Clapp of the *Boston Advertiser;* but even the renowned Mr. Clapp, whose word on dramatic matters had been law for so many years to the inhabitants of Beacon Hill, mingled praise with his blame: "*Shore Acres* is not a play in the accepted sence of that brief but inclusive word. Mr. Howells believes it to be a play, but a series of more or less dramatic dialogues do not make a play. . . . On this line, then, it is hard to take Mr. Herne's work seriously. . . . Finally we come to something which is to be and ought to be taken soberly, the character of Nathaniel Berry, the sweet spirited and big hearted old man. This character approaches the dignity of a whole creation and goes far to light up the whole play. . . . The art of the whole piece is very ragged and intermittent, but when it is genuine in respect of a simple character, it deserves support. As for Mr. Herne's assumption of Nathaniel Berry, it was indeed delightful, its style having much of the exquisite ease and smoothness of Mr. Jefferson, much of the rustic naturalness of Mr. Denman Thompson, with an added and peculiar sweetness which is all Mr. Herne's own. . . . Mr. Herne showed the whole man, as if he had entered into the very body and nature of his hero. A finer illustration of the beauty and power of dramatic impersonation where the movement of the will and intelligence seem to be from the inside out, not from the outside in, has seldom been given on our stages. The monologue in the first act would not have discredited the finest artist in the house of Molière."

On February 25, a few days after the opening, an interview with Herne by the critic, William E. Bryant, appeared in the *Boston Journal:* "Mr. Herne believes that there is no term so often misapplied and generally misunderstood as realism. There is as much realism, Mr. Herne insists, on Beacon Hill as on the farm, and each phase of society should be treated by the dramatist as artistically and as accurately as the other, omitting, of course, that which is degrading and offensive."

Before the first week was over, Herne realized that he had a hit. People were crowding to see his play, and the advance sale was the largest in the history of the Museum. Field quietly dropped all talk of a "tryout," and *Shore Acres* settled down for a run which lasted more than one hundred nights. The news that Herne had a hit soon reached New York, and most of the important managers hurried to Boston to see the play they had once refused. Herne could have had his choice of almost any theatre on Broadway for the coming season. The agreement between Field and Herne was for the run of the Museum only. Nothing had been said about continuing it for another season, but Herne felt that he was morally, if not legally, bound to give Field the first refusal of the play and his services. On the other hand, he was determined that he would not accept the unfair "tryout" terms, which Field had not offered to change and by which he was making enormous profits, as the Museum continued to be crowded night after night.

What Herne asked of Field for the coming season was an adequate share of the profits, a New York run of at least six weeks, and an opportunity to put on *Margaret Fleming* with Katharine in the title role, for as Herne told Field, "I have artistic as well as financial ambition.' Herne, as we have seen, had unbounded faith in the success of *Margaret Fleming* if it were properly presented to enough of the right people, a faith that remained undiminished as long as he lived. The failures in Boston, in New York, and in Chicago had not altered his belief in the least that it was "a great play" and that Katharine was great as Margaret. The fact that he might imperil the money success of *Shore Acres* by insisting that if Field took the one he must also take the other is indicative of depth of his conviction. That he was a full generation ahead of his time in *Margaret Fleming* and that he could not make his generation accept that kind of realism, he could never see, not even when the critic of the Boston *Budget* (Feb. 24, 1893) called it plainly to his attention: "One cannot but wonder that the author of *Shore Acres* is the same James A. Herne who wrote *Margaret Fleming*. The latter play, Zolaesque in motive and Ibsenesque in treatment is realistic and repellent; the former is realistic and attractive. The same man wrote both; but where in the first, he carried his hearers into the depths, in the second we see him struggling to reach the heights." But because his own sympathies and those of literary people like Garland, Howells, and Mary E. Wilkins were catholic enough to embrace both plays, Herne assumed that the general public would show the same breadth. Mary E. Wilkins, for example, was one of the great admirers of *Margaret Fleming,* and she was equally enthusiastic about *Shore Acres:* "I must really tell you how delighted I am with *Shore Acres.* Of course it appeals to me very strongly since it deals with my own New England characters and scenes, but it is not that feature alone which pleases me. It seems to me that Nathaniel Berry is a great dramatic creation, and the last scene is simply extraordinary in its originality and simplicity."

Negotiations with Field for the next season continued for some time, Field and Herne eventually coming to a financial agreement and Field getting Herne time at Miner's new Fifth Avenue Theatre. Henry C. Miner was of German ancestry — stout, stocky, and ruddy of face — and an enterprising business man. He owned four theatres in New York, one in New Jersey, a drug business, and a lithographing company. His new Fifth Avenue Theatre was a little jewel-box of a place, all white and gold inside, with hangings of dark red velvet and seats upholstered in the same shade of plush. It had been built on the site of the old Fifth Avenue, destroyed by fire on January 2, 1891, the scene of many triumphs of Booth and Barrett, Modjeska, Mrs. Langtry, Fanny Davenport, Slavini, Julia Marlowe, and other famous players. It was truly hallowed ground, and Herne, who always preferred small theatres, had a special preference for the Fifth Avenue. Miner would have liked to become Herne's manager, but Herne preferred Field because of his professional standing. The financial agreement eventually decided upon was as follows: Herne to receive as actor a salary of $250 per week, and as author, royalties of 50 per cent of the net profits up to $25,000; 60 per cent over and above $25,000 up to $35,000; 70 per cent up to $45,000, and 75 per cent of all profits over the last amount.

Since the early fall rehearsals were to be in Boston, the Hernes spent the summer at Squantum, a small seashore resort on a rocky headland three miles from the town of Atlantic, Massachusetts, with a fine view of Boston Harbor. Here they rented a rambling, weather-beaten old house with an orchard and a dilapidated barn. Both the parents and children had a glorious summer, swimming and picnicking on the beach, in the afternoons reading beneath the orchard trees, or from the verandah watching the steamboats and sailing ships in the harbor. Herne rented a horse and phaeton, and the family made trips to the charming old towns in the neighborhood — Milton, Hingham, and Quincy.

Meantime Herne was selecting his cast for *Shore Acres,* not realizing at the time that the cast he selected that summer would remain intact for the next five years. The plans were for a brief tour in several Eastern cities before the New York opening late in October. Then disaster struck — the panic of 1893. By early September it was in full swing. This terrible panic, the worst the country had ever undergone, had begun with the failure of the National Cordage Company; then in the spring the Reading Railroad failed, in July came the failure of the Erie, and shortly afterwards the Northern Pacific, the Union Pacific, and the Santa Fe railroads went into the hands of receivers. Other railroads followed, and banks began to call in their loans. This was followed by the failure of thousands of smaller business firms and the bankruptcy of countless numbers of individuals. Then the banks themselves began to fail, by the scores, and finally by the hundreds. Millions of men were thrown out of work as factory after factory closed down for lack of orders. Hordes of hungry men began to roam the countryside in search of food or work.

To the Hernes in their idyllic retreat at Squantum that summer, riding the crest of the first wave of prosperity they had ever known, and engrossed in the casting of the *Shore Acres* company, the panic had seemed far away. *Shore Acres* was to open in Providence early in September, and Katharine and the children accompanied Herne there for the opening, then went on to New York while Herne embarked on his tour of the East. The receipts at Providence were disappointing and Herne's letters home were chronicles of calamity. The panic was having a disastrous effect on the theatres. Herne wrote home: "Formerly, in times of panic, the theatres were crowded, for people flocked to them to forget their troubles. Now, they haven't the money."

Katharine went up to Philadelphia for the opening there on October 9. The papers the next day gave the new play high praise, but it did only a fair business at the box office. The critics not only

Shore Acres 107

gave the play the highest praise in their reviews; they repeatedly urged the public to see it. The following are examples: "It has been stated before in these columns that those who do not see *Shore Acres* at the Opera House will miss one of the greatest dramatic treats offered here for many seasons. . . ." "Those who have not seen the greatest drama of the age should embrace the present opportunity and see *Shore Acres* this week. . . ." "The Old Stager, who has seen all the plays, good, bad and indifferent, which have been presented in Philadelphia for the last thirty years, must say, in justice to Mr. Herne's fine ability as author and actor, that a more interesting, natural and complete dramatic production he does not recollect. If all the theatre-goers in Philadelphia take Old Stager's advice and see *Shore Acres,* they will not regret it."[60] But despite all this extra effort on the part of the critics, business remained poor. People did not have money to spend on entertainment.

The New York opening of *Shore Acres* took place at Miner's new Fifth Avenue Theatre on October 30, 1893. Herne was showing either great courage or great folly in bringing his play to New York so early in its career. The New York critics had always been notably unfriendly to him and his plays, and their leader, William Winter, hated him. Katharine, and the two eldest of her little girls, Julie and Chrystal, occupied a box. "Children, remember you are in a box," said their mother sternly, "and don't make yourselves conspicuous." So, although their excitement was intense, they sat like graven images throughout the performance.

The "Death Watch" was out in full force. This group of drama critics, men-about-town, artists, literary folk, and dilettantes prided themselves on being able to make or break a play on its first night. Coldly critical and cynical, blasé and sophisticated, they rarely laughed, seldom applauded, and displayed as little emotion as possible. Among them were Gertrude Atherton, Mrs. Frank Leslie, and Marshall P. Wilder. As Katharine looked out over the crowded house she saw Alan Dale, probably the most feared and hated drama critic who ever made actors and playwrights writhe under his barbs. For years he terrorized the theatrical profession. His malignant star was now rising and that of William Winter declining. Katharine saw with a sinking heart that Winter was there, too; his atrabilious face with the big pouches beneath the glaring eyes, topped by the disorderly mop of white hair, were all too conspicuous.

The play began, and it was a glorious performance. Every member of the cast seemed to be in top form, and Herne gave one of the best performances of his career. The sophisticates were moved in spite of themselves by the sheer power of simplicity and sincerity. There was little applause until the end, so completely was the audience in the grip of the play's deep humanity; then cheers mingled with tears. The next morning the reviews appeared. With the single exception of William Winter, the critics had been completely won by the play. Even Alan Dale! He wrote in the *Evening World* (Nov. 1, 1893): "It is truth, the unerring brush with which he paints familiar colors, and his peculiar gift of being able to detect the humorous and pathetic. . . . In *Shore Acres* he has written a play so absolutely satisfying to truth that one marvels at the directness of the touches that are apparently aimed carelessly. I would take criminals in a body to see it, and rely more upon its effect than upon all the sermons that coldly inundate those unfortunates." *The Recorder* (Nov. 5, 1893) said: "In *Shore Acres* we have a play true to nature, and presented by an actor whose methods and personality are absolutely unique. The slow-moving measures of the Maine pastoral are full of the perfume of sunshine, the open air, the ocean breeze. . . ." The *Mercury* said (Oct. 31, 1893): "Once in a decade a marvellous play is born, and when such a play is seen, all our playwrights set to work to model on similar lines. . . . Mr. Herne's play marks an epoch in the drama of the American stage. Mr. Herne enacts the principal character, Nathaniel Berry, and no actor ever received a greater acknowledgment of his genius than the death-like silence that followed the ten minutes of pantomime at the end of the play." The *Journal* said (Oct. 31, 1893): "Last night was seen one of those pieces of theatrical work that comes but a few times in a century — those outbursts of genius that sweep aside old ideas, traditions, remembrances of all that our fathers held dear. One of those plays that mark an epoch as did *Hernani*. Last night's play was *Shore Acres*. James A. Herne wrote it, and it is the best American play that we have had. It is a play that one does not wish to talk about, to discuss; rather, the hearer desires to be alone and ponder over what he has seen and heard."

That morning at breakfast as Herne read the reviews to his wife and children he was a very happy man. He had reached the long-sought and desperately fought-for goal of his life. He had written a play that was acclaimed a success in New York, the literary and dramatic capital of the country. But it seemed as if he was never to know an unalloyed happiness, an unqualified success, for the stark fact had soon to be faced that business at the box office was not good. He had written a play, after all these years, which was a popular as well as an artistic success, and now the people did not have the money to come to see it. Scarcely a week had passed before rumors came to Herne that Field wished to withdraw, and this was an added worry for Herne. He felt that if he kept the play on the stage, conditions would improve, and he was determined to do so if possible. Fortunately, Henry C. Miner was eager to take over the management, and as soon as Field withdrew, Miner became Herne's manager under a contract that ran for five years.

In its fourth week, business began to improve, and Herne was in a hopeful, confident mood when he started for the theatre on the evening of November 22. That night when, after his dash up the lighthouse stairs in the third act of the play, he stepped, as usual, offstage onto the moving platform which was to lower him to the floor, the mechanism broke and the platform crashed to the floor below, carrying Herne with it, and throwing him heavily against a stage brace. The stage crew, seeing that he was badly hurt, carried him to his dressing room and sent for a doctor, who found that Herne had two broken ribs and a badly sprained ankle. The doctor wanted to take him to the hospital at once, but Herne insisted on going through with the last act. Though in great pain, he finished the play without the audience's realizing that there had been an accident. Dr. Tifferington, and Miner's own doctor who was called in consultation, both said that Herne would have to remain in bed for at least two weeks. It was a bitter blow. Herne saw success escaping him just as it was within his grasp. He decided to keep the play going with Charles Craig, who played Martin Berry, in the part of Uncle Nat. The houses dwindled, but Herne made a remarkable recovery, and in ten days was back in the cast. During the final week of *Shore Acres* at the Fifth Avenue, Miner gave a professional matinee. The accident which had almost destroyed Herne's success after his years of struggle was known to his fellow players, and after the third act, he was called upon for a speech. Still limping, he came before the curtain and attempted to respond to the tremendous ovation from the packed house, but he was so overcome with emotion that he broke down and could not go on. The audience of fellow actors wept with him.

Daly's Theatre had become vacant, and *Shore Acres* opened there on Christmas Day, 1893. The play made money from the start, and ran until May 26, 1894, one hundred and twenty-six nights, a record for those days. The run at Daly's established Herne as a Broadway star, and *Shore Acres* became one of the acknowledged successes of its time. Herne played it for the next five years in all of the large cities of the country, while a second company played the small towns. The play made a new fame and fortune for him, and for the rest of his life he was free from financial care.[61]

Shore Acres is generally considered Herne's best play, and this is not entirely due to its popularity with the public. *Margaret Fleming* is more powerful and historically more important, and *Griffith Davenport* is more thoughtful, but *Shore Acres* is the fullest and happiest expression of Herne's spirit: it is filled with his love for humanity and his belief in the essential goodness of human nature. It is likewise the best constructed of his plays. Every line and every situation dovetails neatly into the structure of the whole. Yet so simply is this done, and so artfully, that here is no sense of artifice, nor are there any of the contrivances of the "well-made" play so popular in Herne's time. The play has the flow, the rhythm, and the breath of life.

"The temple of the arts," John Galsworthy said, "should have an altar, but not a pulpit." The theme of *Shore Acres* which impressed the audiences of Herne's day so powerfully is implicit and not explicit in the play. That theme is the lack of imaginative understanding, of human sympathy, which separates parents from children, husbands from wives, fellow men from each other in every relationship of life. The theme radiates from the action of the play as a whole, especially from the character of Uncle Nat, with a warmth, a naturalness, and with an irresistible humor that carries its truth alive into the hearts of the audience.

One explanation of the play's excellence is undoubtedly the fact that it was a slow growth of many years, during which it matured along with its author. As Herne said in his article in *The Arena* for February, 1897: "I did not set myself the task of writing *Shore Acres* as it now stands; it grew, and I grew with it; and while I did not realize all its spirituality until its presentation set that spirituality free, still it must have had possession of me while writing. . . ." One night in Boston an unknown man in the gallery, during the final quiet scene at the end of the last act as Uncle Nat, holding his candle, mounted the stairs to bed amidst dead silence, cried, "Good night, old man, God bless you!" Herne was almost thrown out of character. He feared the remark would get a laugh and the scene would be ruined. But there was not a sound from the audience. The speaker had voiced their thoughts.

10

GRIFFITH DAVENPORT

The winter of 1893-1894 was probably the happiest of Herne's life. His play was an unqualified success; for the first time in his life he was free from financial worry, and he was living at home with his family. He did not regret that his "radicalism" had excluded him from The Players, because he did not enjoy club life — he was always happiest at home with Katharine, and with his three girls, Julie, Chrystal, and Dorothy. Then on October 11, 1894, the fondest hope of his life was gratified — a son was born. To add to his satisfaction, there was compelling evidence that serious American drama of the kind he had fought for so long was coming into its own. His young friend Augustus Thomas had had a New York success with *Alabama* and in September of 1893 another big success with *In Mizzoura*. Then too, his dear friend Hamlin Garland, whose brother Franklin was acting in *Shore Acres,* was living on Morningside Heights, and they saw each other frequently.[62] Herne wrote to him on October 11, the day of his son John's birth: "Way down deep in our hearts — beyond the valued friend — beyond the admired writer — there is a love for you — a love for the man." When *Shore Acres* ended its run at Daly's on May 26, 1894, the Hernes left for Sayville, a delightful little fishing village on the Great South Bay where they had rented a house for the summer.

Early in 1894, an old friend of the Hernes, Helen Gardener, had published a novel, *An Unofficial Patriot,* which had excellent reviews. While it was never a great popular success, it was to go through eight editions, the last publication being in 1922. The Hernes had first met Helen Gardener in the winter of 1891, when she and her husband, Colonel C. S. Smart, were guests at 79 Convent Avenue. She was then a woman in her early forties, scarcely bigger than a child, dainty rather than pretty, with lovely hands and beautiful dark eyes. The Colonel, who was devoted to her, was a strapping, raw-boned, and heavily bearded six-footer. Actually, the dainty little woman was one of the most fiery radicals in the country, the friend of Susan B. Anthony, Elizabeth Cady Stanton, the eminent alienist Spitzka, and Colonel Robert B. Ingersoll, and she was well known throughout the country for her sensational writing and lecturing on such subjects as women's rights, atheism, heredity, and insanity. A southerner by birth, she was an eloquent speaker and, despite her diminutive physique, a fearless and dangerous opponent on the platform, as many a man who had crossed swords with her had discovered. Herne, who liked what he called "brainy" women, was very fond of Helen Gardener, and for many years she was Katharine's closest friend. Her novels, dealing realistically with such social problems as the double standard of morality and "the wrongs which are sapping the vitality of civilization through the cover of conservatism" had attracted a great deal of attention. One reviewer said of her *Is This Your Son, My Lord?*: "It is a book that could not have been written twenty years ago, but wrongs that have existed since the beginning of time are now being assaulted by the shafts of free inquiry."

As early as 1891, Helen Gardener had dropped hints to Katharine about a novel she was planning to write on the life of her father, the Reverend Griffith Chenowith, a Methodist circuit preacher in Virginia who afterwards became a chaplain and guide with the Union forces in the Civil War. In 1891 she was already doing research for the novel in the archives of the War Department in Washington. Her first definite request that Herne dramatize her novel was made to Katharine in the summer of 1893, when it was completed and almost ready for publication. On a trip to New York from Squantum that summer Katharine saw Helen Gardener, read the manuscript of *An Unofficial Patriot,* and returned to Squantum in a state of high excitement. "There's a great play in it, Jim!" she said, "and Helen wants you to dramatize it."

An Unofficial Patriot was a distinct departure from Helen Gardener's usual line — it was not a propaganda novel, nor did it champion women's rights, atheism, nor the single standard of morality. Yet to the generation of the 90's it was a radical departure from any war novel they were familiar with, for instead of a romantic story of adventure and hair-breadth escapes, it was a psychological study of the effect of war on individuals. Of course, that generation had never read De Forest's *Miss Ravenel's Conversion,* which had dropped out of sight a generation before, almost as soon as it was printed, and Stephen Crane's *The Red Badge of Courage* had not yet appeared.

At first Herne could not see a play in the novel, but Katharine pleaded with him so earnestly that he finally consented to undertake the work. He had the initial advantage of having lived through the Civil War period as a young man, and he now proceeded to do a great deal of reading about it, making copious notes on historical or political points. This was the first novel he had ever attempted to dramatize, and because he tried to follow the novel faithfully he found that he had a difficult time trying to make a play of it. Only when he took Katharine's advice to "forget the book, throw it away" did he begin to have any success with the project. Out of his own experience came the principle with which he was later to shock Howells with respect to the projected dramatization of *The Rise of Silas Lapham*. *Griffith Davenport* retained the spirit and atmosphere of *An Unofficial Patriot*, but Herne made many changes in the novel's plot and characters.[63] Nonetheless, Hamlin Garland always maintained that Herne adhered too closely to the book.

Herne wrote two versions of *Griffith Davenport*. The first was completed at Sayville in 1894; and the second, which was the version produced, he wrote at Herne Oaks during the summer of 1898. During the four years which intervened between the writing of the first version and the second, when he was on the road in *Shore Acres,* he worked from time to time on *Griffith Davenport,* revising and rewriting.[64] To understand the changes Herne made, it will be necessary to give a brief resumé of the novel.

It will be recalled that the book is based on the life of Helen Gardener's father, and deals with the religious, humanitarian, and patriotic problems of the hero, the Reverend Griffith Davenport, from his youth, when he becomes a convert to Methodism, to his death after serving the Union in the Civil War. Helen Gardener depicts Davenport as a dreamer and a mystic, deeply religious, and with a strong sense of duty. The opening chapters describe the youth of Davenport, a scion of a wealthy and aristocratic Virginia family, his conversion, his circuit riding through the mountains, preaching religion to the poor whites and thus becoming familiar with every road, trail, and footpath in that wild region. At this time he makes a friend of the uncouth but devout mountaineer, Lengthy Patterson, whose devotion to him is unfailing throughout the story.

Hating slavery, Davenport early in life vows that he will never buy or sell a human being. But when his father dies, he inherits his large estate with its numerous slaves, and the young heiress whom he marries brings him more slaves as part of her dowry. Although he and his wife Katharine are ideally happy, Davenport is convinced that slavery is inconsistent with Christianity, and his life becomes a struggle between his traditions as a slave-owning aristocrat and his principles as a Christian. The climax of this part of the novel occurs when Sallie, his wife's maid, to whom Katharine is devoted, is about to be torn from her husband, John, owned by a neighbor, Bradley, whose need of money forces him to sell John to a plantation owner in Georgia. Sallie implores her master to buy John, but Davenport cannot bring himself to violate his vow never to buy or sell a human being, even when the slave girl, in an impassioned scene, flings her baby at his feet. But when Katharine adds her plea to that of the nearly frantic Sallie, Davenport's resolve is broken, and he consents to buy John.

The episode proves to him that he can no longer tolerate slavery, and he decides to free his slaves. But the Negroes who have devoted their lives to his family and are proud to belong to it cannot understand why their master is turning them adrift. A "free nigger" to them is an outcast, and they indignantly spurn their manumission papers. It develops that by his humanitarian act Davenport has not only made his slaves miserable, but he has broken the law of Virginia, and he is forced to leave the state. Davenport, his wife and their children together with their freed Negroes, depart for Washington, enroute to a small town in Indiana, where he has obtained a teaching post in a college. In Washington he learns that Indiana law forbids the bringing of Negroes into the state. Davenport is forced to leave his former slaves in Washington; he pensions off the older ones, leaves the younger ones to shift for themselves, and departs with his family for Indiana. One faithful old Negress, Aunt Judy, follows the family on foot, and Davenport and his wife, in order to keep her with them, declare that she is a guest.

Up to this point, Helen Gardener is chiefly occupied with the irony of Davenport's situation, the sociological problem faced by a just and humane man who is also a Christian in trying to live with slavery in the South before the war, and his equally difficult problem when he takes refuge in the North. These problems are abruptly resolved when the country is plunged into war.

By this time Davenport and his loyal, devoted wife and family have become adjusted to the peaceful but humdrum life of a small Indiana town. The members of the family, of course, are all ardent abolitionists. Beverly, the elder son, has established an abolitionist newspaper in one of the Western border states, and Roy and Howard enlist in the Union Army. The war is not going well for the North. The Army of the Potomac is floundering helplessly in the Virginia wilderness, greatly handicapped because of its unfamiliarity with the terrain. Davenport's friend, Governor Morton of Indiana, who is much disturbed over the situation, knows that Davenport has spent the best part of his life riding circuit in the Virginia wilderness and that he is familiar with every mile of the terrain. Morton informs Lincoln of this fact, and the President wires Davenport to "report to me immediately."

Then follows the scene in which Lincoln overcomes Davenport's scruples and convinces him that he must guide the Union Army through the Virginia mountains, an advance which will mean a victory for the North and, Lincoln hopes, an early end of the slaughter. This is the great scene of the novel. Lincoln, a master of the art of persuasion, appeals to Davenport's patriotism and humanity, and at last wins his consent to guide the Union Army against his own people. Davenport reluctantly performs this duty until he reaches the outskirts of his old home; then he cannot go on. But Lengthy Patterson, his old mountaineer friend, who has been taken prisoner by the Union Army, offers, out of devotion to Davenport, to take his place as guide. Davenport returns to his home in Indiana, and dies of a heart attack as the war comes to a close.

The most dramatic scenes in the book are the scenes in which Davenport buys the slave, John; the one in which he frees his slaves; and the scene with Lincoln. All these scenes depict a struggle of conscience. The description of the retreat after the Battle of Bull Run, Beverly's escape from the angry mob which burns his printing office, and a description of the Battle of Shiloh have only an indirect bearing on the main story. Read now, the book still has great emotional and dramatic strength, as well as authentic atmosphere. But as a story covering, as it does, the passage of many years, it is rambling and discursive, and after the scene with Lincoln it declines to a tame and unsatisfactory ending. Structurally, it has the usual defects of the novel based too closely upon biography. From the standpoint of drama, Herne saw at once that it lacked personal conflict, since the forces opposing Davenport were the abstract ones of social conditions, always difficult to portray on the stage. The characterization, too, suffers from being based too closely on characters near and dear to the author. Such characters tend to become shadowy and conventional, as the history of fiction shows, for the author inevitably idealizes them and unconsciously removes them from reality.

As can be seen, the problems which faced Herne in dramatizing the novel were not simple ones, and a less determined man would certainly have given up. The book had, it is true, a great theme, a colorful historical background, and some dramatic scenes, and there was the always inherently dramatic figure of Lincoln. But the story was biographical and episodic, extending over a period of years, and the principal characters were without any strong emotional appeal since they lacked reality.

Katharine used to say that the play she first saw in the book was not the one Herne wrote. What she had visioned was a romantic play of plot and situation on the order of *The Minute Men,* with a great deal of excitement and action, with the picturesque figure of the circuit preacher dominating the play — something like the play *Davy Crockett,* which, as acted by his friend Frank Mayo, Herne had always found entertaining. But Herne had outgrown his romantic period years before, and he was not interested in doing that sort of thing. His approach was dictated by his deeply held convictions of the supremacy of character over plot and situation, of the supremacy of truth and realism in art. His treatment was foreshadowed in a talk he had had with Hamlin Garland many years before, when they were discussing the Civil War and the plays that dealt with it, such as Gillette's *Held by the Enemy* and Bronson Howard's *Shenandoah.* Herne contended that the Civil War as a subject for the drama of romantic adventure had been worked out, and that the next important play about it must of necessity deal, not with heroes and battles, defeats and victories, but with the effect of the war upon the lives of a single family or group of people. At that time he had no idea of writing such a play, but the remark was prophetic. It was because Helen Gardener's novel represented this new approach that he was interested in dramatizing it, despite the obvious difficulties the book presented.

In the play, Herne eliminated the early scenes of the book dealing with Davenport's youth, his conversion to Methodism, his life as a circuit preacher, and his courtship of his wife, Katharine. He opened his play in the autumn of 1859, when Davenport and Katharine were already in middle life, with grown sons, and the threat of approaching war was casting its shadow over the country. As in the book, his Griffith Davenport is an idealist and a mystic, but he makes him more real and human by giving him a sense of humor. The manuscript of the play was lost in the fire that destroyed Herne Oaks, but the copy of Act III, found among her father's papers by Julie A. Herne in 1952 and published in November of that year in *American Literature,* clearly reveals this quality in Herne's recreation of the character of Griffith Davenport. Herne's character is more vital, cheerful, and human than his saintly but doctrinaire original. In the play, as in the book, Katharine is a devoted wife, but Herne gives her a mind of her own and a firm belief in the aristocratic traditions of the South.

In Herne's play, the first act took place in the charming garden of the Davenport estate and showed the mansion, with its pillared verandah on the left, and the iron entrance gates on the right. The act opened with a comedy scene between the Negro house servants. In this scene Herne used some material from the novel and some from his own unproduced Negro play, *Coon Hollow,* but its distinctive quality was its authenticity and reality, stemming from Herne's accurate knowledge of Negro character, a knowledge he had previously demonstrated so successfully in his creation of the character of the Negro in *The New South.* This scene was not only entertaining in itself, but it established the almost ideal conditions under which the Davenport slaves lived. Most of them had grown up with "Mas' Grif" and "Mis' Kate;" they were humored like a lot of children, and were merry, happy, and devoted. That such conditions were not entirely exceptional in the pre-war South we know from Joel Chandler Harris's descriptions of "Turnwold," the plantation on which he lived during his youth, and from accounts of such plantations as Colonel Robert E. Lee's "Arlington." In contrast to the comfort and security of the slaves on the Davenport plantation was the wretched condition of the freed Negroes, Free Jim and his boy, who lived in a poor cabin on the marsh and who were treated with contempt by the Davenport slaves. Free Jim was not in the novel, nor was the scene in which he rescues his son from the infuriated slaves who find him with the Davenport child Margaret, who has run away from her Mammy and has been found and brought back by Free Jim's son. Free Jim, although ignorant, clothed in rags, and savage-looking, has dignity, poise, and shrewd native intelligence, and is a convincing character creation.

At this point some of the chief characters, Katharine Davenport, her sons Beverly and Roy, and the two girls whom they were courting, Emma West and Sue Hardy, entered. Emma and Sue were hardly more than bits but they supplied a note of youth and girlish charm which Herne felt was a necessary contrast to the serious tone of the play as a whole. The lovely and lovable Sue was played by Chrystal Herne, who at sixteen made her first stage appearance in this part, and Emma was played by Julie Herne.

In the scene which followed, Herne made the first important departure from the novel in which, as has been pointed out, Katharine and Beverly, as well as Roy, are in full sympathy with Davenport's hatred of slavery. Since Herne in the play conceived of the Davenport family as symbolizing the American people, he had them divided on the question of salvery. Katharine and Beverly, the proud, impetuous elder son, representing the South, upheld the institution, while Roy and his father, representing the North, opposed it. Moreover, Herne thus established at the outset of his play the personal conflict so essential to drama.

In the first act the family rift was foreshadowed in a scene in which Beverly objected to Roy's reading of *Uncle Tom's Cabin* to the Negroes, but there was no open quarrel. Then a neighboring slave owner, Squire Nelson, a harsh, cruel man, appeared, bringing with him Jack, one of his slaves who had tried to run away, handcuffed to another Negro to prevent a second attempt. Nelson showed him to Davenport as an example of how the easy-going ways of his slaves were corrupting Nelson's and demanded that Davenport keep his "niggers" off the Nelson plantation. This episode, a briefly mentioned incident in the book, Herne built up into a highly dramatic scene which foreshadowed Davenport's later serious difficulties with his neighbors. Then followed the poignant scene in which the slave, Sallie, begged Griffith to buy her husband, John. This scene, which proved deeply moving on the stage, Herne expanded, but its main features — Sallie's pleas as she knelt with her baby at Davenport's feet, Katharine's tearful entreaties, and Davenport's horror at the idea of breaking his vow never to buy or sell a human being, climaxed by his final compassionate capitulation, were taken from the book. The act ended with a scene between Griffith and Katharine in which he voiced his detestation of slavery and his wish to leave Virginia in order to get away from it. Katharine could not understand her husband's scruples, but she came to realize for the first time that the question of slavery was dividing them and threatening to destroy their marriage, and she decided to go with her husband. They went into the house to talk the matter over, and Beverly, Roy, and Lengthy Patterson, who have witnessed the scene, appeared on the stage in a scene which showed the deepening conflict between the brothers. These two scenes were Herne's in their entirety.

Act II took place in Davenport's study in May, 1860. It opened with a charming love episode between Roy and Emma, which was followed by a brief but powerfully affecting scene between the brothers, Beverly and Roy, in which the breach between the two was widened. This not only represented the tragedy of the divided family, but in a wider sense symbolized the fratricidal strife of the nation. Both these scenes were original with Herne. Then followed the highly emotional scene of the freeing of the slaves, one of the important episodes in the novel. As in the book, the Negroes were puzzled and frightened when they learned they were free and did not belong to anybody. With one voice they rejected their new and anomalous status, and Davenport was so dejected by the failure of his altruistic gesture that Katharine urged him "to give up for tonight," and dismissed the Negroes, who broke into a hymn as the curtain fell.

Act III, as originally written, was in two scenes. The first one took place in December, 1861, in Davenport's home in a small town in Indiana, where he and his wife had settled after being forced to leave Virginia. The Civil War had begun and Beverly was fighting on the Confederate side. Roy was editing an abolitionist newspaper in a Missouri border town, but was forced to flee when enraged Southern sympathizers burned his printing office. At the opening of the act he arrived home to announce that he had joined the Union forces. In this scene Herne introduced the reading of Beverly's letter to his mother, in which the young Southern officer voiced his bitter regret over the war, wishing "it had never been," but in which he also declared his conviction that the South would win, since the decisive battles would have to be fought in the valley of the Shenandoah, where the Union Army was trapped. This scene established in the minds of the audience the perilous situation of the Union forces and prepared them for what was to follow. It was one of the most moving episodes in the play, for in a few swift strokes Herne set before the audience all the heartsickness and war-weariness of the soldier and all the hopeless, futile tragedy of war.

Then came the scene in which Governor Morton tried to persuade Griffith to act as a guide to the Northern forces in Virginia, and gave him Lincoln's peremptory order to "report to me immediately." In all this, Herne followed the novel closely. But now he made an important change. In the book, except for one brief speech of indignation, Katharine acquiesces when her husband tells her he must obey Lincoln's order, but in the play she tells him that if he leads an army against her people she will return to the South and become an army nurse. The scene closed with the husband and wife at odds. The second scene of this act took place in President Lincoln's study in the White House and embodied the great scene in the book in which Lincoln, desperately in need of Davenport's help, tried by persuasion, argument, and all the force of his great intellect and will power to induce Davenport to act as guide to the Northern armies which are at an impasse in Virginia. This scene, the high point of the novel, Herne kept practically intact. His own contributions to Act III were the scene of the break between Griffith and Katherine, and the scene of the reading of Beverly's letter.

Act IV was originally in two scenes. In the first one, in April, 1862, Davenport was guiding a detachment of troops commanded by General Lamoine (the "swearing general" of the book, and a comedy character) through the Shenandoah Valley. The scene was chiefly atmospheric, and Herne introduced a touching episode of his own invention — the capture of a young Confederate soldier who had deserted his regiment because his mother was dying at home, and who was permitted to go on his way by the sympathetic Union soldiers. The second scene took place the following morning. The detachment was approaching Davenport's old home, and, as in the book, Davenport refused to lead the Union troops further. His old friend, Lengthy Patterson, who had been captured by the Union forces, volunteered to take his place. The troops marched away, and Davenport was left standing alone. So far, this act did not differ essentially from the book, but from this point on Herne departed radically from the novel. In the play, Davenport was arrested as a spy by Beverly and other Confederate soldiers who had been awaiting the opportunity to capture him ever since he entered their lines. Davenport protested that he was not a spy and produced his commission to prove it; he was nevertheless marched off to headquarters, after being told that Katharine was at their old home, which had become a hospital.

Act V showed the exterior of the Davenport mansion as in Act

I, but with convalescent soldiers sitting under the trees. Young Mrs. Beverly Davenport (Sue) entered with her baby, attended by a colored nurse, and several of Davenport's neighbors were present. A half-crazed young woman, the widow of a Confederate soldier, wandered in, followed by her mother, who tried to calm her. There was an atmosphere of bitterness and tension as Davenport appeared. He had been cleared of the charge of being a spy, but had been ordered to Libby Prison under a guard headed by Beverly, to await exchange as a prisoner of war. After a tender scene of reconciliation with Katharine, the play ended on a note of near tragedy. As Griffith was being marched off, the the crazy girl rushed forward and fired at him. The shot went wild, but there was a yell of hate from the crowd, then a sudden, dead silence as the curtain fell.

From this analysis of the first version, one may see that all of Herne's departures from the story in the book intensified the conflict and heightened the dramatic suspense. He finished the first draft that summer at Sayville, but was not completely satisfied with it. However, there was no immediate chance of production, since his *Shore Acres* contract with Miner still had several years to run, but there seems to have been a definite understanding that when the play was produced, Miner would do it. Herne would play the part of Griffith Davenport, Mrs. Herne the part of Katharine, and Julie and Chrystal the parts of Emma and Sue. But at the moment, Miner was busy launching a second *Shore Acres* company to play the one-night stands. This company continued on the road for several years after Herne's death and made almost as much money as the original one.

Herne loved Sayville and the peaceful outdoor life he could live there. Every morning he was out for a bicycle ride as day was breaking, often accompanied by Julie or Chrystal. He returned at eight to a bountiful breakfast prepared by Katharine. He loved the early morning hours, and liked to get to bed early. At Sayville he was in bed at nine o'clock every night. After breakfast, and until one o'clock, he worked on the play; in the afternoons he went swimming or boating with Julie and Chrystal; in the evenings he read. Katharine, knowing her husband's love of the sea, decided that they should buy a place of their own, and the vicinity of Peconic Bay, Long Island, was chosen for the future site of Herne Oaks.

It was early in January, 1895, while Herne was on tour, that the real estate agent wrote Katharine that he had found just the place she and her husband wanted, and he was waiting for her in a sleigh when her train arrived at Southhampton. Dusk was falling as they drove for miles through the leafless woods and then along the shore of the bay. Finally they reached what seemed to be a virgin forest, with giant trees and the rising moon faintly gleaming on the snow and the water beyond. Katharine was breathless at the beauty of the scene, and before she returned to New York she had bought thirty acres of land, and taken an option on an additional fifty acres which adjoined it. She likewise had decided on a name — Herne Oaks. As soon as the frost was out of the ground in the spring, work was started on the new house, and in May, at the end of Herne's tour, the family moved in, although it was still unfinished. It was the conventional "Queen Anne" summer cottage of the nineties, complete with gables and dormer windows, and quite without claims to architectural beauty, its best feature being a wide verandah which commanded a lovely view of the bay framed in tall trees. But in time its cedar shingles turned a silvery gray, the house blended into the landscape with an effect that was pleasing and mellow. Herne was soon installed in what Katharine called "The Tower Room," a semi-circular room on the second floor whose six windows overlooked the woods and the bay. It was his summer work room for the rest of his life. From Miner, who had a farm at Red Bank, Herne bought a Jersey cow, some prize poultry and a handsome team of horses and a carriage and in a small way became a gentleman farmer. But best of all was a forty-foot sloop, the *Gretchen*, which he acquired along with her skipper Captain John Peterson of Jamesport. Herne's happiness reached its peak with his ownership of the *Gretchen*, in which he sailed for the next four summers.

Success had a happy effect upon Herne. Respected as the leading exponent of realism in the American drama even by those who disagreed with him, freed from worry over money and able to pay his debts, blessed with a congenial home and with the opportunity to spend more time with his family, he could relax for the first time in his life and enjoy the good that each day brought. And it seemed to his family that there occurred in him, as a result, a kind of late flowering of character — he seemed to grow in dignity, thoughtfulness, and gentleness under the beneficent sunshine of prosperity. But Herne could not rest upon his laurels; whenever he could he continued to work on *Griffith Davenport,* and wherever possible he continued to give talks on the Single Tax.

There is little doubt that Herne could have continued to play for years in *Shore Acres*. Public interest in the play continued strong, and critical comment favorable. It opened in San Francisco on February 22, 1897, and the next day the *Chronicle* said that the play "was deserving of all the praise which it has received from all kinds of authorities;" the *Examiner* praised its "simple, direct setting forth of vital issues with an unconscious, utter defiance and disregard of hackneyed stage methods and traditions;" the *Daily Report:* "For once a play has come to us that justifies every advance word in its favor. . . . Mr. Herne's Uncle Nat is beyond criticism;" the *Bulletin:* "It is unlike anything we have yet received from the hands of an American author;" the *Call: "Shore Acres* . . . . was warmly received at the Baldwin Theatre last night. . . . The reasons for this were no doubt the perfect truth to life of Shore Acres, both in the characters and the way they were put on the stage, added to the exquisitely artistic acting of James A. Herne himself." But the idea of continuing in one role year after year was intolerable to Herne; besides he wanted a repertory of plays which he could play the big cities and avoid the tedium and the hardships of the road. In the fall of 1897 he decided that the coming season would mark his last regular appearance in *Shore Acres* and that he would make every effort to produce *Griffith Davenport* during the season of 1898-99. When Joseph Jefferson, who was then about to begin his thirty-third season in *Rip Van Winkle,* heard of Herne's decision, he said, "He's got a success — why doesn't he stick to it?"

During the New York engagement of *Shore Acres* in January of 1898, Herne gave a reading of *Griffith Davenport* for Miner. One result of this reading was that Katharine, who was there, decided that Lincoln as a character must come out of the play.[65] She saw now that Lincoln with the magic power he has always exercised over the imagination was too powerful a character to appear in a play of which he was not the central character and that he threw the play off balance. After Herne's initial consternation at his wife's criticism he saw that she was right, and decided to try to alter the play in accordance with Katharine's further suggestion to "fill the play with the spirit of Lincoln, and make his influence felt in every scene without his ever appearing on the stage." Another result of this reading was not revealed to Herne at the time — Miner had no confidence in the play as a money-maker, and probably decided then and there that he would never risk a penny on it.

The sinking of the battleship *Maine* in Havana Harbor on February 15, 1898, occurred soon after the *Shore Acres* company had started on a long tour of the South. The disaster shocked the entire country, and a great wave of patriotism was soon sweeping across the nation. The Spanish-American War which followed had the effect of eliminating much of the emotional and psychological effect of secession and the Civil War on the South, and two sections joined hands in an outburst of fervent nationalism that the country had not seen in a hundred years. The mood of the nation was to forget old differences, forget the Civil War and everything connected with it, as the two sections, brothers in arms, joined forces against the common foe. As Herne on tour in *Shore Acres* traveled blithely through the South, it never occurred to him that this new national mood would be fatal to the success of *Griffith Davenport*. He was too much interested in making observations and in absorbing atmosphere for the play.

When he returned to Herne Oaks early in the summer of 1898, he began rewriting the play. He wished the influence of Lincoln to permeate the play, and one of the first things he did was to alter the dates of the acts so that they would coincide with the important events in Lincoln's career. The dates of the first version were advanced, and the acts were now dated as follows: Act I. Virginia, April, 1860. Coming Events Cast Their Shadows. Act II. Virginia, May, 1860. The Nomination of Abraham Lincoln. Act III. Virginia, November, 1860. The Election of Abraham Lincoln. Act IV. Washington, March, 1862. An Unofficial Patriot. Act V. Virginia, April, 1864. First Scene, The Shenandoah Valley. Second Scene, The Next Evening. Another device he employed was that of having the characters make frequent references to Lincoln throughout the play, thus keeping Lincoln's personality vividly before the audience.

Act II, he felt, had a weak ending, which he changed into a powerfully climatic one by using an actual incident that had occurred to the veteran actor, F. F. Mackey when he was playing in Memphis. He was strolling along the street one morning when a fine-looking young Negro, evidently an escaped slave, with a group of white men in hot pursuit, ran up to him and implored his help. Before he could interfere, the pursuers caught up with the Negro and attempted to seize him, but the slave ran a knife across his throat and fell dead at Mackey's feet. In the play the Negro is Jack, previously treated cruelly by the brutal Squire Nelson. In Act II of the revised version, as Davenport's slaves are being dismissed after their rejection of freedom, the sounds of men shouting and dogs barking are heard outside, and Nelson's Jack, in another attempt to escape, bursts into the room, a broken chain dangling from his ankle, a pruning knife in his hand. Nelson and his men are at his heels, and as they close in on him, Jack holds up his knife. "Ef yo' comes neah me, I'll cut mah froat," he cries, and then turns pleadingly to Davenport, "Yo' buy me sah, please!" Davenport, forgetting all his scruples, cries impulsively, "I'll buy him, Mr. Nelson!" "I won't sell him!" the infuriated Nelson says. "Take him, boys!" As the men move towards Jack, the Negro, with a quick movement, plunges the knife in his throat and falls dead before them all. There is a wail of horror from the assembled Negroes. Nelson kicks the body. "There goes fifteen hundred dollars!" he cries bitterly, and then to Davenport, "This is what your damn abolition theories have come to!" Katharine faints, and Griffith stands dazed and speechless as the curtain falls.

Herne's finest contribution to the revised version of *Griffith Davenport* was the new third act which he wrote during the summer of 1898, and which, supposedly destroyed in the fire at Herne Oaks in 1909, was later found among his papers, as has been previously mentioned. In this act, which takes place in Virginia on the evening of election day, 1860, Davenport's neighbors, infuriated because he has voted for Abraham Lincoln, invade his home, threaten to burn it, and demand that he leave Virginia. The act ends as Davenport gathers his family and servants about him and prays for help and guidance in the new life which they all face and for the preservation of his country in the ordeal through which, he forsees, she must pass. This act in its charm and humor, its atmosphere, its suspense and drama is one of the finest things Herne ever wrote. It greatly improved the play, since the audience could actually see Davenport being forced to leave his home instead of, as in the first version, merely hearing about it. Likewise the conflict between Davenport and his neighbors heightens the dramatic tension, and emphasizes the powerful influence of Lincoln that pervades the play.

Herne's main change in Act IV (Act III of the first version) was, as we have seen, the elimination of Lincoln, with the consequent building up of the character of Governor Morton. But he made other changes which greatly strengthened this act. Instead of having the opening scene take place in Davenport's home in Indiana, he kept the action in Washington, where Davenport is the pastor of a church, and the entire act passes in the Davenport living-room, with no change of scene and no interruption in the action, which rises steadily to a moving climax. Herne undoubtedly worked harder over this act than over anything else he ever wrote. William Archer, among whose papers the act was found many years later, called it "a masterpiece." The last two acts were altered little at this time except to merge them into one act of two scenes, Act V. Later, as we shall see, he made drastic cuts and changes in this act.

Meanwhile Miner was going through the motions of getting "time" for the new play, apparently with the idea of keeping on good terms with Herne until the *Shore Acres* contract ran out. Herne, thinking that Miner intended to produce the play, asked Ernest Albert, the noted scene designer, to submit models for the stage sets. The 1898-99 theatrical season was probably the most successful from a financial standpoint that the American theatre had witnessed up to that time. The victorious termination of the war, from which the United States emerged as a world power, had keyed her citizens to a high pitch of optimism; business was booming and the theatre reflected the country's mood. The richness and variety of the theatrical fare offered to the public was amazing; there were big musicals such as Victor Herbert's *The Fortune Teller;* there was classical repertory; there were melodramas, farces, and romantic comedies. Nearly everything was a smash hit. Joe Jefferson in *The Rivals,* Maude Adams in *The Little Minister,* Charles Coghlan in *The Royal Box,* E. H. Sothern in *The Adventure of Lady Ursula,* Richard Mansfield in *Cyrano de Bergerac* — all were playing to packed houses. "What a time this would be to do my play!" Herne thought, but Miner, still refusing to reveal his real intentions, continued to keep him dangling in suspense.[66]

The season in New York never opened officially until John Drew appeared at the Empire, generally about the middle of September, when Society, returning from Bar Harbor, Newport, and Southhampton, turned out *en masse* to see their favorite. It did not matter what the play was; people went to see John Drew. The position he occupied in the New York social and theatrical world of the day was unique, and nothing like it exists today. In an era when people of the stage were still socially taboo, Drew was received in the most impregnable fortresses of the elect, and his audiences were filled with his personal friends. Quiet and unassuming in his private life, impeccable in conduct and taste, Drew by his prestige helped his profession attain a dignity and standing it had never had before. He typified the gentleman that was every woman's—and every man's—ideal. His poise, his elegance, his ease of manner, and the way he wore his perfectly tailored clothes would have made him a distinguished figure anywhere; in addition, he was a finished artist, an actor of charm, wit, intelligence and restrained pathos, and in his manner of delivering comedy lines, he has never had an equal. His charm and good breeding were not merely surface attributes; they arose from the true goodness and kindliness of his heart. We had then, and have now, many actors of facility and grace — but there has been only one John Drew. That fall he was appearing in Henry Arthur Jones's brilliant comedy, *The Liars,* with a glittering cast, of which Drew himself was the most scintillating member. Herne, a great idmirer of Jones, as well as of Drew, was thoroughly delighted by the play and the performance. He and the family saw the play at a matinee, and occupied a stage box near which was a door which led backstage. At the end of the play this door opened, and as if by magic, John Drew entered, still in his make-up, and greeted the Hernes, whom he had never met before, as if they were old friends. He lifted little Jack up in arms and kissed him, and afterwards, whenever the child was asked who was his favorite actor, he always replied, "John Drew."

The Liars was a great success, as indeed almost everything was on Broadway that fall. When Herne and the family went to see Mansfield's magnificent production of *Cyrano de Bergerac,* which was playing to packed houses at the Garden Theatre, A. M. Palmer, the manager, visited them in their box. "We would not have dared to risk doing a play like this a few years ago," he said. "There would have been no audience for it. We owe a great deal to you, Mr. Herne." The effect of this praise on Herne was bitter-sweet just then, for Miner had finally revealed that he would have nothing to do with *Griffith Davenport,* and Herne knew that he would have to finance the production himself.[67]

Shore Acres closed in Boston on December 3, 1898, and this marked Herne's last appearance in the play which had brought him fame and fortune. On his return home, he immediately began preparations for the new production. *The Mirror* of December 10, 1898, carried the announcement that *Griffith Davenport* would open at the Herald Square Theatre on January 30, 1899. In the same issue was a statement that Miner and Herne had ended their long association and that Herne would be the sole producer of *Griffith Davenport*. Herne was once more on his own. It was apparent at the beginning that it would be a most expensive production, for there were four full-stage, solidly built sets and forty-two speaking parts, each one a distinct type, as well as a large number of extras. While the cast that Herne finally assembled had no big names, with the possible exception of Sidney Booth, nephew of Edwin Booth, its members were players of standing who had all done creditable work, and William Archer said after he had seen the play (*Morning Leader,* Dec. 22, 1900): "Never did I see a play better acted than *Griffith Davenport*. The individual actors, with the exception of Mrs. Herne, were not specially distinguished, but Mr. Herne has a genius for instructing his company, which enabled them, in this case, to achieve the perfection of naturalness."

Herne was an excellent teacher, for his temper was always under control, his voice never raised in anger or sarcasm; he had the faculty of inspiring his actors with his own ideals of perfection and the patience to repeat and repeat until those ideals were as nearly realized as possible. To him, the most important quality in acting was "repose," which to him comprehended almost the entire realm of acting technique — authority, poise, precision, timing, control of the voice and body, and of facial expression. Unless a man acquired repose, he said, he could not hope to be a finished actor. He was a stickler for good diction, and maintained that the only way to attain clear, distinct utterance was to go over one's part, line by line, pronouncing each word pedantically, first slowly, then faster and faster, until clear enunciation becomes second nature. He constantly told his actors: *"Think* what your lines mean first. When you have their meaning clearly in your mind, you can't help but express it in your voice, your face, and your action." He believed in expressing emotion through suggestion, with a minimum of facial expression and gesture, and he did not think an actor should lose himself in his part to the point where he could not control his emotion. On the other hand, he deplored the casual, almost indifferent attitude of some actors towards their work, the laughing and joking in dressing rooms and behind the scenes. "In the ideal theatre," he often said, "no talking behind the scenes should be allowed. From the moment the actors entered the theatre, absolute silence should prevail." "Not speak?" asked Julie. "What would they do?" Herne replied, "Think about their parts and get into the atmosphere of the play." He greatly disliked the habit some players had of chatting backstage while waiting to go on, and then rushing on the scene at cue, completely out of character. To him, to be "out of character" at any moment of a performance was a serious artistic offense. When Julie first began to act, he instructed her, "Sit quietly in your own dressing room and concentrate on your part, and don't go out on the stage until just before it is time for you to go on." He himself followed his own counsel. No matter how harassed he was by the problems of stage production, curtain-time always found him dressed and made up and seated in his dressing room, calm, poised, and unhurried. He frowned upon the practice of actors deliberately playing their scenes for applause as part of the artificiality of the old-fashioned theatre; he wished that applause, except at the end of a performance, could be abolished, and he himself went out of his way to discourage it.

The regular rehearsals of *Griffith Davenport* took place on the stage of the Herald Square Theatre, and from the start they went as smoothly as though everyone had played his part for years. Herne was so familiar with the script that he hardly ever referred to it, and he had worked out the mechanics of the long, complicated play in his mind beforehand and carried them in his head. He had thought out every reading, every movement, every gesture for every character. No actor had to stop and ask, "What do I do here?" and then wait until the director invented some stage business for him on the spur of the moment. Chrystal Herne was making her debut in the part of Sue Hardy. Slender and graceful, a "tall lily" as Augustus Thomas once described her, her delicate beauty, her musical voice, and her lovely personality made a deep impression on the company, and one knowing old actor was prophetic when he predicted her future success on the stage.

Hamlin Garland attended one of the rehearsals. Garland was unhappy about the play, because he thought that it was not authentic Herne.[68] He said later in *Roadside Meetings* (pp. 395-6): "I could not tell him so, but I was less interested in this play than in any of his others, mainly for the reason that it was based on a book by another writer. . . . I marvelled at his patience and endurance and in the end came away as limp as a rag. My brain echoed for hours with his hammering drill. For me, it was all a waste of time. It served no purpose. I could not tell him what I really thought, which was that the last act was feeble and inconclusive and that it ought to be entirely reconstructed. That he would not do this was certain, for he was too deeply enmeshed with the facts of the novel."

The first performance of *Griffith Davenport* took place at the Lafayette Square Opera House in Washington, D. C., on January 16, 1899. The performance was well received by a large audience, but the theatrical people who had come up from New York saw at once that the last act was wrong and would have to be re-written. Herne had a new last act ready for the opening in Baltimore the following week. The final scene of the new last act was laid, as formerly, in the garden of Griffith's old home. Formerly the act closed with the departure of Griffith for Libby Prison amid the yells of an enraged mob. The new ending, which was very quiet, struck a note of idyllic tenderness which was reminiscent of the final scene in *Shore Acres*.[69] Night has fallen, and Griffith Davenport stands alone and forsaken in the old garden, which is empty and silent except for the sentry who paces to and fro. Davenport is waiting for the guard that is to take him to Libby Prison. Then Katharine, dressed in somber gray, enters from the house and speaks to him gently. The two old lovers sit together on the steps of the house in the moonlight, as they used to do, and talk over all that has happened. Katharine is no longer bitter, but softened and full of understanding. There is a full renewal of their love for each other, and they plan to take up their life together after the war is over.

The play opened in New York at the Herald Square Theatre on January 31, 1899. The critical reaction was mixed, and is perhaps best typified by the New York *Mirror* (Feb. 11, 1899): "It is a work of splendid art, superb construction, and magnificent dramatic force . . . however, the last two acts are weak and sadly uneventful. Poetic they are, simple and direct, but these qualities do not atone for lack of action. The audience that had sat spellbound by the exquisite strength of the preceding scenes, wearied under the closing dearth of movement and superabundance of talk. . . . As an example of dramatic writing the work is a thing of beauty." Of Herne's acting, and of Mrs. Herne's, the *Mirror* had only the highest praise. Garland saw the play and his opinion formed at the rehearsal was confirmed. He says in *Roadside Meetings* (pp. 402-3), after praising the acting as "masterly": "The play moved the audience powerfully, and yet I confessed to a feeling of disappointment. I saw no future for it. It failed to clinch the nail. The audience went away admiring the Hernes, but not in praise of the play. There was not enough of Herne in the writing. 'He has been too loyal to the historical novel from which he has taken the story,' they said, and they were right." [70] By the end of the first week, Herne knew that he had a failure.

In *Griffith Davenport* Herne had essentially a thesis play, and its theme, as far as the American public at the moment was concerned, was not only dead, but actually antagonistic in the new era of good feeling towards the South, the South that had so magnificently rallied to the Stars and Stripes in the Spanish American War. No one was in the mood to dig up old skeletons. And despite Herne's most heroic efforts in the script and on the stage he could not make the Reverend Griffith Davenport a sympathetic character. He remained an idealist and a martyr, and while Herne did much to humanize him, he was not really interesting to the great masses of the public. They might respect him, but he made no appeal to their emotions — they did not love him, as they loved Uncle Nat.

William Archer voiced the opinion of the discriminating few in his article in the London *Morning Leader* (Dec. 22, 1900).[71] He said, in part, that the play was "the most interesting, the most artistic, the most characteristic, and, above all the most truly American thing I saw in the American theatre . . . if I had seen nothing else in America, my visit would not have been barren. . . . *Griffith Davenport* is a piece of really national dramatic literature." On February 18, 1899, the American Dramatists Club gave a supper in honor of Herne, and forty well known American dramatists and actors were present to pay tribute. Bronson Howard presided, and Augustus Thomas spoke. It was a signal honor by the men of his own profession, and it meant much to Herne. There were some American dramatic critics who gave the play unqualified praise, and among these was Hamilton Ormsbee, the drama critic and later the editor of the Brooklyn *Eagle,* who said in an address delivered in Brooklyn later that spring: "The important element of an American dramatic season should be the American plays. It has not been so this year. Few American plays have been produced, and of these by far the most beautiful has failed in a way that is highly discreditable to the American public. That was Mr. James A. Herne's wonderfully artistic picture of slavery and of the causes that led to the Civil War, Griffith Davenport. . . . the whole town settled down complacently under the judgment of the Manhattan critics that the new play was 'not dramatic.' [72] It was not in the way that *Secret Service* and *The Three Guardsmen* are dramatic; but its character drawing is so fine, its selection of incidents is so thoroughly typical of the forces involved in the war, its atmosphere is so natural and its acting on the part of Mr. and Mrs. Herne was so nearly perfect, that for any auditor who takes his brains and artistic sense to the theatre it was worth almost any three of the season's successes — outside of *Cyrano*." In Boston, where the play opened on April 17, it was an artistic triumph. The Boston critics, especially Lewis Strang, gave it high praise, and a few days after the opening Barrett Wendell gave a luncheon at the St. Botolph Club in Herne's honor. Such honors as these did much to compensate Herne for the heavy financial loss he had taken.[73]

He always regarded *Griffith Davenport* as a greater play than *Shore Acres*. He said in *The Coming Age* for August, 1899: "I consider *Griffith Davenport* a much greater play than *Shore Acres*. Not that it will ever appeal as largely to the people, because *Shore Acres* is so simple, and deals with the life of a farmer . . . . but *Griffith Davenport* is largely a sociological study, dealing with a great historic epoch now more than a generation past." [74] Later he came to recognize what was perhaps the principal cause of its lack of popular success, and in an interview with E. F. C. Boddington of the Brooklyn *Eagle,* published on July 29, 1900, admitted that "it was put on at a bad time." Now that the third and fourth acts of this "lost play" have been recovered, we can better understand why such men as William Archer and Barrett Wendell thought it so important a contribution to the American drama.

Professor Richard Moody of Indiana University in his *America Takes The Stage* (1955) summarizes the historical importance of the play: ". . . it was not until *The Reverend Griffith Davenport,* by James A. Herne, was produced on January 16, 1899, that a Civil War play received an almost completely realistic treatment. The problem of slavery had hardly been mentioned in previous Civil War dramas, whereas in Herne's play it was the starting point.[75] The military operations in the earlier plays had been clearly defined actions, depending for success only on the skill and fortitude of the men and their commanders, but in *The Reverend Griffith Davenport* the enormous complexity of the military problems was at the center of the drama. Where motives and feelings had been clear and unmistakable in the plays of Howard and Gillette, the emotions and thinking of Herne's characters were complex and confused. Katharine Davenport was an ardent believer in the Southern cause, but her feeling of loyalty to her husband was so strong that not until the final scene was she able to break from him and act in behalf of her Southern compatriots. The Reverend Griffith Davenport was one of the most intricate realistic character studies of nineteenth-century American drama."

11

SAG HARBOR

In the summer of 1899, Herne was invited to join the recently organized National Institute of Arts and Letters. This was an honor that he esteemed very highly. He fastened the list of members to the wall of his study at Herne Oaks and it remained there for the rest of his life. Among others, the list contained the names of W. D. Howells, Henry James, George W. Cable, Samuel L. Clemens, John Hay, Henry Cabot Lodge, T. R. Lounsbury, Charles Eliot Norton, S. Weir Mitchell, Theodore Roosevelt, Woodrow Wilson, Owen Wister, Joel Chandler Harris, Augustus Thomas, Joseph Jefferson, Lafcadio Hearn, William James, Hamlin Garland, James Ford Rhoades, W. C. Brownell, John LaFarge, Augustus St. Gaudens, John Singer Sargent, James McNeil Whistler, Winslow Homer, Edwin A. Abbey, Daniel French, Walter Damrosch, and Reginald DeKoven.

During the previous summer, W. B. Gross, Herne's manager, had suggested a revival of *Hearts of Oak* for the one-night stands, and Herne had agreed.[75] But on re-reading the play he realized that the dialogue and certain other aspects of the play had become old-fashioned, and he decided to modernize it. He changed the locale from Marblehead to Sag Harbor; he introduced several new characters and filled the revised version with the local color he had absorbed while visiting the little towns about Peconic Bay on his sailing trips in the *Gretchen*. He was especially fond of the picturesque little shipyards at Greenport, which did a thriving business with the local yachtsmen and "baymen," who made their living "scallopin' winters and sailing comp'ny summers." The first act of the new version of *Hearts of Oak,* Herne decided, would take place in a country shipyard instead of, as formerly, on the beach.

Herne always enjoyed talking with Captain Peterson, the *Gretchen's* skipper, and often attempted to draw him out. But the Captain, bronzed and blue-eyed, was quiet and self-contained, and almost never emerged from his protective shell of reserve. A few days after Herne started work on the revised version of *Hearts of*

Oak, he remarked casually to the Captain, as they were sailing one afternoon, "I'm writing a play which opens in a shipyard, with a small sailboat on the ways. Her owner and the boss carpenter are talking over the repairs to be made on her. Can you give me an idea what they might be?" The Captain, who was at the wheel, kept his eyes straight ahead, and not a muscle of his face moved, but his voice when he spoke betrayed his pride in being consulted, and he named a number of things that might be wrong with a small boat. Herne took it all in, occasionally asking a question or noting some mechanical detail. Unknown to Captain Peterson, Herne had also collected a number of the old sailor's dryly humorous remarks, many of which helped to build up the character of Cap'n Dan in *Sag Harbor*. It soon became evident that Herne's changes were so extensive that he had a new play. Katharine was the first to notice this, and Herne, taking her advice, devoted the rest of the summer to the new play, later to be called *Sag Harbor*. The humble, rugged, rural character and background was the thing he most enjoyed doing, and his family had never before seen him so engrossed in anything. As soon as he had finished a scene, he would call them all together and read it aloud. He wrote rapidly and by the end of September had finished the first draft. Then it had to be laid aside, for he was busy with the production of *Griffith Davenport*. After the production and brief tour of *Griffith Davenport* came another interruption, which, if Herne could have foreseen its effect on his health, he would never have undertaken.

This was the stage direction of Israel Zangwill's *Children of the Ghetto*. Herne had first met Zangwill in the winter of 1898, during the last Boston run of *Shore Acres*. Zangwill, then only in his early thirties, was bent and twisted like an old man, and because of his poor eyesight had a habit of thrusting his head forward in a groping, purblind manner. His clothes were well made, but he wore them carelessly, and a pair of eyeglasses teetered perilously upon his nose. A shock of jet black hair curled tightly all over his head, and altogether he looked like a figure from an Assyrian frieze come to life and dressed in modern clothes. But when he began to talk one forgot the misshapen body and the ugly features, for his speech was clear, terse, and incisive, his mind was brilliant, and his wit had the flash and swiftness of lightning. Herne liked him at once, particularly when he said, "I have been criticized for calling the theatrical managers shopkeepers. I mean nothing uncomplimentary by this. The fault

I find with them is that, unlike other merchants, they refuse to display new wares."

During the Boston engagement of *Griffith Davenport* in April, 1899, Herne received a letter from George Tyler of Liebler and Company saying that the firm was going to do Zangwill's dramatization of his novel, *Children of the Ghetto,* with an all-star cast, and asking Herne to direct it. Zangwill, Tyler said, had been so much impressed with *Griffith Davenport* that he insisted no one but Herne should direct his play. Herne was highly complimented, but he wanted to spend the summer polishing *Sag Harbor,* for he was now certain that he could get a production for it in the fall, so he declined the offer. But Zangwill and Tyler were determined, and persuaded Herne to read the script. Herne asked Julie to read it aloud to him and the rest of the family one night in the Adams House. Zangwill's novel was a vast panorama of the London Ghetto of the 60's, full of color and throbbing with life, and it would have been impossible to transfer it and its numerous characters to the stage *in toto* and to maintain its sweep and breadth. Zangwill had wisely confined the play to one story of the many in the book—the love affair between David Brandon and Hannah Jacobs, the daughter of the beloved Reb Shemuel. Interwoven with their story were some of the chief characters and episodes of the book. Herne could not see a success in the play, and again he declined to direct it, but on his return to New York after the closing of *Griffith Davenport,* he was once more importuned by Tyler to undertake it. Tyler finally offered him such a large salary, that Herne, who had suffered a heavy financial loss in the failure of *Griffith Davenport,* was tempted, and he signed an agreement on May 17, 1899. Zangwill had sailed for London, but planned to return for the rehearsals. On his return to America he was to spend a week or two at Herne Oaks working out the details of the production with Herne.

Tyler, a relative newcomer to Broadway, had had a meteoric rise as a producer. Beginning as a manager for James O'Neill in a road tour of *Monte Cristo,* he had had a respectable success starring Charles Coghlan in *The Royal Box* and had hit the jackpot when he starred Viola Allen in Hall Caine's *The Christian,* which had been a sensational success. His specialty was lavish productions and all-star casts, and he was a born salesman and publicity man. Sometimes, however, he oversold his productions. First, though, he had oversold himself on them. He worshipped James O'Neill, fell so madly in love with Viola Allen that he had to be forcibly restrained from jumping out of his hotel window when she did not return his affection, and he called Zangwill the greatest genius of the age.

In the early part of the summer Herne worked hard revising *Sag Harbor* until, except for the bare outline of the plot, it had no resemblance whatever to *Hearts of Oak*. Then he had to hurry to New York in a summer of terrific heat to make plans for the production of *Children of the Ghetto*. The production was a heavy one, with four sets and thirty-six speaking parts. He soon found that he was to have little to say about the selection of the cast. Tyler had engaged Wilton Lackeye, Blanche Bates, and Frank Worthing, three of the highest salaried people in the country, for the parts of Reb Shemuel, Hannah, and David. He was also paying exorbitant salaries to other prominent actors for mere bits. Herne returned home discouraged. He felt that given half the money that Tyler was throwing about, he could have cast the play better.

While in New York, Herne had casually mentioned to Tyler that he had finished his new play, and the producer seemed interested. A few evenings later Tyler arrived unexpectedly at Herne Oaks, accompanied by his business manager, William Connor. Tyler was short, stocky, and voluble; Connor was tall, quiet, and reserved. "I've come to hear your play," announced Tyler. Herne read the play, which took him about two hours, while Tyler listened attentively, with a poker face. At the end, he said, "I'll do it. We'll open in October at the Park Theatre, Boston, for a run." The rest of the evening was spent listening to Tyler tell about his plans for making Liebler and Company the greatest theatrical firm in America.

A few days before Zangwill arrived from London, Herne went to New York on business, saying he would bring the noted author with him on his return. The family was thrilled at the idea of entertaining such a distinguished guest, and they were all on the verandah to greet him on his arrival. The carriage drove up, and Herne and the little bent figure alighted. When the introductions were over, Zangwill lifted his head and sniffed several times. "Why," he remarked, "this is as good as our best English air!" Herne told the family that Zangwill had been surrounded by reporters ever since he landed and that one enterprising young man had journeyed down to Southhampton on the same train in order to get an interview with him. Zangwill was as delighted as a child with all this attention. He subscribed to a clipping bureau and appeared at supper that evening with a large envelope full of press notices which he passed about. The caricatures afforded him great amusement, for he was not at all sensitive about his appearance.

The Hernes soon discovered that Zangwill was a delightful guest. In spite of his fame and success, there was a simplicity, and even a kind of pathos about him that were very endearing. He fell in with their free and easy ways as though he had known the family for years. He had been everywhere, met everyone, and seen everything, and his table talk was a constant flow of wit and wisdom. With the young people he was a beloved companion and entered into all their fun. He played croquet and tennis with them and went swimming with them. When Herne drove him to Southhampton village, he always bowed and smiled cordially to every passer-by. He was especially fond of Chrystal; he called her the "naiad" because, when they went swimming, of the graceful way she would dart swiftly out on the wharf and take a flying leap into the water. Months later, when Herne was reading *The Mantle of Elijah* aloud to the family, a book Zangwill was working on while he was at Herne Oaks, he came to the passage in which Zangwill described the heroine, Allegra, with her "pointed chin," her "clear gray eyes," and her air of being "a woman half out of her shell," and they all recognized it as a lovely and truthful description of Chrystal.

A sincere friendship sprang up between Herne and Zangwill, which made Herne all the more anxious to make Zangwill's play a success. They held daily consultations about the play. Zangwill knew very little about the practical side of the theatre, and gladly left all technical details to Herne. It was said afterwards that Herne had rewritten and vastly improved *Children of the Ghetto,* but he denied this in a curtain speech on the opening night. Such changes and improvements as were made in the play were due simply to Herne's suggestions, which Zangwill adopted, and to his masterly stage direction. About the middle of August, Zangwill and Herne departed for New York to begin rehearsals. The heat was terrific, and Herne always suffered severely in hot weather. Actually he was trying to do two jobs—direct the Zangwill play and prepare for the production of *Sag Harbor.* It was too much. The rehearsing of a new play is always fraught with anxiety, and tension develops sooner or later. Herne had never encountered too much of this with his own plays because he was in the position of author and star as well as director. Zangwill, despite his kindness, displayed the novelist's usual aversion to cuts. When a cut was suggested he was as concerned as a fond parent over the amputation of an arm or leg of a favorite child. Finally he would demand, "Is it for the good of the play?" When Herne assured him that it was, he would sigh, "Very well. Then you may cut the line. I will consent to any change that is for the good of the play. But I will not take out *one line* just for the sake of getting the curtain down at eleven o'clock!"

Herne had never approved of all-star casts, because, he said, the stars all played for themselves and vied with one another for the center of the stage, which made teamwork almost impossible. Now he found he was directing a cast of primadonnas—all temperamental, all jealous of their rights, and every one of them determined to occupy the limelight to the exclusion of the others. He discovered that several members of the company were reading Zangwill's novel assiduously with an eye to enriching their own parts; when they found scenes in which the characters they played shone to advantage, or had good lines, they demanded that these be incorporated in the play, whether they fitted into the general scheme of the drama or not. When Herne declined to entertain their suggestions, they appealed to Zangwill, and although he always upheld Herne, this division of authority led, inevitably, to confusion. In the end, however, by employing all his firmness, good temper, and tact, Herne succeeded in keeping the company under his control and in winning their trust and co-operation. His patience under these trying conditions was the marvel of all who witnessed it. What all this cost him in the expenditure of nervous energy no one, perhaps not even he himself, realized.

Wilton Lackeye, who had the important part of Reb Shemuel, appeared to resent the fact that Herne was in charge of the play. Lackeye had the reputation of being a deadly wit, and his overbearing egotism was notorious. There was no open clash, however, until the final rehearsals, which took place in Washington. Although the opening was only a week away, Lackeye had still not learned his lines, and was "fluffing"—fumbling his lines and substituting his own words for those in the script. Zangwill was terribly upset. Willard Halcomebe, who was watching the rehearsal, later related what happened (*Washington Post,* Jun. 23, 1901): "Herne called Lackey to book several times, whereat the actor, who was accustomed to dictate rather than be disciplined, waxed wroth and replied sharply, 'The words are synonymous, and one is just as expressive as the

Sag Harbor 141

other.' 'If the author had wanted to use that word, he would have so written it,' rejoined Herne calmly but firmly. 'It is his right to have his words delivered exactly as he wrote them, for he is held responsible for them by the critics and the public. A generation ago, when we used to change the bill every night, it was permissible to fake and paraphrase, since no memory could hold all the lines exactly, but nowadays when plays are classed as literature, and we devote months of study and rehearsal to them, there is no excuse.' Whereat the actor aforesaid became sulky and whiled away his time upstage by growling sullen asides to the scenery, or to whoever was near enough to hear him. The air was electric with foreboding ... and the company was on the *qui vive,* expecting a clash of authority. Herne apparently paid no attention to the irate player's asides, but at the close of the scene he arose from his seat in the orchestra, and began in that deliberate Down East drawl which characterized his Uncle Nat in *Shore Acres*: 'Ladies and gentlemen of the company,' said he, 'I want to explain my position. I am here on a salary, just as you are, and my sole interest in this play is to give it the best possible production. There is this difference, however; while my interest in the play ends with the first performance, yours does not. You remain, and will be held responsible by the public for your individual and collective performances. Therefore, it is even more to your interest than to mine to get this thing right. And what I tell you to do is right'—this with a shade more of firmness in his voice. 'I have spent more years of study and hard work on the stage than any of you, and I know. I have consulted with the author, and am endeavoring to help you interpret his ideas to the public through this play. Whatever comes of it, whether it proves a failure or a success, it deserves our best endeavors.' Then relapsing into his accustomed drawl, 'Now, I don't want to have trouble with anybody—and what's more I won't. I have the reputation of being the most even-tempered stage manager in America, and whether it is true or not, I'm not going to lose it now. But I know that I am right, and I am not here to be bulldozed. Call the next act.' This little speech was like oil on troubled waters. Everybody drew a breath of relief. Even the belligerent actor, calmed by words which embodied the acme of common sense, without a sign of irritation or personal animus, came down to make his peace with the suave old stage manager, and everything went smoothly after that."

The play opened on September 18, 1899, at the National

Theatre in Washington. Although it never became a popular success, it was greeted with enthusiasm, and the New York *Mirror* reported that Zangwill made a speech in which he paid tribute to the admirable stage direction of James A. Herne.[76]

His work finished, Herne returned to New York, arriving at 79 Convent Avenue in time for Sunday breakfast. He was in high good spirits and spent most of the day telling Katharine and the girls about his amusing experiences with Zangwill and the company. But they were shocked to see how worn and thin he was; the rehearsals and the grilling heat had taken something out of him that he was never to regain, and he seemed to have aged in a few weeks. Katharine urged him to return with her to Herne Oaks for a brief rest, but there was no time, for *Sag Harbor* was to open in Boston in just four weeks. Exhausted as he was, Herne immediately plunged into the arduous task of producing a new play. The next morning when he started downtown to begin the selection of his cast, he could hardly drag himself along. Katharine and Julie, watching at the window, marked his slow, lagging step, and turned to look at each other, while a fear they hardly dared express revealed itself in their eyes.

Fortunately, the production of *Sag Harbor* went smoothly and with no more than the usual amount of worry attendant on a new production. Liebler and Company were financing the production on the most generous scale and gave Herne everything he asked for without imposing any conditions. He had a free hand with the scenery, the cast, and the entire production. The atmosphere of harmony and good will had a beneficial effect on Herne's spirits, and he regained a measure of his lost strength and cheerfulness. But his old vigor was gone, never to be recovered, and he was noticeably gentler and quieter. The first week after his return was devoted to casting and consultations with the scene designers, and every evening, as was his wont, he would tell the family what he had done. He engaged Forrest Robinson and Sidney Booth for the two brothers, Ben and Frank Turner; Marion Abbott, an excellent character actress, was his choice for Elizabeth, Cap'n Dan's middle-aged sweetheart; Mrs. Sol Smith, one of the grand old ladies of the theatre, was Mrs. Russell; Julie and Chrystal, much to their delight, were given the parts of Martha and Jane. Critics and audiences later agreed, whether they liked the play or not, that Herne's casting had never been better and that the company was excellent. Most of the cast were old friends of Herne, but an unknown named William Hodge,

Sag Harbor 143

who had been playing small parts in musical comedy, created a sensation at the first rehearsal as Freeman Whitmarsh, the village housepainter. He was a tall, gangling young man with a shock of red hair, an incredibly homely face, and the dry, off-hand manner of the born comedian.

The stage rehearsals took place at the Herald Square Theatre. *Sag Harbor,* with its small cast, was a much simpler play to produce than *Griffith Davenport,* and Herne directed it in the easiest, most casual manner possible. He always tried to make the actors feel at home on the stage. As a rule, he had planned every move ahead, but occasionally a new bit of business occurred to him during a scene at rehearsal. In the second act of the play, Julie, as Martha, had to stand and listen while Ben and Frank had a long scene. She felt awkward with nothing to do, and Herne must have observed it, for one day he said,"Suppose, during this scene, you stroll over to that work bench, and while you listen to what the men are saying, you absentmindedly pick up a pencil and begin scribbling on the drawing board." This is one example of the way Herne obtained the simple, natural effects for which he was noted. In the third-act supper scene any pre-arranged plans which Herne had made were cast aside when he saw that Hodge, as Freeman Whitmarsh, simply walked away with the scene without half trying. When Herne realized that the actor knew what he was doing, he gave him free reign, and the company followed suit and played up to him. The result was one of the funniest episodes in the play.

Sag Harbor opened at the Park Theatre, Boston, October 24, 1899. The play was a hit from the moment the curtain rose. The reviews the next morning confirmed the enthusiastic verdict of the first night audience. Henry Arthur Clapp of the *Advertiser* said: "Much of the value and most of the popular charm of the play are to be found in its easy, shrewd, and natural touches of ordinary conditions of ordinary life.... The red blood of men and women constantly colors the text and the sympathy and observation of the dramatist in dealing with common weaknesses and passions, and his fluent gift in mild but expressive humor are almost steadily interesting." John J. McNally of the *Herald* said: "America has not his equal in producing perfect illusion in scenes of simple country life." Charles S. Howard of the *Globe* said: "In dramatic situations or strong 'acting scenes' the play is truly lacking, but there is a constant heart interest which holds the audience's unwavering attention, and the humor of the play is constantly delightful." Lewis C. Strang of the *Journal* said: "He puts humanity into his plays, and one always finds the old stories the most touching when they are adorned with sincerity and truth. With remarkable fidelity to nature he has transferred to the theatre the quaint atmosphere of a typical New England seaport, not by means of an elaborately bedecked stage... but by means of the simple honesty that shines through the characters. There is not a melodramatic touch in the whole play, and mere theatrical artifice is so far away as never even to be thought of." [77] E. H. Crosby of the *Post* said: "Mr. Herne has come to be recognized as the apostle of realism... and he has given proof of his skill in more instances than one. His *Shore Acres* came as a revelation to the satiated theatre-goers... and it has taken high and possibly lasting rank among the classics of the American stage. In *Sag Harbor* Mr. Herne has carried his creed to such an extreme that even his friends gasp at his temerity. *Sag Harbor* has a meagre and not particularly novel plot... most of his scenes, in fact all of them, occur when the main thread of the story is lost sight of." George T. Richardson of the *Evening Traveler* said: "Mr. Herne is the foremost American representative of realism in dramatic art. He believes that the doings of the stage should resemble those of everyday life as closely as is possible within the limitations of the footlights. *Sag Harbor* is a second *Shore Acres* in many respects.... To some it will appear monotonous.... Yet its very quietness has a power, and a convincing spirit which many plays more showily dramatic do not possess." On the following Sunday, the *Post* said in its editorial columns: "He stirs our nature to its depth, because he pictures things as they are and feelings as they manifest themselves in those relations of life which are tenderest and commonest. His art is homely but convincing. We yield to its charm without need of analysis and without thought of resistance." In an editorial, probably written by Strang, the *Journal* said: "He is a man with an ideal and the world admires that. It may scoff, but it admires just the same.... To quote Israel Zangwill: 'Nothing will alter my admiration for a man who has for years fought almost single-handed in the cause of artistic sincerity.' "

Sag Harbor was so entirely different from *Hearts of Oak* that not a single critic mentioned the older play, even though both plays were available for comparison, for a revival of *Hearts of Oak* had opened at the Metropolitan Theatre in the Bronx on September 25,

1899, and the old play continued on the road successfully for some years after Herne's death. To the Herne of 1899, the old play seemed melodramatic, crude, and often silly, as he said in an interview in *The Coming Age* for March, 1899. All that he really drew from it for *Sag Harbor* was the central situation of two brothers in love with the same woman and some of the attendant circumstances. All the "strong" scenes of *Hearts of Oak* such as the shipwreck and the church scene, are missing from *Sag Harbor;* and the simple, natural dialogue of the latter play shows the enormous progress towards truth and realism that Herne had made in twenty years. That the two plays had an almost equal popular success simultaneously at the end of the century is perhaps indicative of how little the general public is interested in art in the drama if a play has genuine human interest.[78]

Sag Harbor settled down into one of those prosperous, comfortable, steady runs that every actor dreams of, and a feeling of content, shared by every member of the company, was apparent as soon as one entered the stage door. Herne had written fine acting parts for all of them; even the smallest character had his moment, his chance to score, so that the professional jealousy which disrupts so many companies was noticeably absent. One person who was exceedingly puzzled by the hit she made was Mrs. Sol Smith, who played Mrs. Russell, the widow of an old-time whaling captain. She was a diminutive old lady, dressed in quaint costumes of her own design, and Chrystal Herne always called her "The Fascinator." She won the audience on her first entrance, and got a round of applause every time she went on or off the stage. "I don't understand it," Mrs. Smith said, "Mrs. Russell is only a bit, and has nothing to do with the plot." Part of her success was undoubtedly due to her lovable personality and finished acting, but part also to the fortunate placement of the character. Mrs. Russell always entered at the right moment, and every line she spoke registered with the audience. It was Chrystal Herne's theory that the position, or placement, of a character in a play is of the utmost importance to the actor.

Herne received many complimentary letters from people who saw *Sag Harbor* in Boston, but one especially pleased him.[79]

350 Marborough Street,
3 December, 1899

My dear Mr. Herne:

May I express the great pleasure which *Sag Harbor* gave me last evening.

It is not as serious a work at *Griffith Davenport,* of course, —and so perhaps in the deeper sense of the word is not so interesting. Superficially, though, I found it even more so. It had the power of pleasantly and firmly holding attention from beginning to end; and of leaving, at the end, the impression that it was worth every bit of attention it called for.

During the summer I have been at work on a rather elaborate essay on American Literature. In the course of this I have found myself more and more disposed to think that our next serious literary expression—now that the literary period of New England is a thing of the past—will take dramatic form. Such work as yours goes far to confirm this feeling.

Sincerely yours,
Barrett Wendell

Shortly before the holidays Herne became ill with a severe attack of rheumatism which settled in his knees. His doctor prescribed the usual remedies of that time, and a rigid diet—no red meat and no sweets. Herne became weak and thin under this regimen, and suffered excruciating pain. The girls, who had scarcely ever seen their father ill, were greatly concerned, and Katharine hurried on from New York. She begged Herne to close the play and rest, but he refused to do this. He was making more money than he had ever made in his life, he said, and he could not afford to stop working. Had he given up then, he might have prolonged his life.

In November, 1899, Hamlin Garland had married Zulime Taft, the beautiful sister of his friend Lorado Taft, the sculptor, and early in the New Year he came to New York with his bride. Katharine wrote enthusiastic letters to Herne about Mrs. Garland, and Garland wrote later of their meeting in *A Daughter of the Middle Border* (p. 161): "Mrs. James A. Herne, who had meant so much to me in my Boston days, was one of our very first callers, and no one among all my friends established herself more quickly in my wife's regard. Katharine's flame-like enthusiasm, her never-failing Irish humor, and her quick intelligence, made her a joyous inspiration." Soon afterwards, the young couple arrived in Boston, where Garland was to deliver a lecture, and Julie and Chrystal, in high excitement, went to call on them at the Parker House. Herne was too ill to accompany them. Mrs. Garland was a lovely blonde, with a graceful figure, a low, sweet voice, and a quiet manner that concealed a keen sense of humor. Garland's love and pride were overflowing; he wanted all his friends to know his bride, and although meeting so many strangers must have been an ordeal for her, she carried it off with remarkable poise and self-possession. "It's Zulime's first visit to Boston, and I've been showing her the sights," said Garland exuberantly. The girls were about to ask his wife what she thought of the State House and Faneuil Hall, when he added with a twinkle in his eye, "Yes, we've visited all the places where I nearly starved to death in my youth." He laughed joyously, for those hard days were now behind him. The Garlands went to see *Sag Harbor,* of course, and of it Garland wrote in *A Daughter of the Middle Border* (pp. 162-3): "Herne was growing old and in failing health, but he showed no decline of power that night. His walk, his voice, his gestures filled me with poignant memories of our first meeting in Ashmont, and our many platform experiences, while the quaint Long Island play brought back to me recollections of his summer home on Peconic Bay. How much he had meant to me in those days of Ibsen drama and anti-poverty propaganda!" It was the first time since their meeting nearly twenty years before that Garland had come fresh upon one of Herne's plays knowing nothing about it beforehand, and he told Katharine afterwards what a delightful experience it was and that Howells had said the same thing.

Sag Harbor closed in Boston on January 20, 1900, after an engagement of thirteen weeks, a run, according to the Boston *Journal* (Jan. 16, 1900) that was "not only the longest, but the most prosperous in the history of the Park Theatre." The company then embarked on an eight-week tour that took them through New England from Connecticut to Vermont. With the exception of one week in Providence, they played nothing but one, two, and three-night stands. Financially the tour was a triumph, for Tyler, as usual, had advertised the play like a circus, and the theatres everywhere were packed to the doors. But it was sheer martyrdom for Herne. The New England winter was cruelly cold, the hotels were primitive and poorly heated, and the travel was exhausting. With only brief stops in each town, there was no opportunity for him to get proper medical treatment, and his rheumatism grew steadily worse, until stepping on the stage became a torture. Whenever possible, he and the girls spent their Sundays at the Adams House in Boston, where they could get brief respite from the horrors of the road, and decent food and rest. But these interludes were few and far between, and for the most part the tour was a nightmare. The girls were able to endure it, for they were young, but their hearts bled for their father. He bore it uncomplainingly, but he rarely joked, ate little, and slept less, and his face was often drawn with pain. More than ten years previously, Herne, then in the fullness of his power, had played that same territory in *Drifting Apart,* but no one would come to see him. Now he was old and broken, and they were crowding into the theatres.

On they went, through the small towns of New Hampshire and Vermont, sheeted with ice and snow, and then into the still relentless cold of Northern New York. From there they went to Chicago, where Herne and the girls settled down at the Sherman House for a much-needed rest. It was not a moment too soon. Herne had developed an inflammation in his foot, which the doctor who was called in diagnosed as gout. He advised rest, but Herne had centered all his hopes on the Chicago opening of his play. He could not cancel it now.

Sag Harbor opened at the Grand Opera house, Chicago, on March 19, 1900. How Herne managed to give a performance was a miracle. But that night he seemed inspired and he inspired the company. The audience was enchanted. The critics raved. Business grew by leaps and bounds until by Saturday night the theatre was playing to standing room only. Herne had never played to so much money. There, in the city where he had made his first success with *Hearts of Oak* and had failed with *Shore Acres,* he had his greatest triumph.

The critics joined in a paean of praise. Tiffany Blake in the *Journal* (March 20, 1900) said: "What a strange, unwonted delight this is—to find upon the stage, between the painted canvas wings, in the yellow glare of the footlights, human life! Just plain, human life, your life and my life, and the life of those we love or hate, or pass unknowing in the streets . . . truly *Sag Harbor* is a triumph of wholesome naturalism. The story is simple . . . it is not of the lurid sort known to the mimic life of the stage, and it has none of the complexities of the stage-built plot. It is just such a common human catastrophe as might befall in any family, and Mr. Herne's method of telling it is original because it is natural." Lyman B. Glover of the *Times-Herald* (March 21, 1900) said: "Mr. Herne strikes the note of homely feeling and unpretentious life at the outset, and remaining true to the key, conquers by this one touch of nature, which cynics may decry, but sincere men and women must find irresistible. And thus we bow at the shrine of Herne's moving and illuminating realism...." Errol Hart in the *Chronicle* (March 20, 1900) said: "Mr. Herne has achieved the acme of naturalness." L. H. Bickford of the *Inter-Ocean* (March 20, 1900) said: "There is not a character in *Sag Harbor* that lacks verity. Each is distinct, and what is better, each may be recalled from life." Amy Leslie in the *Daily News* (March 20, 1900) said: "The finest thing in art that Herne has ever done." Edgar F. Sisson of the *Tribune* (March 20, 1900) said: "Set against the bulk of the season's cargo of imported stage stuff, *Sag Harbor* is a pearl of price. It is an American play and a good one."

But neither the critics nor the audiences—nor Herne himself— knew that *Sag Harbor* was his swan song. His health grew steadily worse. His foot was ulcerated and he suffered agonies. He could not sleep, and spent his nights sitting in a chair with his foot on a hassock. Towards morning the pain would become unbearable and he would give an involuntary groan. His daughter Chrystal would waken from her sleep, hurry to him, and dress the sore. Her devotion was tireless, and she would sit at his feet with her head on his knees. Herne's hand would stroke her hair gently as they sat silently, waiting for the dawn. A specialist was consulted, and announced that Herne's toe must be amputated; otherwise blood poisoning might set in. This meant the knell of all Herne's hopes, but he took the news with absolute calm. He said he wanted to go home for the operation. "You know, doctor," he said, "I've got an awfully good wife." It was decided to keep the play running with Frank Monroe, who played William Turner, in Herne's part of Cap'n Dan Marble. The girls wanted to return home with their father, but he insisted that they remain with the company. It was a sad little party which accompanied Herne to the train the next morning. Julius, Herne's faithful colored servant, who was to go with him, looked worried, and the girls could hardly keep back their tears. As they stood on the platform and watched the train pull out, they said nothing to each other; but they feared they would never see their father again.

12

FAREWELL

The operation was successful, and when the girls returned to New York after the closing of the play in April, they found their father much improved. As he gained in health, his spirits rose, and the family life resumed for a brief time its old air of happy bustle. Katharine made plans for the annual pilgrimage to Herne Oaks, but suddenly towards the end of May, Herne announced that he was going to Hot Springs, Arkansas, to take the baths and that Katharine and the family were to proceed to Herne Oaks without him. They looked at him in consternation. Hot Springs was where Uncle John, Herne's brother, had died. The very name of the place had a sinister sound to Julie. She wondered if her mother felt as she did, but she did not dare to ask. For a reason that they could not bring themselves to voice, the family, always so open in discussing their plans and feelings, had become reticent, and they feared to confide their thoughts to one another.

The evening before his departure, Herne and Julie sat together by the open window in his study on the second floor. He sat in his wooden arm-chair. In the corner stood his desk with its favorite pictures and nicknacks—the big brass inkstand and the little silver box in which he kept his pens and clips. On the desk were two pictures—one of Katharine as Margaret Fleming and one of Henry George. On the wall hung Chrystal's first water color sketch. It was the middle of May and very warm; they sat in the dark because of the mosquitoes, and the only light came from the lamp in the street below, "Papa," said the girl, for once overcoming her awe of him, "Why are you going to Hot Springs?" "To get well," he replied quietly, but with such finality that she was silenced. The next day he started on his lonely journey.

He remained at Hot Springs for about six weeks, taking the baths as well as the medical treatment. It was a dull, monotonous routine, but he went about the business of getting well with the same systematic thoroughness that characterized everything he did, and, in spite of the uncertainty of his health and the collapse of his brilliant prospects in Chicago, he contrived to retain his sense of humor. His letters showed an increasing cheerfulness as his health improved. When he returned to Herne Oaks early in July, he was very thin, but his color was good, and he seemed to have regained his health. His rheumatism was gone and never returned. His spirits were high, and he entered heartily into all the family activities, especially Katharine's plans for remodeling the house. He was overflowing with enthusiasm and ambition regarding his own future work. With Gross, he mapped out a season of repertory to begin as soon as his contract with Tyler expired, including besides *Sag Harbor,* a revival of *Shore Acres* and possibly of *Griffith Davenport.*

The era of the dramatized novel was at its height, and Charles Frohman had just returned from Europe with the dramatic rights to about 150 novels in his portfolio. Tyler, in an attempt to emulate Frohman, was buying up every novel that escaped his rival's clutches, and had obtained the rights to F. Marion Crawford's *In the Palace of the King.* He engaged Lorimer Stoddard to dramatize it for Viola Allen, but when the play was submitted to her, she refused to do it. Tyler was in a terrible predicament. With scenery and costumes contracted for, and an expensive cast engaged, he was in danger of having no star. In his dilemma, he appealed to Herne. Would he hear the play read and give Miss Allen and Tyler the benefit of his advice? Herne, who hated the cloak-and-dagger romance fully as much as Howells did, groaned inwardly at the prospect, but he reluctantly consented, and invited Miss Allen and Tyler to spend the day at Herne Oaks and bring their play along. The girls were wild with excitement at the thought of actually meeting one of their favorite stars.

Tyler and Miss Allen arrived on a day of grilling heat. But neither the weather nor the almost equally warm admiration of the girls had any effect on the cool detachment of the self-centered Viola Allen. Her icy politeness, her frigid courtesy, quenched all enthusiasm. She didn't quite snub the girls, but she conveyed the impression that she was there for one purpose only — to get advice on the play — and she had no time to waste on stage-struck juveniles. Katharine was impressed by the calm, unhurried manner in which Miss Allen ate her dinner; she thought it showed tremendous poise.

As soon as the mid-day meal was over, Tyler began to read the play in his harsh, raucous voice, in the most perfunctory manner, without the slightest feeling or expression, hurrying through the scences at break-neck speed. To Herne the play seemed heavy and boring, and its exotic atmosphere and complicated yet conventional plot of court intrigue in the Spain of Philip II represented all that he most detested in the novel or drama. The fact that the book was one of the best sellers for the year 1900 made no difference to him, nor that it was one of the most popular books in England during that year. The work of the exotic and cosmopolitan Mr. Crawford disgusted him quite as much as it did Henry James, who called it "six-penny humbug." Unlike Robert Louis Stevenson, who "could always get a happy day out of Crawford," Herne was in acute mental misery as he listened to Tyler in silence. *The Outlook* on December 1, 1900, had called the novel "dramatic, picturesque, and deeply interesting," and in eulogizing Crawford had compared him to Balzac, Dickens, and Thackeray; but to Herne, the clever and versatile Crawford represented everything he had fought against all his life. When Tyler finally paused, exhausted, and Herne and Julie went out to the kitchen to prepare drinks, he let himself go. "Good God, Julie!" he cried. "What horrible stuff! Tyler must be mad to produce this thing! What can I say? What can I tell him?" Julie, who was not such a devoted realist as her father, suggested that the play might be rewritten. "What's the use of rewriting such trash? It's hopeless!" replied Herne. He tried to temper his criticism with kindness, but he could not conceal his intense dislike of the play, and Miss Allen and Tyler departed very much depressed. Whether it was Herne's dislike that determined Miss Allen to do the play will never be known, but she changed her mind, or Tyler, pleading his heavy investment, induced her to change it, and the play was produced. It was one of the big hits of the season.[80]

Late in August Herne went to New York to rehearse the road companies in *Shore Acres* and *Hearts of Oak,* which he was sending out under the management of Gross. *Sag Harbor* could not open until the new Republic theatre, which Oscar Hammerstein was building, was completed. After a series of maddening delays and disappointments it was announced that the Republic would be ready by the last week in September, and the company assembled for rehearsals. The season had already started. Augustus Thomas's *Arizona* was a smash hit at the Herald Square, and at the Empire John Drew was delighting audiences in *Richard Carvel,* based on Winston Churchill's novel. On September 17, E. H. Sothern opened at the

Garden in *Hamlet,* in a magnificent production. Physically the ideal Hamlet, Sothern's creation was a masterpiece of intellect, poetry, and beauty. The Herne girls saw it and were enthralled. The season opened with romanticism the dominant mood of the public. Liebler and Company's *Monte Cristo* was to be a big financial success. Likewise *Quo Vadis,* and Sarah Bernhardt and Coquelin in *L'Aiglon, Cyrano Bergerac,* and *Camille* were popular.

The first-night audience, when *Sag Harbor* opened on September 27, was not in the mood to appreciate the simple, rural realism of the play and was extremely hostile, even for Broadway. They did laugh at Hodge as Freeman Whitmarsh, and they gave Chrystal an ovation after her last act scene, but otherwise the play fell flat. Several circumstances probably contributed to the failure, besides the general mood of the audience. During the long delay over the opening of the theatre the company may have been over-rehearsed and as a result have gone stale. The actors may have been disconcerted by the hammers of the carpenters which were still pounding as they were making up backstage. Fresh paint and varnish ruined costumes, and even some of the women's dresses in the auditorium. The actors, sensing the mood of the audience, may have over-acted in an attempt to overcome its antagonism. It was, admittedly, the worst performance of the play ever given. On the second night, the company got into its stride, and by the end of the week it was giving a fine performance. But by then the damage had been done. Even the favorable reviews were not sufficient to counteract the bad impression created on the opening night. There was no denying the fact that *Sag Harbor* had failed on Broadway.[81]

Herne, who should have been resting at Herne Oaks that season anyway, had to take this shocking blow when he was not physically capable of absorbing the punishment. To add to his worry, there was a big argument with Tyler, who wanted to close the play at once and send it on the road. Herne would not consent to this. He believed he could build the play into a success as he had built *Shore Acres.* Finally they reached a verbal agreement whereby Tyler would keep the play on if Herne did not collect his salary until after the play went on the road. But Herne could not build *Sag Harbor* into a popular success as he had with *Shore Acres.* The moment was not right for it, and besides he was physically exhausted. His fellow actors—William Gillette, Maclyn Arbuckle, and Leo Ditrichstein—went up and down Broadway proclaiming the play a work of art, but the theatre remained half-filled. After two months, even Herne was convinced that the play could not be built into a Broadway success, and it closed on December 1, 1900, after a run of only nine weeks. Herne took it on the road to recoup his fortunes, Tyler having booked a tour which was to last until the end of June. The play did fairly well on tour, but it was never a financial success.

Herne's health now began to decline again. He seemed very tired and had a racking cough. But, foolishly, he refused to rest. During the first week in January in Ohio, he was forced to give up for a week, and his understudy, Monroe, took his place. In Cleveland he was able to take over his part again, but his spirits were not raised when *Sag Harbor* barely broke even, and the plays he regarded as trash, *In the Palace of the King* and *When Knighthood was in Flower,* played to phenomenal business. Early in February, when the Hernes were playing the Walnut in Philadelphia, William Gillette, playing in *Sherlock Holmes,* attended a matinee, and between the acts visited backstage to greet his old friends. The next morning a note arrived for Herne asking if he and his daughters would dine with Gillette that evening at the Stratford Hotel. Herne at first felt too ill to go, but when he saw the looks of disappointment on the faces of Julie and Chrystal, he had not the heart to refuse the invitation. Gillette was in his middle forties, tall, distinguished, handsome, with an inscrutable, indescribably fascinating personality, and that night he exerted every bit of his devastating charm upon his guests. He made the girls feel like royal princesses, and Herne forgot his illness under the spell of their host's graciousness.[82]

Tyler, who had always admired Chrystal and thought her very talented, now made her an offer to star in *The Christian,* which he was going to send on the road the following season. She was not quite nineteen, and it was her first great opportunity. She was eager to accept it, but first she asked her father's consent. Herne was troubled; he felt that Chrystal was too young and inexperienced to play such a demanding part, but when he saw how much she wanted to do it, he told her that she might accept the offer. Tyler lost no time in making the news public, and Herne's company came in a body to congratulate the happy young girl. Tyler's offer meant that Herne's best-loved child was leaving the parental nest to try her wings for herself, and he took it deeply to heart. He had always had a special tenderness for Chrystal, for he knew her to be more sensitive and more highly emotional than his other children, but with a great capacity for suffering. Once he said to Julie, "I hate to think of Chrystal having to go through the struggles that everyone has to meet in life." Yet, when the time came, Chrystal developed an inner strength and spiritual power that sustained her through many bitter ordeals.

Emboldened by Chrystal's success, Julie asked her father to obtain an interview for her with Charles Frohman. Herne was stunned. He expected to continue in *Sag Harbor* for at least another year, and now both girls wanted to leave him! He said, half-humorously, half-sadly, "You girls had better not be in such a hurry to desert the old man. I'm going to write a lot of good plays yet." But he wrote to Frohman, who replied that he would be glad to see Julie when he returned from Europe in the fall. The girls did not mean to be selfish. They were devoted to their father, but like all young people they felt the urge to strike out for themselves, and they did not realize until too late how much their father had depended on them.

All through the winter, Herne had counted on his reappearance in Chicago, where he felt sure of repeating his former success. But his cough still bothered him, and in Baltimore during the week of February 18, he was obliged to have a doctor in attendance every evening at the theatre, giving him oxygen treatments. During the first week in March, while the company was playing one-night stands in Pennsylvania, he was again forced to stop acting, and the tour was temporarily closed. Instead of returning home to rest, however, Herne decided to go to West Baden, Indiana, for the ten days that remained before the Chicago opening. By this time even Katharine did not dare oppose him in anything he wanted to do, and his doctors neglected to warn him that the resort was not the best place for one in his run-down condition. So to West Baden he went, and it proved to have tragic results.

On March 16, 1901, the Saturday before the opening, Julie and Chrystal, who had been at home with their mother, arrived with the rest of the company in Chicago. Herne, who had reserved rooms at the Victoria Hotel, was to arrive from West Baden on Sunday morning, and the girls went to the train to meet him. They were horrified when they saw their father. He was thinner than ever; his clothes hung upon him; he could scarcely walk, and his voice had sunk to a whisper. He looked, as indeed he was, a dying man.

March 18, the opening night, was a disaster. The critics descended upon Herne like a flock of vultures and tore his performance to pieces. They gave him no credit for his courage in playing while mortally ill; indeed, they berated him, and commented cruelly on his weakened voice and enfeebled appearance. This reception, after his former triumph, hurt and humiliated Herne deeply, although in justice to the critics it must be said that he had no right to appear in his condition. But he was a favorite with Chicago audiences and his houses, while not as large as formerly, were excellent. The Chicago climate, however, was at its worst; and day after day, rain, sleet, and snow descended upon the city. Herne came down with a heavy cold. But he continued to play, urged on by Askin, Tyler's representative, and by the theatre manager, and by a doctor who made light of his illness, calling it just a touch of grip, when in reality Herne was on the verge of pneumonia.

By the beginning of the third week, Herne was so ill that he went up in his lines during his long speech in the last act. Julie, seated near him on the scene, prompted him in a whisper, and he was able to finish the play. He told her afterwards that he did not know what he would have done if she had not given him the line. It was the last time he ever played Cap'n Dan. He was driven back to his hotel, where he collapsed. A nurse was called in. Frank Munroe, his understudy, went on in his place. Meantime, both girls fell ill with grip, but they continued to play because their father begged them to remain in the cast. Herne had forbidden them to tell Katharine of his illness, for he did not want to worry her. But now Julie, frightened, took matters into her own hands and wrote to her mother. Katharine replied in a series of frantic letters, begging her husband to come home.

Herne sent word to Tyler that he had not the strength to undertake the long Western tour. Tyler was angry. He thought Herne, to use his own expression, was "faking," and he rushed to Chicago, accompanied by his factotum, Connor, determined to bully Herne into making the trip. The doctor had given orders that Herne was not to be disturbed, but Tyler forced his way past the nurse and into the sick room. He must have realized then that Herne was very ill, for he emerged greatly subdued. George Woodward, a capable character actor, was summoned to Chicago, and took over the part for the rest of the season. As was usual in those days, no announcement was made of the change in the cast, and Herne's name was still prominently displayed in the billing and in front of the theatre. Sick men have strange fancies. The night that Woodward made his first appearance as Cap'n Dan, Herne insisted on going to the theatre and playing the small part of George Salter. The girls, and even the members of the company, knowing how ill he was, tried to dissuade him, but he was adamant. "I must go on," he said. "My name is up. Even if I go in a small part, I'll still be in the cast." They had to let him have his way, but it was agony for them all to watch his pitiful attempts to speak his few lines. That night marked Herne's last appearance on any stage.

He arrived home on April 7. Katharine was horrified at his condition. But with the rest and good nursing at home, he began to show some improvement. His illness, which was diagnosed as pleuropneumonia, baffled his doctor, and several specialists were called in consultation. Meanwhile, Katharine was almost breaking under the double strain of his illness and the absence of her daughters. She wrote for Julie to come home, and Julie returned from Denver to find him somewhat better. But early in May he suffered a serious relapse, and Chrystal was summoned home from San Francisco, where the play had just opened. Throughout his illness, Herne had been worrying over Chrystal's engagement in *The Christian,* and he begged Katharine to cancel their daughter's contract with Tyler. Katharine did not dare oppose him, and although it was a blow to Chrystal, she was too devoted to her father to make any protest.[83] After his relapse in May, Herne's illness became front page news, and friends called daily to inquire about him, sent flowers, or wrote notes of comfort and cheer to Katharine.

Herne's illness lasted for eight weeks after his return home. They were weeks of anguish for Katharine, who hardly ever left his side, and whose hopes rose or fell with his daily gain or loss. Everything was done that could be done. Eminent specialists came, looked grave, and prescribed this or that medicine or form of treatment. But the antibiotics that might have saved his life had not yet been discovered, and when he finally developed abscesses of the lungs, the doctors gave up hope. On Sunday afternoon, June 2, 1901, Herne's long fight ended.

The word spread quickly that the famous actor and dramatist was dead, and friends rushed to condole with Katharine. The first to arrive was young Samuel Seabury, who lived nearby, and who hastened to offer his help. He and another kind neighbor, James R. Brown, took charge of the funeral arrangements, for Katharine had collapsed completely and remained secluded in an upper room of the house where she gave herself up to her grief. She would see no one, she was incapable of speaking or planning. She sat and wept uncontrollably.

The funeral took place on Tuesday, June 4. In deference to Herne's wishes, there was no formal religious ceremony. One of his favorite songs, *All Through The Night,* was sung, and three musicians played the haunting melody, *Do They Think Of Me At Home,* which always accompanied the final scene of *Shore Acres.* Augustus Thomas, in an address memorable for its eloquence and beauty, spoke of Herne's work as a dramatist, and said, "As a dramatist he won his high place in the esteem of his countrymen as much by a personal quality that showed through his work as he did by his art, which was rare and of fine perfection. . . . For useless convention of any kind he had that disregard which is a mark of genius. . . . His fidelity in every work was compelling, and he added a gentle ideality, hopeful and uplifting as the breath of morn. In all he has ever written, affection and charity dominate. His men have moral bravery; his women abiding trust, for he himself had the courage of the truth and an enduring faith in humanity. . . . James Herne was a poet of the poor. He saw and knew the sublimity of plain living. He was the apostle of simplicity. . . . He was strong because he was attuned to Nature's will, and because his efforts were enlisted in not perverting but in expressing it. He had a spiritual magnetism that drew to him souls of his kind, and without robe or sceptre he swayed an empire that had sworn no allegiance, yet which gave its unconscious tribute of laughter and of tears where he raised the standard of his art. He made his character, Margaret Fleming, take the babe from the arms of a dead girl, who had enticed the husband, and put its famishing lips to her own maternal breast. No evangel ever framed a higher concept of charity and fraternal love. James Herne loved his fellow men. Into this world he brought a kindliness that it does not teach. He was a medium through which an exalted tenderness found voice. He spoke for the children, for the slave, for the oppressed of toil. To the weary, worn, and sick of heart he sang a sustaining patience that was not of time alone. . . ."

Farewell 159

Among the hundreds of letters to Katharine from people in all walks of life — from William Gillette, from Julia Marlowe, from R. H. White of Boston, from Adlai Stevenson of Chicago, from Israel Zangwill in England—there was one that spoke not only of personal sorrow but spoke for American literature and the future. For in this letter Hamlin Garland wrote: "Had he died in 1890 how much sadder it would have been! He had put himself among the first of our dramatists — and you will see his fame suddenly bloom out now."

Garland's words were prophetic, even though he was mistaken when he predicted a sudden growth in Herne's fame. The recognition of the importance of Herne in the history of the American drama has been a slow growth, like his own long struggle for truth and realism, but the passage of time has at last established his true significance.

NOTES

CHAPTER 1—BEGINNINGS

1. The biography of Edwin Forrest by Richard Moody (Knopf 1960) is now the definitive book on the first great American actor.
2. Patrick Aherne eventually found the stern Calvinism of the Dutch Reformed church more congenial to his temperament than the Catholic faith of his boyhood, and became a member of the former church. Herne's life-long prejudice against organized religion may have been stemmed from Patrick's excessive strictness.
3. An important source of information about the theatre conditions of the time from an actor's point of view is Herne's article, "Old Stock Days in the Theatre," published in *The Arena* in September, 1892.
4. In the above article Herne describes the complex system that governed the casting of parts at the time:
   Companies were engaged for a season of forty-two weeks, and were classified as follows:

Leading Man	2nd Old Man	2nd Heavy Woman
1st Juvenile Man	1st Comedian	1st Old Woman
2nd Juvenile Man	2nd Comedian	2nd Old Woman
1st Heavy Man	Respectable Utility	1st Singing Chambermaid
2nd Heavy Man	General Utility	
1st Walking Gent.	Leading Lady	2nd Singing Chambermaid
2nd Walking Gent.	Juvenile Lady	
1st Singing Walking Gent.	1st Walking Lady	Utility
2nd Singing Walking Gent.	2nd Walking Lady	Ballet
1st Old Man	1st Heavy Woman	

5. Most of the information about Herne's early life is derived from Julie Herne's biography and was related to her by her father. It agrees substantially with Herne's later autobiographical articles about this period published in *The Arena* and *The Coming Age*. From about the time when she made her first appearance in *Shore Acres* she began to plan her biography of her father and made extensive notes of his conversations with her and others. Later she was to receive considerable assistance in her projected book from her mother and Chrystal. John T. Herne has given Julie's manuscript to the University of Maine and it is now in the Folger Library, University of Maine.

CHAPTER 2—THE WESTERN SISTERS AND THE OLD MELODRAMA

6. The photographs of Herne and his family on stage and off were given to me by the late Julie A. Herne.
7. *Charles II, or The Merry Monarch,* A Comedy in Three Acts, was written by Payne and Irving in 1824 and was still popular thirty years later.
8. Julie Herne's information about the Western sisters and her father's relationship to them was derived mainly from her mother, Katharine

Herne. Herne, as Julie said, was always silent about this phase of his life, and it may be supposed that Katharine acquired her information about the sisters from their mother, Jane Sharples Western, who all her life remained a friend of the Herne family. Herne's only mention in print of Lucille Western was a passing reference in his article, "Forty Years Before the Footlights," in *The Coming Age* for August, 1899.
9. A valuable source of information about the history of the theatre in San Francisco is Edmond W. Gagey's *"The San Francisco Stage—A History* (New York, 1950).

CHAPTER 3—LITTLE MISS CORCORAN

10. Katharine's early life history was later told to her daughter, Julie.
11. Julie comments on her mother's love of children: "She spent hours playing with the babies on the tenement block. All her life she never passed a child in the street without stopping to speak to it." The remarkable authenticity of her portrayal of the mother-and-child scenes in *Margaret Fleming* years later impressed the critics.
12. Katharine designed and made her costume for the part of Peg Woffington. She had an instinctive feeling for line and color. Julie relates, and throughout her career on the stage made all her costumes.
13. Katharine's deeply religious nature is revealed by the following extract from a letter to Herne: "I am beginning to realize for the first time in my life what a great benefaction Christ was to the world, and how noble and yet simple were the truths that He taught, and how by that greatest of all methods, Example, He impressed upon the people the God-like laws of humanity."

CHAPTER 4—HEARTS OF OAK

14. William Winter's adulatory biography of Belasco (1918) is untrustworthy in some respects; Craig Timberlake's (New York, 1954) is more reliable. A recent, and realistic, estimate of Belasco is in Allen Churchill's *The Great White Way* (1962).
15. Mrs. Thomas Whiffen, who with her young husband was a member of the New Theatre company of which Herne was manager and Belasco stage director, says in her book, *Keeping Off the Shelf* (1928): "Mr. Herne was an inspiring man to work with, and we both learned a lot from his direction. He had formerly played with Lucille Western ... and he taught me all the older actress's business...."
16. Mrs. Whiffen mentions "a new play adapted by Mr. Herne and a young man named David Belasco, who was just beginning to come to the fore in San Francisco—*Lighthouse Cliffs*...." This was the earliest mention of Herne as a playwright.
17. Among Herne's papers was a play called *Agnes,* partly written by him and adapted from Sardou's *Andrea.* Herne's collaborator was probably Belasco. In the summer of 1886 Belasco produced at the Baldwin Theatre in San Francisco a play supposedly written by him, *Anselma,* and which he describes as "from Sardou's *Andrea,* via the German."

18. Julie Herne wrote: "But, if Broadway was cold to *Hearts of Oak,* on the road a vast and ever-growing public eagerly flocked to see it, and the critics outside New York were warm and enthusiastic. They called it, 'A charming and beautiful drama... and praised its 'scenic pictures, wonderful in their realistic effects.' The dramatic critic of the *St. Louis Republican* said. 'It is a strong and thoroughly absorbing domestic drama, and embraces several scenes of distinctly original cast and treatment. It is an idyl of the seacoast, and the sea is an element in the movement of the drama.'"
19. An editorial in *The Peorian* (Peoria, Illinois) expressed the satisfaction of the hinterland with the play: "It is great and grand in every sentiment and no man or woman can look upon or listen to it without being the better for having done so. Patience, love, sublime devotion and unflinching obedience to duty shine out in every scene."
20. Julie Herne stated that her father said that the play had grossed "well into the hundreds of thousands," but this is probably an exaggeration. She also tells of her father traveling about "with a theatre trunk packed to the lid with greenbacks, his share of the weekly receipts" from *Hearts of Oak.* At any rate, this was the family legend.

CHAPTER 5—BOSTON

21. Katharine was devoted to her children. Her own childhood had been so wretched that she was determined that her children should have a happy childhood. "No matter what they have to meet later in life," she wrote, "I want them to be able to say they had a happy childhood."
22. A few days after the opening of *The Minute Men of 1774-1775,* Henry C. Miner, owner and manager of the Bowery and People's Theatres, offered Herne $25,000 for a half-interest in the play, but Herne, certain that the play would be a success, refused the offer.
23. Herne did not understand why *The Minute Men of 1774-1775* failed. One fact that he failed to take into consideration when he wrote the play was that to date no play about the American Revolution has ever been really successful on the American stage.
24. Herne may have been influenced to write *Drifting Apart* by the continuing success of the dramatization of T. S. Arthur's *Ten Nights in a Barroom.* This play had been a box office success since 1858.
25. Later in *Roadside Meetings* (1930) Garland was to describe the powerful effect *Drifting Apart* had upon him. He wrote: "All through the scene [the second act], which was charmingly set, Herne moved unaffectedly, joking, chuckling, making quaint gestures with a naturalism I had never before seen upon a stage; and Katharine was almost equally delightful as the wife, and when at the close of the joyous act her sailor husband returned from the village, his arms full of holiday presents, hopelessly drunk, her expression of grief, of shame, of despair formed a complete and piteous contrast for the homely comedy which preceded it."

CHAPTER 6—HAMLIN GARLAND

26. Garland, Julie Herne relates, could quote pages verbatim from Spencer and Darwin.
27. Garland at this time, says Julie Herne, was "an intolerant realist, who had no use for the classic or romantic schools ... Ibsen, Zola, Howells and James were his gods."
28. After Garland had seen Beatrice Cameron (Mrs. Richard Mansfield) in a Boston matinee performance of Ibsen's *The Doll's House,* he "burst into the Ashmont living room, shouting triumphantly, 'No more of Shakespeare's hash!' " wrote Julie Herne.
29. Garland's statement that "in all matters concerning the American Drama we were in accord" needs some qualification. Herne once told Katharine, Julie states, that "Garland's idea of a drama is a scene in which two people discuss, for instance, the purchase of a ton of coal. One says, 'I think we are running short of coal.' The other replies, 'We have enough to last until next week.' To him, that is realism. To me, it is not drama."
30. Julie Herne says: "Garland did not rest until he had brought Herne's work to the attention of Howells, Flower, Enneking, Chamberlin, Perry, and others in the Boston literary and artistic world. For the next two years, whenever the Hernes were at home, a parade of Boston intellectuals, proudly escorted by Garland, made pilgrimages to Beale Street."
31. Herne and Garland collaborated on an Ibsenesque play called *Fall River,* which they copyrighted on April 15, 1890, but which was never produced.
32. Julie Herne states that Garland was much interested in "psychic research" and spent much time going to spiritualistic seances and investigating mediums. One evening Garland arrived at the Hernes' in a state of unusual excitement and announced that he had had a most remarkable experience at a seance the previous night: the medium had balanced a walking stick between his knees, where it stood upright, unsupported by any visible means, controlled only by the magnetism of the medium's waving hands. "That's an old trick, Garland," said Herne. "I'll do it for you after supper." That evening the family gathered in the study, which was lighted only by a lamp, turned low. Herne seated himself in a chair, took his walking-stick, rubbed it several times impressively "to set the magnetic currents flowing," placed it between his knees and rubbed his hands. The stick remained upright, swaying a little to the right or left as Herne waved his hands. Garland was dumbfounded. Katharine turned up the lamp for a better view, and moved it to the edge of the table. Her eyes caught the gleam of a black silk thread fastened low down on either side of Herne's trousers. The thread kept the stick upright. Garland saw it at the same time. He never mentioned "psychic research" again.

CHAPTER 7—MARGARET FLEMING

33. Garland was to write of *Margaret Fleming* forty years afterward in *Roadside Meetings*: "Without question it was the most naturalistic, the

most colloquial and the most truthful presentation of a domestic drama ever seen on the American stage up to that time, and I am free to say that in some regards I do not think it has been surpassed since."

34. There is no record of the exact date on which Herne started work on *Margaret Fleming*. Garland later wrote in *A Son of the Middle Border* that Herne "was at this time (1889) working on two plays which were to bring lasting fame and a considerable fortune. . . One became *Shore Acres* and the other *Margaret Fleming*."

35. Julie Herne felt that the character of Margaret was based on that of Katharine Herne. Margaret voices a number of Katharine's ideas and sayings.

36. Katharine suggested to Herne the scene which forms the climax of Act III, in which Margaret nurses the starving child of her husband's dead mistress.

37. A critical controversy later arose over Herne's indebtedness to Ibsen in *Margaret Fleming*. See "Ibsen and Herne's *Margaret Fleming*: A study of the Early Ibsen Movement in America," in *American Literature* for January, 1946, by Dorothy S. Bucks and Arthur H. Nethercot; "Ibsen and Herne, Theory and Facts" in *American Literature for* May, 1947, by Arthur H. Quinn, and "Howells and Herne," in *American Literature* for January, 1951, by Herbert Edwards. Quinn states in his *History of the American Drama* that Herne, like Howells, was "authorized rather than inspired by the continental realists." (Vol. I, p. 159). Julie Herne felt that "Herne was inspired by Ibsen, but he did not deliberately set out to imitate him. . . He would have been a realist had he never heard of Zola or Ibsen, just as he would have continued to seek new paths in the theatre, even if he had never had the valuable encouragement of such men as Garland and Howells." Garland stated in his article, Mr. and Mrs. James A. Herne," in *The Arena* for October, 1891; "Epoch-making as it was, *Margaret Fleming* was only a logical, latest outcome of the work the Hernes have been doing for the last ten years."

38. Among those who saw the play was Lucy Stone, the remarkable champion of women's rights. She invited Katharine to tea at her beautiful old house in Roxbury.

39. As soon as *Margaret Fleming* closed at Chickering Hall, Herne began work on *My Colleen*. His familiarity with the large number of sentimental Irish plays that followed Boucicault's *Arrah-na-Pogue, The Colleen Bawn,* and *The Shaughran* was a help, as well as his memories of his father and mother, but he worried because he had never actually lived in Ireland. Finally, after much searching of Boston book shops, he found a travel book, *Picturesque Ireland,* in three enormous, profusely illustrated volumes, carried it home and devoured it almost in one reading. Julie Herne relates the following incident in connection with *My Colleen*: "One of the children begged permission to read the play to Maggie Kenny, the Herne's Irish maid, recently arrived from 'The ould country.' In the midst of the reading Maggie gave a choking cry and covered her face with her hands. 'What's the matter?'

asked the somewhat dismayed child. 'It's so Irish,' cried Maggie, between laughter and tears."

CHAPTER 8—WILLIAM DEAN HOWELLS

40. Walter J. Meserve's *The Complete Plays of William Dean Howells* (1960) is an indispensable work on Howells as a dramatist. In his introduction, Meserve states that Howells had been interested in the theatre from early youth and that this interest never abated. Meserve mentions several reasons why Howells' plays were not successful on the stage: They are mainly one-act plays, with largely a Boston Back Bay background, with characters drawn from Back Bay society. Most of them are farce-comedies, with the emphasis on situation rather than character. While they are often witty and clever, they lack the forceful impact of the novels. The women characters are stronger and more interesting than the men, but none of them achieve the distinction of his fine portraits in the novels.
41. Meserve says that Howells had an opportunity to collaborate with Augustin Daly and that if he had accepted he might have written a successful play.
42. Meserve quotes a letter from Herne to Howells on June 1, 1890, in which Herne suggests that Howells write a comedy to be presented on the same program with *Margaret Fleming*.
43. *Bride Roses* is included in *The Complete Plays of William Dean Howells*. In his introduction to the play Meserve includes an analysis and critical estimate of it.
44. Meserve states that Howells refused to conform to the requirements of the theatre, and that his dramatic methods were ineffective.
45. Although Howells and Herne corresponded for some years, only one of Howell's letters to Herne has survived.
46. When Herne was directing *The Country Circus*, which ran in New York between December 29, 1891, and March 26, 1892, he made a special effort to get Howells behind the scenes. Herne received $100 a week from Klaw and Erlanger for directing this play.
47. Julie Herne said that when she was a girl in her early teens she and her parents had read all of Howell's novels that had then been published.
48. Howells was, nonetheless, Katharine's favorite novelist. She wrote to Herne when he was on the road in 1896, after she had finished Howell's *The Day of Their Wedding*: "Do read this fine book, if you have any leisure or inclination at all. You will be deeply moved by its unaffected honesty and sincerity, and by its wholesomeness and sanity."
49. Julie Herne's ms.

CHAPTER 9—SHORE ACRES

50. The lighthouse scene was to undergo changes after Herne's later visit to Lamoine and his opportunity to observe the interior of an actual lighthouse on the Maine coast.
51. As the play grew slowly in Herne's imagination, he added new situations

and characters, among the latter the old farmer, Joel Gates. When Herne first told his wife about Gates, Katharine said, "Jim, why don't you give him a little girl, a pathetic, neglected little thing, who follows her father about all through the play?" Herne was quick to see the value of her idea, and thus was born the character of little Mandy Gates, who never spoke a word, but whose forlorn, bedraggled appearance, as she trailed after Joel, never failed to arouse laughter and tears."

52. The high esteem for McVicker by actors and managers is indicated by Leavitt in his *Fifty Years of Theatrical Management* (p. 35): "James Hubert McVicker was the most kindly, tender-hearted and gentle of men, while at the same time he was an unflinching and uncompromising combatant for what he believed to be right."

53. McVicker was prominent in the civic life of Chicago, and his address at Central Music Hall on November 28, 1892, "The Press, The Pulpit, and The Stage," had been given wide publicity.

54. Indicative of the radical changes Herne made in the play is the fact that Sam was a blacksmith instead of a doctor in the early version of the play and was named Philip.

55. Two changes suggested by McVicker were adopted by Herne in the final version of *Shore Acres*: (1) The first scene of Act II, a "front" scene which took place on a country road and featured the guests driving to Berry's house in various quaint old carriages, was dropped. (2) Audible dialogue was eliminated from the second scene of Act III, in which the sloop *Liddy Ann* is seen drifting towards the rocks in the storm.

56. One of McVicker's objections to the play was that it did not "possess a positive meaning for all," as *Hearts of Oak* did.

57. As Herne had originally written the play, the character of Blake was consistently evil. McVicker insisted that Blake undergo a change of heart at the end of the play, and wrote: "He is not viciously bad, so give him a chance to show that there is something good in human nature after all." McVicker then suggested some dialogue for Blake's exit, which Herne considered hackneyed and did not adopt, but he did accept McVicker's suggestion that a change for the better take place in Blake before his exit.

The extent to which Ibsen was becoming known is shown in the closing paragraph of a letter McVicker wrote to Herne on March 14, 1892: "Are you familiar with Ibsen's plays? I have just read *The Pillars of Society*, which, properly cut, would be strong in the line of human plays. If you have not read it, do so. You can buy a volume for 60 cents in Lovell's Series of Foreign Literature which contains *Doll's House, Ghosts, Rosmersholm,* and *The Pillars of Society*. With a slight alteration, and a woman capable of grasping and acting the part in *The Doll's House* it's a fortune to the woman—but where is she?"

58. Amy Leslie not only liked *Uncle Nat*, but had high opinion of Herne: "To look upon, James Herne is a commonplace, unpretentious man, suited to the plodding conditions of existence. But in the dreamy deeps of his eyes and in the kindly half smile that plays about his lips, there

is nothing commonplace; there shows the thoughtful mind that has learned the world by heart, not bitterly, but sympathetically, compassionately, lovingly, with a sorrow for its infirmities, and a joy for its virtues, for Mr. Herne is something of the philosopher and much of the poet, and out of the abundance of his knowing he makes plays that utter the eloquence of nature, simply, modestly, but positively."

59. Howells' letter to Field recommending *Shore Acres* stated: "I was delighted to hear from Mr. Herne, the other day, that you had decided to produce his *Shore Acres* at the Museum. I read the play not very long ago, and I thought I saw in it a success like that of *The Old Homestead,* or *The County Fair.* It seems to me that it has all the popular elements of those plays, and there is a strain of finer poetry in it."

60. On his last tour in *Shore Acres,* Herne had an enjoyable visit with his old friend, James Whitcomb Riley, in Indianapolis. Julie Herne says: "They were drawn to each other through their love of common, simple things, and whenever Herne was in Indianapolis they spent a great deal of time together. There was a deep vein of sentiment in both men, which, combined with a keen sense of humor, made them congenial. Riley always had a fund of stories, both funny and sad, to tell Herne, and Herne treasured them to repeat to his family. Some of them became household sayings. Herne liked to read Riley's poems aloud, bringing out the music of his verse, as well as its pathos and humanity. He was especially fond of *The South Wind and the Sun,* and *Jim.* Riley gave Herne a set of his works, each volume inscribed in his fine, old-fashioned handwriting. These books were destroyed in the fire at Herne Oaks."

On the last tour of *Shore Acres,* in Fort Worth, then largely a cattle town, a cattlemen's convention had attracted a large number of cowboys to the town and they crowded the theatre where *Shore Acres* was being shown. During the first-act love scene between Sam and Helen, which Herne had directed should be played very quietly, with the lovers hiding their emotion beneath typical New England restraint, a great commotion broke out in the audience. On the stage, Sam and Helen, like good troupers, tried to ignore the interruption and go on with the scene, but their words were drowned by the increasing uproar. Suddenly Herne, in his Uncle Nat make-up and costume, stepped out on the stage. He waited for quiet, and then said: "Ladies and gentlemen, we are giving the same performance tonight we have given in all the big cities of the country. Those of you who are dissatisfied may have your money refunded at the box office, but we cannot allow those who wish to hear the play to be disturbed. We must have quiet."

At this point someone in the audience shouted, "We don't mean any harm, old man! We want Sam to kiss the gal—jes' once—that's all."

From all over the house came the cry, "Yes, go ahead, Sam! Kiss her! Kiss her!" Herne smiled, but ignored the plea, and said, "If there is any further noise, I must order the curtain rung down." The audience suddenly became silent. "Now," Herne said, "we will go on with the performance."

For the rest of the evening, the cowboys were as quiet as mice. If anyone started to laugh or applaud, he was quickly hushed by the rest of the audience. The thrilling lighthouse scene in the third act was always good for several curtain calls, but the frightened cowboys didn't dare give it a single hand.

61. Although Herne was later to lose a considerable amount of money on his unsuccessful play, *Griffith Davenport* and was to spend large sums in developing his Long Island estate, "Herne Oaks," he was still regarded as a wealthy man at the time of his death.

CHAPTER 10—GRIFFITH DAVENPORT

62. Garland's current enthusiasm at this time was Stephen Crane, an admiration which Herne shared. Before Herne completed the final version of *Griffith Davenport* he had read Crane's *The Red Badge of Courage,* published in 1895.
63. "Herne was fonder of *Griffith Davenport* than of anything he ever wrote, except *Margaret Fleming.*" Julie Herne said.
64. A letter from Herne to Julie from Chicago in the winter of 1895, stated, in part: "I am to read a couple of acts of 'Rev. Grif' this afternoon to select listeners, among whom will be your favorite authors, Hamlin Garland—he of *Main Travelled Roads,* and Henry Fuller, he of *The Cliff Dwellers.*"
65. Katharine may have made a serious error in insisting that Herne remove Lincoln as a character in the play. Plays about Lincoln or plays in which he appears, have rarely been unsuccessful.
66. Miner never shared Herne's sympathy for Negroes. In this connection it might be noted that Herne was probably responsible for the first important critical recognition received by Paul Laurence Dunbar. When Herne was in Toledo, Ohio, playing in *Shore Acres* on one of its last tours, a Dr. Robey gave Herne a little book of poems entitled *Majors and Minors* by Paul Laurence Dunbar, a young Negro who had run an elevator in a Toledo office building. Herne was greatly impressed by the youth's talent, and sent a copy of the book to Mr. Howells, who wrote in praise of it in *Harper's Weekly* for June 27, 1896. This was the first important critical recognition that Dunbar received.

On July 13 Dunbar wrote to Howells expressing his deep appreciation and said: "I have written to thank Mr. Herne for putting the book in your hands. I have only seen the man on the stage, but I have laughed and cried with him until I love him."

67. Miner always regarded Herne as impractical and extravagant. Herne wanted the actors and actresses in the *Shore Acres* company to have a share in the play's prosperity, but Miner opposed all of Herne's efforts to raise salaries. Typical is a letter of April 27, 1896, which Miner wrote from New York when the company was playing in Detroit. Herne had evidently asked that the salary of an actress in the company should be raised and Miner replied: "I think $50 a week is all she is worth, Jim. Why should she jump up $15 a week? Because she has been playing the part

and has no clothes to buy and no rehearsals? I am blamed if I think we should let her impose upon us."
68. Garland was never happy at Herne Oaks, presumably because the luxury of the place, with its servants and yacht, disquieted him. A horror of extravagance had been bred in him by his Down-East Yankee father, and he could not help feeling that the money Katharine and Herne were spending so freely at Herne Oaks should have been saved and wisely invested. In July, 1896, when Garland visited Herne Oaks, he was working on his *Life of Grant.* He read parts of it aloud to the Hernes, with, they thought, a perceptible emphasis on Grant's extravagance and unwise management of his financial affairs.

Garland later wrote of *Griffith Davenport* in *Roadside Meetings*: "Herne's return to speculative producing seemed foolish to me, for it had plunged him once again into the morass of anxious toil from which *Shore Acres* had lifted him."
69. "In the ideal theatre," Herne told Julie, "there will be no applause, except perhaps at the end of the performance. Instead, the audience will show their appreciation by their silence, and the strict attention with which they follow the play." Once, before a performance of *Shore Acres,* he told Julie he would show her how easy it was to get applause. He chose the scene in which Uncle Nat is proudly displaying to his brother, Martin, the Christmas presents he has bought for the children with his pension money. Martin, gloomy and sullen, suggests it would have been better if he had bought himself an overcoat. *Uncle Nat:* What's the matter with the one I got?
Martin: That old army cut? It's patched from one end to t'other.
Uncle Nat: Thet makes it all the warmer. *(With humor)* 'Sides, yeh mustn't never despise a man jes' because he wears a ragged cut."

When Herne came to the last line of this speech, he always "threw it away," as actors say, that is, spoke it casually, almost carelessly. But on that night he paused before he spoke the last line, then with all the pathos he could command, he spoke the line directly to the audience in a quavering voice. He was rewarded with an instantaneous round of applause. He had shown Julie the difference between the artistic and the theatrical.
70. In early March of 1898, Garland appeared at 79 Convent Avenue and announced solemnly to Katharine and the children that he was going to the Klondike. They stared at him in consternation. They knew that the Klondike, where gold had been discovered two years before, was a perilous Arctic waste where many had lost their lives. Garland knew that he was going to face cold, hunger, and possibly death, and as he paced about the room with a tense face, describing the dangers of the journey, he suddenly paused, and said to Katharine in a voice trembling with emotion, "In case I don't come back, I have dictated a record of my life, and the story of my meeting with you and James A., and our association in the production of *Margaret Fleming.* I consider that one of the most important things that ever happened to me."

71. William Archer and Herne became good friends. Archer asked to read the manuscript of *Margaret Fleming, Shore Acres,* and *Griffith Davenport.* Later Archer assigned Herne a significant place in the development of modern American drama.
72. The New York engagement of *Griffith Davenport* lasted only four weeks. Despite the all too evident signs that it was a commercial failure, Herne was determined to take it on the road.
73. At the annual benefit for the Actor's Fund at the Fifth Avenue Theatre on Thursday afternoon, March 23, 1899, Herne and his wife, appearing in the fourth act of Griffith Davenport, were given an ovation.
74. The last performance of *Griffith Davenport* was at Stamford, Connecticut, May 13, 1899.

CHAPTER 11—SAG HARBOR

75. Herne's revival of *Hearts of Oak* opened on September 25, 1899, at the Metropolitan Theatre in New York. The play was then over twenty years old, but it still retained its appeal.
76. Julie Herne said: "Probably the person who took the faliure of the Zangwill play most deeply to heart was Tyler—on Zangwill's account, not on his own. He related, with a voice shaking with emotion, how the author, on his departure, shook the producer's hand and said, 'I'm going to write you a play that will earn you all the money you've lost on this one.' Some years later, Zangwill wrote *The Melting Pot,* which Tyler produced and which made a fortune for them both. The actress who played the leading part was Chrystal Herne."
77. Although Lewis C. Strang of the Boston *Journal* praised *Sag Harbor* highly, he felt that it was inferior to *Shore Acres.*
78. "*Sag Harbor* and *Hearts of Oak* are the only plays by Herne in which not one important line or scene was changed after the opening night," Julie Herne said.
79. Herne was always more impressed by praise from the intelligentsia than were his daughters. Also playing in Boston at the same time as *Sag Harbor* was the first important "Western" to reach the American stage— Augustus Thomas' *Arizona.* Herne did not care for it, but his daughters —and the public—loved it. It had excitement, romance, and suspense, and the following year became a Broadway hit. Some years later, in an all-star revival, Chrystal Herne played the part of Estrelle Bonham.

CHAPTER 12—FAREWELL

80. George C. Tyler became one of the most important producers of the period. When he brought the Irish Players to the United States in such plays as Synge's *The Playboy of the Western World* he introduced modern Irish drama to the American public. He brought Mrs. Patrick Campbell and Eleanora Duse to the United States, and had specially written for George Arliss his great starring play, *Disraeli.* He promoted such stars as Helen Hayes, Lynne Fontanne, Laurette Taylor, Alfred Lunt, and Jeanne Eagels.

81. "The New York failure of *Sag Harbor,* coming just when his expectations had reached their peak, was the greatest disappointment ever suffered by Herne, and undoubtedly contributed to his death," Julie Herne said.
82. Gillette played in *Sherlock Holmes* until he was seventy-five years old, and made a fortune out of it for himself and Charles Frohman, who first had the idea of a stage version of Sir Arthur Conan Doyle's famous detective and his exploits.
83. Although Chrystal Herne was the only one of Herne's children to make a success on the stage, all of them were connected directly or indirectly with the theatre. John T. Herne, the only boy in the family, married Carolyn Thomson, who starred in a number of musical plays. Carolyn Thomson was a soloist with the Minneapolis Symphony Orchestra when the great operatic soprano, Mme Nellie Melba heard her sing and urged her to continue her career. Her first starring role was in the operetta, *Adele,* in London, where she met John T. Herne, then an officer in the United States Navy. Later she sang in *Maytime* with John Charles Thomas, and in a number of other successful musicals. Perhaps her greatest success was in *The Vagabond King,* which played at the Casino in New York from September, 1925, to August, 1927, before beginning its long career on the road.

    Dorothy married Montrose J. Moses, well-known writer and drama critic.

BIBLIOGRAPHY—BOOKS AND PERIODICAL ARTICLES

Ahnebrink, Lars, *The Beginnings of Naturalism in American Fiction*, Upsala, 1950.
Anderson, John, *The American Theatre*, New York: Dial Press, 1938.
Archer, William, *Playmaking—A Manual of Craftsmanship*, Boston: Small, Maynard, and Company, 1948.
Belasco, David, "My Life's Story," *Hearst's Magazine*, October, 1915.
Belasco, David, *Plays Produced Under the Direction of David Belasco*, New York (privately printed), 1925.
Brown, T. Allston, *A History of the New York Stage*, 3 vols., New York: Dodd, Mead, 1903.
Bucks, Dorothy S. and Nethercot, Arthur H., "Ibsen and Herne's *Margaret Fleming*: A Study of the Early Ibsen Movement in America," *American Literature*, January, 1946.
Churchill, Allen, *The Great White Way*, New York: Dutton, 1962.
Creahan, John, *Life of Laura Keene*, Philadelphia: Rogers Publishing Co., 1897.
Dictionary of American Biography, New York: Scribner's, 1928.
Downer, Alan S., *American Drama*, New York: Crowell, 1960.
Edwards, Herbert, "Howells and Herne," *American Literature*, January, 1951.
Freedley, George, and Reeves, John A., *A History of the Theatre*, New York: Crown, 1941.
Gagey, Edmond M., *The San Francisco Stage—A History*, New York: Columbia University Press, New York, 1950.
Gardener, Helen, *An Unofficial Patriot*, New York: R. F. Fenno, 1894.
Garland, Hamlin, *Companions on the Trail*, New York: Macmillan, 1931.
Garland, Hamlin, *A Daughter of the Middle Border*, New York: Macmillan, 1921.
Garland, Hamlin, "Mr. and Mrs. James A. Herne," *The Arena*, October, 1891.
Garland, Hamlin, "On the Road with James A. Herne," *The Century*, August, 1914.
Garland, Hamlin, *Roadside Meetings*, New York: Macmillan, 1930.
Garland, Hamlin, *A Son of the Middle Border*, New York: Macmillan, 1921.
Gassner, John, *Masters of the Drama*, New York: Random House, 1940.
George, Henry, Jr., "James A. Herne," *Single Tax Review*, July 15, 1901.
Hapgood, Norman, *The Stage in America*, New York: Macmillan, 1901.
Herne, James A., "Act III of *Griffith Davenport*." (Prefatory Note by Arthur H. Quinn and Commentary by Julie A. Herne). *American Literature*, November, 1952.
Herne, James A., "Art for Truth's Sake in the Drama," *The Arena*, February, 1897.
Herne, James A., *The Early Plays of James A. Herne, with Act IV of Griffith Davenport*, edited with an Introduction by Dr. Arthur Quinn, Princeton, New Jersey: Princeton University Press, 1940.
Herne, James A., "Forty Years Behind the Footlights," *The Coming Age* v. II, No. 2.

BIBLIOGRAPHY

Herne, James A., "Old Stock Days in the Theatre," *The Arena,* September, 1892.
Herne, James A., *Shore Acres and Other Plays.* Revised by Mrs. James A. Herne, Biographical Note by Julie A. Herne, New York: Samuel French, 1928.
Herne, James A.,*"Margaret Fleming,"* in *Representative American Plays,* edited by Arthur H. Quinn, New York: Century Co., 1930.
Howells, William Dean, "Editor's Study," *Harper's Magazine,* August, 1891. (Margaret Fleming)
Howells, William Dean, "Editor's Study," *Harper's Magazine,* July, 1889.
Howells, William Dean, *Life in Letters of William Dean Howells,* edited by Mildred Howells, Garden City, N. Y., Doubleday, Doran, 1928.
Howells, William Dean, *The Story of a Play,* New York: Harpers, 1898.
Howells, William Dean, "Bride Roses," *Harper's Magazine,* August, 1893.
Irving, Laurence, *Henry Irving,* New York: Macmillan, 1952.
Kirk, C. M. and Kirk Rudolph, *William Dean Howells,* New York: American Book Company, 1950. (American Writers Series)
Josephson, Matthew, *The Robber Barons,* New York: Harcourt, Brace, 1934.
Leavitt, M. B., *Fifty Years in Theatrical Management,* New York: Broadway Publishing Co., 1912.
Meserve, Walter J. (ed.), *The Complete Plays of William Dean Howells,* New York University Press, 1960.
McVicker, James H., *The Press, The Pulpit and the Stage,* Chicago, 1882.
Moody, Richard, *America Takes the Stage,* Bloomington: Indiana University Press, 1955.
Moody, Richard, *Edwin Forrest,* New York: Knopf, 1960.
Morris, Clara, *Life on the Stage,* New York: McClure, Phillips, 1901.
Morton, Frederick, "James A. Herne," *Theatre Arts,* December, 1940.
Moses, Montrose, J., and Brown, John Mason, *The American Theatre As Seen By Its Critics,* New York: W. W. Norton and Company, 1934.
Moses, Montrose J., *The Fabulous Forrest,* Boston: Little, Brown and Company, 1929.
Moses, Montrose J., *The American Dramatist,* Boston: Little, Brown, 1911.
Mowatt, Anna Cora, *Autobiography of an Actress,* Boston: Reed & Fields, 1854.
Odell, George C. D., *Annals of the New York Stage,* New York: Columbia University Press, 1927...
Quinn, Arthur H., *A History of the American Drama from the Civil War to the Present Day,* New York and London: Harper, 1927. 2 vols. (Revised edition, in one volume, 1936.)
Quinn, Arthur H., "Ibsen and Herne, Theory and Facts," *American Literature,* May, 1947.
Rees, James, *Life of Edwin Forrest,* Philadelphia: 1874.
Smith, Henry Nash, and Gibson, William M., editors, *Mark Twain—Howells Letters,* Cambridge: Harvard, 1960.
Sobel, Bernard, editor, The Theatre Handbook, Preface by George Freedley, New York: Crown, 1941.

Spiller, Robert E., *et al.*, *Literary History of the United States,* New York: The Macmillan Company, 1948.
Strang, Lewis, C., *Famous Actors of the Day in America,* Boston: L. C. Page, 1900.
Sullivan, Mark, *Our Times: I. The Turn of the Century,* New York, London: Scribner's, 1926.
Thomas, Augustus, "Address at Funeral Service of James A. Herne." *The Single Tax Review,* July 15, 1901.
Tompkins, Eugene, *The History of the Boston Theatre,* Boston: Houghton, Mifflin Co., 1908.
Waggoner, Hyatt A., "The Growth of a Realist: James A. Herne," *New England Quarterly,* March, 1942.
Whiffen, Mrs. Thomas, *Keeping Off the Shelf,* New York: Dutton, 1928.
Winter, William, *Life of David Belasco,* New York: Moffat, Yard, 1918.

BIBLIOGRAPHY—NEWSPAPERS

Anaconda (Montana) *Standard,* April 24, 1898.
Anaconda (Montana) *Standard,* June 11, 1901.
Boston *Advertiser,* February 1, 1893.
Boston *Advertiser,* October 25, 1893.
Boston *Budget,* February 24, 1893.
Boston *Commonwealth,* February 25, 1893.
Boston *Courier,* February 24, 1893.
Boston *Globe,* February 21, 1893.
Boston *Globe,* October 25, 1899.
Boston *Herald,* October 25, 1899.
Boston *Journal,* February 25, 1893.
Boston *Journal,* October 25, 1899.
Boston *Post,* February 21, 1893.
Boston *Post,* October 25, 1899.
Boston *Times,* February 26, 1893.
Boston *Transcript,* February 21, 1893.
Boston *Transcript,* October 25, 1899.
Boston *Transcript,* May 22, 1920.
Boston *Traveler,* October 25, 1899.
Chicago *Chronicle,* May 17, 1897.
Chicago *Inter-Ocean,* July 8, 1892.
Chicago *Inter-Ocean,* May 17, 1897.
Chicago *News* (No date)
Chicago *Record-Herald,* June 4, 1901.
Chicago *Record-Herald,* January 30, 1907.
Chicago Tribune, July 8, 1892.
Chicago *Tribune,* January 30, 1907.
London *Morning Leader,* December 22, 1900.
London *Tribune,* May 22, 1906.
New York *Advertiser,* December 31, 1893.
New York *Clipper* (No date)

BIBLIOGRAPHY

New York *Dramatic Mirror,* January 4, 1896.
New York *Dramatic Mirror,* February 22, 1896.
New York *Dramatic Mirror,* March 14, 1896.
New York *Dramatic Mirror,* April 26, 1896.
New York *Dramatic Mirror,* May 16, 1896.
New York, *Dramatic Mirror,* August 22, 1896.
New York *Dramatic Mirror,* November 16, 1896.
New York *Dramatic Mirror,* July 17, 1897.
New York *Dramatic Mirror,* January 29, 1898.
New York *Dramatic Mirror,* February 11, 1899.
New York *Dramatic Mirror,* February 25, 1899.
New York *Dramatic Mirror,* September 23, 1899.
New York *Evening World,* November 1, 1893.
New York *Herald,* October 31, 1893.
New York *Herald,* January 12, 1877.
New York *Journal,* October 31, 1893.
New York *Mercury,* October 31, 1893.
New York *Recorder,* October 31, 1893.
Peoria (Illinois), *The Peorian,* (c. 1879-1880).
Philadelphia *Times,* June 3, 1901.
St. Louis *Republican,* January 9, 1881.
San Francisco *Bulletin,* (No date.)
San Francisco *Call,* February 23, 1897.
San Francisco *Chronicle,* February 23, 1897.
San Francisco *Daily Report,* February 23, 1897.
San Francisco *Examiner,* (No date.)
Washington *Post,* June 23, 1901.

PLAYS BY JAMES A. HERNE
(With Dates of First Performances)

Charles O'Malley. Adapted from the novel by Charles Lever. Maguire's New Theatre, San Francisco, November 11, 1874.

Oliver Twist. Adapted from the novel by Charles Dickens. Maguire's New Theatre, San Francisco, November 26, 1874.

Rip Van Winkle. Adapted from the story by Washington Irving. Maguire's New Theatre, San Francisco. About 1874-75.

Robert Macaire. Adapted from *L'Auberge des Adrets.* No date.

Within an Inch of His Life. Adapted from *La Corde au Cou,* by Emile Gaboriau. In collaboration with David Belasco. Grand Opera House, San Francisco, February 17, 1879.

Marriage by Moonlight. Later entitled *Hap-Hazard.* Adapted from *Camilla's Husband,* by Watts Philips. In collaboration with David Belasco. Baldwin Theatre, San Francisco, June 30, 1879.

Agnes. Adapted from *Andrea,* by Victorien Sardou. Never produced. Although part of the manuscript is in Herne's handwriting, it does not appear to be his work. It may possibly be by Belasco, although he does not mention it in his list of plays.

Hearts of Oak. First entitled *Chums.* Adapted from *The Mariner's Compass,* by Henry J. Lealie. In collaboration with David Belasco. Baldwin Theatre, San Francisco, September 9, 1879.

The Minute Men of 1774-1775. Chestnut Street Theatre, Philadelphia, April 6, 1886.

Drifting Apart. First entitled *Mary, The Fisherman's Child.* People's Theatre, New York, May 7, 1888.

Fall River. In collaboration with Hamlin Garland. Not produced. Copyrighted, April 15, 1890.

Margaret Fleming. Lynn, Massachusetts, July 4, 1890.

My Colleen. September, 1891.

Shore Acres. First title, *Shore Acres Subdivision.* Second title, *Uncle Nat.* McVicker's Theatre, Chicago, May 23, 1892.

Griffith Davenport. First entitled, *The Reverend Griffith Davenport.* Lafayette Square Theatre, Washington, January 16, 1899.

Sag Harbor. Park Theatre, Boston, October 24, 1899.

INDEX

Abbey, Edwin A., 135
Abbott, Marion, 142
Actress of Padua, The, 12
Adams, Mr. and Mrs. Henry, 74, 75
Adams, Maude, 28, 33, 127
Adventure of Lady Ursula, The, 127
Agatha, 99
Age of Innocence, The, 88
Aherne, Charles, 2
Aherne, James A., 2, 3, 4, 5
Aherne, Patrick, 2
Ahnebrink, Dr. Lars, 48
Aiken, George L., 5
Alabama, 69, 112
Albert, Ernest, 127
Aldrich, Mildred, 66, 102
Aldrich, Mr. and Mrs. Thomas Bailey, 68
Allen, C. Leslie, 97
Allen, Viola, 137, 138, 151, 152
America Takes the Stage, 40, 133
American, The, 30
American Claimant, The, 80
American Senator, The, 14
Annie Kilburn, 75
Anthony, Susan R., 112
Arbuckle, Maclyn, 153
Archer, William, 54, 93, 94, 96, 129, 132, 133
Arizona, 152
As You Like It, 9, 19
Atherton, Gertrude, 107
Baker, George, 35
Balzac, Honoré de, 29, 152
Banks, Maude, 71
Barrett, Laurence, 16, 22, 76, 78, 79
Barrett, Wilson, 61
Barron, Elwyn, 71
Barrymore, John, 10
Bates, Blanche, 138
Beau Brummel, 57
Beginning of Naturalism in American Fiction, The, 48
Belasco, David, 20, 27, 28, 29, 31, 32, 33, 34, 35, 36, 39
Ben My Chree, 57
Bennett, James O'Donnell, 73
Bernhardt, Sarah, 153
Berry, James, 86
Bickford, L. H., 149
Bishop, Charles, 4, 9
Bissell, Arthur, 72
Bjornson, Bjornstjerne, 74
Blake, Tiffany, 148
Blinn, Holbrook, 100
Boddington, E.F.C., 133
Bond Holders and Bread Winners, 47

Booth, Edwin, 3, 8, 13, 48, 129
Booth, John Wilkes, 9
Booth, Junius Brutus, 3, 9
Booth, Sidney, 129, 142
Boucicault, Dion, 9, 27, 88
Bradley, Sculley, 57
Brady, Alice, 100
Brady, William A., 99, 100, 101
Brass Monkey, The, 57
Bride Roses, 77
Brown, James R., 158
Brownell, W.C., 135
Brutus, 3
Bryant, William Cullen, 1
Bryant, William E., 103
Buchanan, McKean, 13
Buchanan, Thomas Read, 35
Buckstone, John B., 12
Butcher of Ghent and His Dog, The 4
Byron, George Gordon, 21
Cable, George W., 74, 135
Caine, Hall, 57, 137
Cambridge, Arthur, 17
Cameron, Beatrice (Mrs. Richard Mansfield), 51
Camilla's Husband, 28
Camille, 12, 13, 153
Charles O'Malley, 19
Chamberlin, E.B., 45, 64, 102
Charles the Second, 11
Chatfield, Taylor, H. C., 72
Chenowith, Rev. Griffith, 113
Child Stealer, The, 17
Children of the Ghetto, 136, 137, 138, 139
Christian, The, 137, 154
Chums, 32, 33
Churchill, Winston, 152
Clapp, Henry A., 103, 143
Clark, John Sleeper, 13
Clemens, Samuel L., 80, 83, 84, 135
Clement, E. H., 64
Coghlan, Charles, 127, 137
Coghlan, Rose, 28
Colonel Sellers as a Scientist, 80
Complete Plays of William Dean Howells, 76
Connor, James, 4, 5
Connor, Mrs. James, 4
Connor, William, 138
Coon Hollow, 89, 118
Cooper, James Fenimore, 2, 30, 31
Coquelin, Benoit C., 153
Corbett, James J., 99
Corcoran, Edward, 20
Corcoran, Elizabeth, 20

Corcoran, Katharine, 18, 20, 21, 22
Corcoran, Mary Nolan, 20, 21, 22, 23 24, 25
Corcoran, Michael, 20
Corcoran, Mollie, 20
Corsican Brothers, The, 15
Count of Monte Cristo, The, 38, 137, 153
Counterfeit Presentment, A, 76, 78, 79
Country Circus, The, 69, 88, 89
Courtleigh, William, 97
Crabtree, Lotta, 22
Craig, Charles, 109
Crane, Stephen, 113
Crane, William H.,7, 80, 81, 83
Crampton, Charlotte, 4
Crawford, F. Marion, 151, 152
Crosby, E. H., 144
Crumbling Idols, 45, 64, 102
Cushman, Charlotte, 3, 9
Cymbeline, 19
Cyrano de Bergerac, 127, 128, 153
Daisy Miller, 30, 31
Dale, Alan, 107, 108
Daly, Arnold, 72
Damrosch, Walter, 135
Darling of the Gods, The, 29
Darwin, Charles, 45, 91
Daughter of the Middle Border, A, 146, 147
Davenport, E. L., 13, 14, 16
Davenport, Fanny, 105
David Copperfield, 25
Davy Crockett, 117
Deemster, The, 59
DeForest, J. W., 30
DeKoven, Reginald, 135
Descent of Man, The, 47
Devilish Good Joke, A, 15
Dickens, Charles, 2, 3, 16, 21, 74, 152
Dillingham, Charles, 72, 73
Ditrichstein, Leo, 153
Dog of Montargis, The, 4
Doll's House, A, 48, 51, 54
Dombey and Sons, 25
Don Juan, 57
Donoho, Thomas S., 8
Dostoevsky, Fédor M., 75
Drew, John, 10, 127, 128, 152
Drifting Apart, 40, 41, 43, 44, 45, 49, 50, 53, 54, 58, 85, 86, 148
Dr. Jekyll and Mr. Hyde, 57
East Lynne, 13, 15, 17, 57
Eggleston, Edward, 30
English, Jane, 11, 15
English, William B., 11
Enneking, John J., 64, 66, 75

Erlanger, Abraham Lincoln, 61, 62, 63, 69, 94
Europeans, The, 30
Fair Rebel, A, 61
Farrell, Tony, 64, 88
Fate of a Coquette, The, 14
Fawcett, George, 71, 96
Field, R. M., 8, 99, 100, 104, 105, 107
First Principles, 47
Fiske, Harrison Grey, 13
Fiske, James, 16, 17
Fiske, Minnie Maddern, 13
Flaubert, Gustave, 29, 57, 74
Flockton, C. P., 65, 66
Flower, B. O., 47, 48, 64, 65, 66, 67, 69
Flowers of the Forest, The, 12
Ford, John T., 7, 8, 9
Forrest, Edwin, 1, 2, 3, 8, 10, 14, 16
Fortune Teller, The, 127
Four Legged Fortune, A, 61
French, Daniel, 135
French Spy, The, 12, 14, 15
Frohman, Charles, 151, 155
Frohman, David, 83
Gaboriau, Emile, 28
Gagey, Edmond, 16, 19
Galsworthy, John, 110
Gardener, Helen H., 47, 112, 113, 114, 117
Garland, Frank, 87, 112
Garland, Hamlin, 42, 43, 44, 45, 46, 47, 48, 49, 50, 51, 52, 53, 54, 55, 56, 57, 63, 64, 65, 66, 67, 68, 69, 74, 75, 79, 80, 87, 88, 95, 96, 98, 102, 105, 112, 114, 117, 130, 135, 146, 147, 159
Garland, Zulime Taft, 147
Garrison, William Lloyd, 66
George, Henry, 46, 48, 49, 54, 55, 61, 70
George, Henry, Jr., 54
Ghosts, The, 54
Gibson, William M., 80
Gilder, Richard Watson, 35
Gillette, William, 36, 69, 76, 134, 153, 154, 159
Girl I Left Behind Me, The, 29, 35
Gladiator, The, 1
Glover, Lyman B., 148
Goethe, Johann Wolfgang von, 78
Gohdes, Clarence, 76
Goldoni, Carlo, 78, 79
Gosse, Sir Edmund, 76
Gould, Jay, 16, 17
Greene, Clay M., 99
Grein, J. T., 54
Griffith Davenport, 7, 83, 110, 112,

Index

114, 123, 124, 125, 126, 128, 129, 130, 131, 132, 133, 134, 136, 137, 143, 146
Grismer, Joseph, 99, 100
Grismer, Phoebe, 99
Gross, W. B., 135, 151, 152
Hackett, James H., 16
Halcomebe, Willard, 140
Hale, Philip, 64
Hamlet, 153
Hamlin, John A., 33, 34
Hammerstein, Oscar, 152
Hannelse Himmellfahrt, 71
Hardy, Thomas, 75
Harrigan, Edward, 78
Harris, Joel Chandler, 74, 135
Hart, Errol, 149
Harte, Bret, 30
Hauptmann, Gerhart, 71, 72, 118
Havisham, Yolande, 79
Hawthornes, The, 50, 85, 87, 88, 89
Hay, John, 135
Hazard of New Fortunes, A, 80, 92
Hazel Kirke, 31
Hearn, Lafcadio, 135
Heart of Maryland, The, 29
Hearts of Oak, 33, 34, 36, 37, 38, 39, 40, 61, 87, 135, 138, 144, 145, 148, 152
Held by the Enemy, 57, 117
Henrietta, The, 7, 80
Herbert, Victor, 127
Hernani, 108
Herne, Chrystal, 2, 6, 37, 66, 72, 73, 107, 112, 119, 122, 130, 139, 142, 145, 146, 149, 155
Herne, Dorothy, 38, 112
Herne, Helen, 15, 17, 18
Herne, James A., 6, 7, 8, 9, 10, 12, 13, 14, 15, etc.
Herne, Julie Adrienne, 37, 43, 49, 55, 66, 76, 77, 83, 107, 112, 122, 131, 142, 146, 155
Herne, Katharine, 25, 29, 32, 37, 38, 40, 41, 42, 43, 49, 50, 51, 55, 61, 63, 64, 65, 68, 69, 72, 76, 84, 85, 86, 88, 89, 95, 101, 104, 106, 107, 112, 113, 114, 117, 122, 123, 124, 142, 146, 155
Herne, Patrick, 7
Heron, Matilde, 13, 16, 24
History of the American Drama, 32, 76
Hoblitzell, Helen, 14
Hodge, William, 142
Homer, Winslow, 135
Hoosier Schoolmaster, The, 30
Howard, Bronson, 7, 39, 80, 132
Howard, Charles, 143
Howard, Cordelia, 5
Howard, George C., 5, 134
Howells, Mildred, 76, 82
Howells, William Dean, 31, 45, 48, 49, 52, 53, 57, 64, 65, 66, 67, 68, 70, 74, 75, 76, 77, 78, 79, 80, 81, 82, 83, 84, 85, 92, 94, 100, 102, 103, 105, 114, 135
Howells, Winifred, 75
Hoyt, Charles Hale, 57
Hubbard, W. L., 72
Hurd, Charles, 45
Ibsen, Henrik, 48, 49, 51, 52, 53, 54, 56, 57, 71, 72, 75, 79
Indian Summer, 74
Ingersoll, Robert, 47, 112
In Mizzoura, 112
In the Palace of the King, 151
Irrepressible Conflict Between Two World Theories, The, 47
Irving, Henry, 7
Is This Your Son My Lord?, 47, 113
James, Henry, 30, 31, 74, 75, 81, 83, 135, 152
James, William, 135
Jason Edwards, An Average Man, 47
Jefferson, Joseph, 9, 10, 14, 16, 20, 22, 38, 76, 94, 103, 124, 127, 135
Jewett, Sarah Orne, 74
Jones, Henry Arthur, 128
Keene, Laura, 16, 24
Keeper of the Lighthouse Cliff, The, 85
Kester, Paul, 80, 81, 82
Kester, Vaughan, 81
King, E. S. Esq., 47
King Richard the Third, 6, 7, 22
Klaw, Marc, 61, 62, 63, 69
Knowles, Sheridan, 24
La Belle Russe, 36
Lackeye, Wilton, 138, 140
La Corde au Cou, 28
LaFarge, John, 135
L'Aiglon, 153
Landlord at Lion's Head, The, 83
Langtry, Mrs., 105
Leah the Forsaken, 13, 17
Leslie, Amy, 10, 15, 17, 97, 149
Leslie, Mrs. Frank, 107
Lever, Charles, 19
Liars, The, 128
Life of David Belasco, 35, 85
Lincoln, Abraham, 8
Lingard, Dickie, 34
Literary History of the United States, The, 36, 57
Literature of the American People, The, 57, 76
Little Minister, The, 127

Lodge, Henry Cabot, 135
Longfellow, Henry W., 1
Lounsbury, T. R., 135
Love Chase, The, 24
Luck of Roaring Camp, The, 30
Lucrezia, Borgia, 13
MacCready, William, 1
Mackaye, Steele, 31
Mackey, Charles, 100
Mackey, F. F., 28, 71, 100, 125
Madame Bovary, 31
Main Travelled Roads, 47, 50
Mansfield, Richard, 57, 127, 128
Mantle of Elijah, The, 139
Margaret Fleming, 57, 58, 62, 63, 65, 66, 67, 68, 70, 71, 72, 73, 75, 80, 88, 94, 95, 96, 98, 102, 104, 105, 110
Mariner's Compass, The, 32, 34
Mark Twain-Howells Letters, 80
Marlowe, Julia, 105, 159
Marriage by Moonlight, 28, 29, 32
Masks and Faces, 24, 25
Mawson, Harry P., 61
Mayhew, Katie, 23
Mayo, Frank, 117
Mazeppa, 19
McCormick, Medill, 72
McCullough, John, 16
McGuire, Tom, 16, 20, 27, 28
McNally, John J., 143
McVicker, J. H., 8, 70, 71, 72, 95, 96, 97, 98, 100
McWade, Robert, 20
Meade, James A., 12, 13, 18
Meade, Lucille, 12, 13, 14, 15
Melville, Emelie, 23
Melville, Mrs. Julia, 23, 24
Member of the Third House, A, 49, 50
Menace of Plutocracy, The, 47
Menken, Adah Isaacs, 16, 19
Merchant of Venice, The, 6
Meserve, Walter J., 76
Meyer, Charles, 100
Midnight Bell, A, 57
Millet, Jean François, 43
Miner, Henry C., 105, 107, 122, 123, 124, 127
Minister's Charge, The, 75
Minute Men of 1774-75, The, 39, 40, 86, 117
Miss Ravenel's Conversion from Secession to Loyalty, 30, 113
Mitchell, Maggie, 22
Mitchell, S. Weir, 135
Modern Instance, A, 30, 74
Modjeska, Helena, 105
Moliere, 78, 103

Monroe, Prof. Richard, 40, 133
Morals of Evolution, The, 47
Mordant, Frank, 9
Morgan, Thomas, 39
Morrison, Lewis, 28
Moulton, Louise Chandler, 66
Mrs. Warren's Profession, 52
Murray, David, 65
My Colleen, 64, 65, 88, 98
Neilson, Adelaide, 19
Neville, Henry, 58
New South, The, 99, 100, 118
Norton, Charles Eliot, 137
Oaken Hearts, 34
Octoroon, The, 57
Olcott, Chauncey, 88
Oliver Twist, 14, 15, 17, 19, 25, 28
O'Neill, James, 20, 22, 28, 38, 137
Origin of Species, 47
Ornsbee, Hamilton, 132
Owens, John E., 13
Palmer, A. M., 69
Parsons, Louella, 10
Perry, Thomas Sargent, 61, 66, 67
Pillars of Society, 54
Playmaking, 93
Prairie Heroine, A, 47
Progress and Poverty, 46, 55
Prom, Miss Jakoban, 66
Quality of Mercy, The, 80
Quinn, Dr. Arthur H., 31, 32, 57, 76, 83
Quo Vadis, 153
Rajah, The, 57
Rankin, McKee, 16
Reade, Charles, 24
Red Badge of Courage, The, 113
René, Marie, 100, 101
Representative American Plays, 31
Rhoades, James Ford, 135
Richard Carvel, 152
Richman, Charles, 65, 71
Richardson, George T., 144
Rip Van Winkle, 17, 19, 20, 22, 38, 124
Rise of Silas Lapham, The, 74, 79, 80, 83, 112
Ristori, Adelaide, 19
Rivals, The, 127
Roadside Meetings, 49, 64, 74, 130, 132
Roberts, J. B., 6
Robinson, Forrest, 71, 142
Robson, Stuart, 7, 9
Rockefeller, John D., 62
Roderick Hudson, 30
Rogers, H. H., 84
Romeo and Juliet, 19
Roosevelt, Theodore, 135

Rose, Edward E., 99, 100
Rosenfeld, Carl, 71
Rosenfeld, Theodore, 71
Rose of the Rancho, 29
Roxy, 30
Royal Box, The, 127, 137
Sabine, Lillian, 83
Sag Harbor, 135, 137, 138, 139, 142, 143, 144, 145, 146, 147, 148, 149, 152, 153, 155
Samson, 76
Sargent, John Singer, 135
Satan in Paris, 14, 15
Savage, Rev. Minot J., 47
Schiller, Johann, C. F. von, 78
Schoeffel, J. B., 64
Scott-Siddons, Mrs., 24
Scott, Sir Walter, 2, 16, 21, 72, 74
Seabury, Samuel, 158
Secret Service, 133
Shakespeare, William, 3, 14, 19, 48, 78, 84
Sharples, Jane, 10
Shaughraun, The, 88
Shaw, Bernard, 55, 56, 72
Shelley, Percy B., 21
Shenandoah, 39, 57, 117
Sheridan, Richard Brinsley, 9
Sherlock Holmes, 154
Shore Acres, 36, 50, 54, 70, 77, 81, 83, 85, 89, 93, 94, 95, 96, 97, 98, 99, 100, 102, 103, 104, 105, 106, 107, 108, 109, 110, 112, 114, 122, 124, 125, 127, 128, 131, 133, 136, 141, 144, 148, 152, 153
Shore Acres Subdivision, 96, 97
Sisson, Edward F., 149
Smart, Colonel C. S., 112
Smith, Henry Nash, 80
Smith, Penn, 12
Smith, Mrs. Sol, 142, 145
Son of the Middle Border, A, 45, 49
Sothern, E. H., 13, 127, 152, 153
Soudan, The, 58, 88
Spencer, Herbert, 45, 49
Spoil of Office, A, 47
Stanton, Elizabeth Cady, 112
St. Elmo, 30
Stevenson, Adlai, 159
Stevenson, Robert Louis, 152
St. Gaudens, Augustus, 135
Stoddard, Lorimer, 151
Stoddard, Richard Henry, 35
Story of a Play, The, 77, 78, 82
Stowe, Mrs. Harriet Beecher, 7
Strang, Lewis, 133, 144
Sudermann, Hermann, 64, 72
Sullivan, Barry, 22, 23
Sweet Nell of Old Drury, 80

Tayleure, Clifford W., 13
Taylor, Bayard, 35
Taft, Lorado, 146
Taft, Zulime, 146
Tempest, The, 16
Ten Nights in a Bar Room, 57
Tennyson, Alfred Lord, 21
Terry, Ellen, 7
Thackeray, W. M., 21, 74, 152
Thomas, Augustus, 69, 112, 132, 135, 152, 158
Thompson, Denman, 103
Thorne, Charles, 9, 16
Thorpe, Willard, 36
Three Fast Men, The or *Female Robinson Crusoes, The*, 11
Three Guardsmen, The, 133
Three Musketeers, The, 9
Tolstoy, Leo, 75, 80
Tom Sawyer, 31
Traveler from Altruria, A, 80
Trollope, Anthony, 14, 15
Turgenev, Ivan, 75
Twain, Mark, 31, 74, 84, 91
Twelfth Night, 9
Tyler, George, 137, 138, 151, 152, 153, 154
Tyrrell, T. M., 4
Uncle Tom's Cabin, 4, 11
Under the Lion's Paw, 55
Under Two Flags, 29
Unofficial Patriot, An, 112, 113, 114
Volunteer, The, 98
Wallack, J. W., 14
Wallack, Lester, 9, 10, 29
Washington, General George, 39
Watts, Phillips, 28
Webster, Daniel, 1
Wendell, Barrett, 66, 133, 146
Western, George, 10, 11
Western, Helen, 10, 11
Western, Jane, 11
Western, Lucille, 10, 11, 12, 16, 17, 22
Wharton, Edith, 88
When Knighthood Was in Flower, 154
Whistler, James McNeil, 135
White, R. H., 159
Whitman, Walt, 3, 6, 50
Widowers' Houses, 52
Wilder, Marshall P., 107
Wilkins, Mary E., 66, 102, 105
Wilson, Woodrow, 135
William Dean Howells: Life In Letters, 81, 83
Willis, N. P., 1
Winter, William, 35, 36, 39, 41, 54,

59, 69, 71, 85, 107, 108
Winter's Tale, The, 9
Wister, Owen, 135
Within an Inch of His Life, 28
Wood, Mrs. Henry, 13
Woodward, Charles, 156, 157
Worthing, Frank, 138

Years of My Youth, 77
Yorick's Love, 76, 79
Zamar, 80
Zangwill, Israel, 136, 137, 138, 139, **140, 142,** 144, 159
Zaza, 29
Zola, Emile, 52, 74

UNIVERSITY OF MAINE STUDIES*
Second Series

Adams, Amy Belle. The Novels of William Hurrell Mallock. 156pp. 1934. No. 30. 50 cents.
Aiken, Pauline. The Influence of the Latin Elegists on English Lyric Poetry, 1600-1650. 115pp. 1932. No. 22. 50 cents.
Anderson, Miriam Sylvia. The History of Secondary Education in Waldo and Piscataquis Counties in Maine. 111pp. 1939. No. 48. 50 cents.
Bailey, Marcia Edgerton. A Lesser Hartford Wit: Dr. Elihu Hubbard Smith. 150pp. 1928. No. 11. 50 cents.
Bartlett, Edmund Hobart. Local Government in Penobscot County. 82pp. 1932. No. 21. 50 cents.
Benner, Helen Frances. Kate Douglas Wiggin's Country of Childhood. 1956. No. 71. $1.50.
Billias, George A. The Massachusetts Land Bankers of 1740. 59pp. 1959. No. 74. $1.00.
Bowen, Howard Lancaster. The History of Secondary Education in Somerset County in Maine. 85pp. 1935. No. 35. 50 cents.
Bragg, Marion Kathryn. The Formal Eclogue in Eighteenth-Century England, 146pp. 1926. No. 6. 50 cents.
Brockway, Philip Judd. Sylvester Judd, 1813-1853: Novelist of Transcendentalism. 121pp. 1941. No. 53. 50 cents.
Cameron, Jean Wallace. The Orchids of Maine. 80pp. 1951. No. 65. $1.00
Chaplin, Leola Bowie. The Life and Works of Nathaniel Deering (1791-1881). 244pp. 1934. No. 32. 75 cents.
Chase, George Davis. Sea Terms Come Ashore. 90pp. 1942. No. 56. 50 cents.
Costrell, Edwin. How Maine Viewed the War, 1914-1917. 101pp. 1940. No. 49. 50 cents.
Creamer, Walter Joseph, Jr. A Study of the Vector Impedance of Two Parallel Circuits. 32pp. 1929. No. 13. 50 cents.
Creamer, Walter Joseph, Jr. Vacuum Tube Amplifiers for Audio-Frequency Currents. 46pp. 1927. No. 10. 50 cents.
Davis, Harold A. An International Community on the St. Croix. 412pp. 1950. No. 64. $2.75.
Davis, Rose Mary. Stephen Duck, the Thresher-Poet. 198pp. 1927. No. 8. 50 cents.
Day, Clarence Albert. Farming in Maine, 1860-1940. 306pp. 1963. No. 78. $2.00.
Day, Clarence Albert. A History of Agriculture in Maine, 1604-1860. 318pp. 1954. No. 68. $2.50.
Dow, Edward F. A Portrait of the Millenial Church of Shakers. 52pp. 1931. No. 19. 35 cents.
Dow, Edward F. and Hormell, Orren C. City Manager Government in Portland, Maine. 119pp. 1941. No. 52. 50 cents.
Eckstorm, Fannie Hardy. Indian Place-Names of the Penobscot Valley and the Maine Coast, 272pp. 1941. Reprinted 1960. No. 55, $3.00.
Edwards, Herbert J. and Hankins, John E. Lincoln the Writer. 117pp. 1962. No. 76. $1.00.
Ellis, Milton—See Pendleton, Emily.
Fassett, Frederick Gardiner, Jr. A History of Newspapers in the District of Maine. 242pp. 1932. No. 25. 75 cents.
Field, Vena Bernadette. Constantia—A Study of the Life and Works of Judith Sargent Murray, 1751-1820. 118pp. 1931. No. 17. 50 cents.
Finley, Raymond Stevens. The History of Secondary Education in Kennebec County in Maine. 119pp. 1941. No. 54. 50 cents.
Golden, Samuel Adler. Frederick Goddard Tuckerman: an American Sonneteer. 74pp. 1952. No. 66. $1.00
Hankins, John E.—See Edwards, Herbert J.
Hatch, Frieda Wardwell. Status of the Social Sciences in Secondary Schools of Maine. 114pp. 1933. No. 27. 50 cents.
Healy, Richard Wyman. The History of Secondary Education in Androscoggin and Franklin Counties, Maine. 165pp. 1949. No. 63. $1.00.
Hempstead, Alfred Geer. The Penobscot Boom and the Development of the West Branch of the Penobscot River for Log Driving. 187pp. 1931. No. 18. $1.50.
Hilton, C. Max. Rough Pulpwood Operating in Northwestern Maine, 1935-1940. 197pp. 1942 No. 57. $1.50.
Hormell, Orren C.—See Dow, Edward F.
Huff, Jean Keirstead. The History of Secondary Education in Aroostook County in Maine. 138pp. 1946. No. 60. 50 cents.
Hylan, John Coffey. The History of Secondary Education in York and Oxford Counties in Maine 78pp. 1933. No. 29. 50 cents.
Hyland, Fay and Steinmetz, Ferdinand H. The Woody Plants of Maine, Their Occurrence and Distribution. 96pp. 1944. No. 59. $1.00.
Jones, Maurice Daniel. Methods Used in Growing Peas for Canning in Maine and the Problems Connected with Their Economical Production. 80pp. 1927. No. 9. 50 cents.
Katz, David. The Vibratory Sense and Other Lectures. 163pp. 1930. No. 14. 50 cents.
Keith, Philip Edward. The History of Secondary Education in Penobscot County in Maine. 249pp. 1948. No. 61. $1.00.
Kelley, Maurice. Additional Chapters on Thomas Cooper. 100pp. 1930. No. 15. 50 cents.
Kellogg, Thelma Louise. The Life and Works of John Davis, 1774-1853. 139pp. 1924. No. 1. 50 cents.
Kirshen, Himy B. Essays in Legal Economics. 73pp. 1932. No. 24. 35 cents.
Knowlton, Thomas Anson. The Economic Theory of George Bernard Shaw. 82pp. 1936. No. 39. 50 cents.
Levinson, Elizabeth Johnson. Retarded Children in Maine. 208pp. 1962. No. 77. $2.00.

Linscott, Edward Lyon. The History of Secondary Education in Washington and Hancock Counties in Maine. 171pp. 1937. No. 41. 50 cents.
McDonald, Dorothy Smith. Union List of Serials in Maine Libraries. 257pp. 1937. No. 40. $1.50.
Mendall, Howard L. The Ring-necked Duck in the Northeast. 320pp. 1958. No. 73. $2.50.
Morse, Frank Leander Staples. The History of Secondary Education in Knox and Lincoln Counties in Maine. 81pp. 1939. No. 47. 50 cents.
Nylander, Olof O. The Lymnaeidae of Northern Maine and Adjacent Canadian Provinces, and Notes on Anson Allen and His Collection. 43 pp. 1943. No. 58. 50 cents.
Ogden, Edith Bolan. The Ferns of Maine. 128pp. 1948. No. 62. $1.00.
Peck, Esther Alice. A Conservative Generation's Amusements. 119pp. 1938. No. 44. 50 cents.
Peck, Henry Austin. Seaports in Maine: An Economic Study. 68pp. 1955. No. 70. 50 cents.
Pedder, Laura Green. The Letters of Joseph Dennie, 1768-1812. 212pp. 1936. No. 36. 75 cents.
Pendleton, Emily, and Ellis, Milton. Philenia—The Life and Works of Sarah Wentworth Morton, 1759-1846. 122pp. 1931. No. 20. 50 cents.
Perrin, Porter Gale. Thomas Green Fessenden. 206pp. 1926. No. 4. 50 cents.
Phillips, Evelyn Butler. An Analysis of the Curricula of the Small High Schools of Maine. 89pp. 1932. No. 23. 50 cents.
Prince, Alton Ernest, and Steinmetz, Ferdinand Henry. Gymnosporangium Rusts in Maine and Their Host Relationships. 111pp. 1940. No. 50. 50 cents.
Ring, Elizabeth. The Progressive Movement of 1912 and Third Party Movement of 1924 in Maine. 68pp. 1933. No. 26. 35 cents.
———— Part II. With an Introduction on Maine Maps, by Fannie Hardy Eckstorm. 261pp. 1939. No. 45, Part II. $1.25.
———— Part III. Index. 211pp. 1941. No. 45, Part III. $1.00.
Sayward, Dorothy S. Comfort Magazine, 1888-1942: A History and Critical Study. 106pp. 1960. No. 75. $1.00.
Segall, Jacob Bernard. Roumanian Folk Tales, Retold from the Original. 105pp. 1925. No. 3. 50 cents.
Shay, Robert P. Regulation W: Experiment in Credit Control. 108pp. 1953. No. 67. $1.50
Snider, Rose. Satire in the Comedies of Congreve, Sheridan, Wilde and Coward. 136pp. 1937. No. 42. 50 cents.
Snow, Charles Augustus. The History of the Development of Public School Supervision in the State of Maine. 99pp. 1939. No. 46. 50 cents.
Stanley, Preston J., Jr. The Economic Feasibility of the Personal Income Tax for Maine. 69 pp. 1964. No. 79. $1.00.
Steinmetz, Ferdinand H.—See Prince, Alton Ernest. Also, Hyland, Fay.
Stevens, James Stacy. Whittier's Use of the Bible. 103pp. 1930. No. 16. 50 cents.
Stuart, Richard Kenneth. Financing Public Improvements By the State of Maine. 188pp. 1957. No. 72. $1.50.
Wixson, Edwin Atwell. An Economic Study of the Production, Destination and Farm price of Maine Potatoes. 75pp. 1929. No. 12. 50 cents.
Wood, Richard G. A History of Lumbering in Maine, 1820-1861. 267pp. 1935. No. 33. Reprinted 1961. $3.00.
Wray, Ruth Arline. The History of Secondary Education in Cumberland and Sagadahoc Counties in Maine. 153pp. 1940. No. 51. 50 cents.
York, Robert M. George B. Cheever, Religious and Social Reform (1807-1890). 240pp. 1955. No. 69. $2.00.

---

* Orders and inquiries should be addressed to the Mail Room, Winslow Hall, University of Maine, Orono, Maine, USA 04473. Prices include postage in the United States when payment accompanies the order. Residents of Maine please add 4% Sales Tax.
Exchanges should be sent to the Raymond H. Fogler Library, University of Maine.